Tax Due Diligence

Matthew Peppitt,
Ernst & Young

Spiramus

Published January 2009 by

Spiramus Press Ltd
102 Blandford Street
London W1U 8AG

Telephone +44 20 7224 0080

www.spiramus.com

Reprinted 2009

ISBN 978 1904905 46 2

Printed and bound by CPI Group (UK) Ltd, Croydon, CR0 4YY

Table of contents

Tables of authorities

Acts of Parliament

Regulations

Rules and Codes

OECD model conventions

Cases

1. Introduction

1.1. Introduction

Tax due diligence is essentially a practical subject and this book is a practical guide to the process of tax due diligence and how to extract the most value from it. Accordingly, this guide will cover areas such as:

- The different circumstances in which tax due diligence is performed and the implications of each
- How to manage the tax due diligence process
- How to plan and define the scope of tax due diligence
- How to focus limited tax due diligence resources on the areas which will make a real difference to the contemplated transaction
- How to deal with limited access to a target company's tax records, management or advisers
- How to make the most of limited information
- Effective reporting of tax due diligence findings
- How to deal with the issues identified by tax due diligence, contractually or otherwise
- Due diligence in relation to specific areas of tax risk
- Tax due diligence in relation to asset deals
- The tax treatment of due diligence costs

But this book is not, and cannot be, an exhaustive guide to all the specific circumstances which can give rise to tax exposures under the tax code of any jurisdiction in which due diligence might be performed. Such a guide would require an exposition of the tax law and practice in each jurisdiction which is clearly outside the scope of this book. For such information, reference should be made to publications on the tax codes of the countries where due diligence is required, although there is no substitute for experience. Tax due diligence can only be effective if it is carried out by someone with experience of the relevant tax law and practice who is familiar with the circumstances and dynamics of the transaction in question. Put simply, to be able to identify a potential tax issue or exposure, one has to know what one is looking for.

1.2. What is tax due diligence – a definition

Tax due diligence is the process by which some or all of the tax affairs of a company or business are independently reviewed in connection with a transaction to identify tax risks and/or benefits inherent in the company or business and/or to establish particular facts or circumstances with regard to its tax position.

Tax due diligence, of course, can be performed in any circumstances where knowledge of a company's or business' tax position is required. But as the term is generally understood, and as the above definition suggests, tax due diligence is normally performed:

- in the context of a transaction;
- with a third party;
- in which one party will directly or indirectly assume liability for, or the benefit of, or otherwise be affected by, some aspect of the tax history of a target company or business.

Accordingly, the circumstances in which tax due diligence is commonly performed include:

- any transaction in which some or all of the shares of a company are to be acquired from a third party, whether for cash, shares or otherwise ('pre-acquisition' or 'buy-side' tax due diligence);
- any transaction in which a seller needs to provide information about the tax position of a company to one or more potential purchasers in connection with a sale of some or all of that company's shares, usually as part of an auction process, where a seller will invite bids for a target business from a number of competing bidders in a managed sale process ('vendor' or 'sell-side' tax due diligence);
- any transaction in which a company needs to provide information about its tax position to one or more potential providers of finance in connection with a refinancing; and
- any transaction in which an independent review is required in order to meet some related compliance obligation, e.g. the due diligence performed by reporting accountants in connection with certain listed company transactions and initial public offerings ('long form' tax due diligence).

There are, inevitably, exceptions to the definition put forward above. In particular:

- limited tax due diligence is sometimes performed in connection with acquisitions and disposals of business assets, even though, in the UK at least, a purchaser of business assets will not generally inherit pre-acquisition tax liabilities associated with the business in which the assets were formerly employed. (With regard to tax due diligence in asset deals, see Chapter 10); and
- tax due diligence is occasionally carried out where an acquisition is made

from, or a disposal is made to, someone who is not strictly a third party, e.g. where the common owners of two companies contribute their respective shareholdings in each to a joint venture such that their effective shareholdings in the company in which each originally had a minority interest is increased. See Example 1.

Example 1

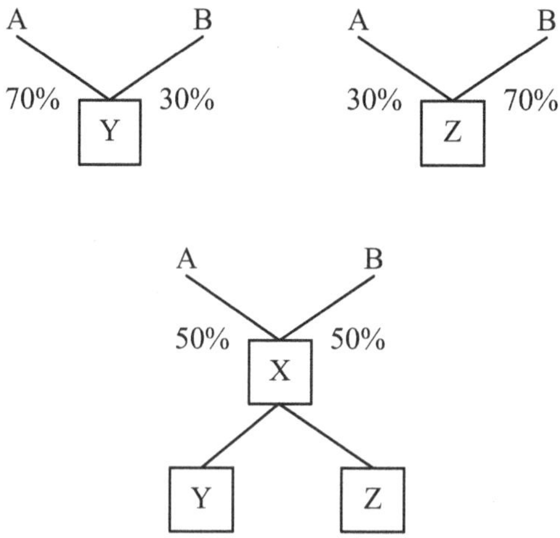

If A and B were to contribute their respective shareholdings in Y and Z to a new jointly owned vehicle, their exposure to the historical tax liabilities of the company in which they currently have a minority interest may be increased.

In whatever context it is performed, tax due diligence should not merely be a fact-finding exercise. Facts without interpretation are of limited value. Users of due diligence require guidance on the implications of those facts and how to address those implications in the context of a particular transaction. So good tax due diligence should be as much about advice and opinion as it is about facts.

Above all, tax due diligence serves a commercial purpose. It should help the person who commissioned it to make the commercial decisions critical to a transaction, in particular:

- whether or not to complete the transaction either in its entirety or even at all;
- how to complete the transaction in question;
- at what price; and

- on what terms.

While the above may seem obvious, it is often overlooked. Tax due diligence will fail in its purpose if it mires the user in too many facts from which no conclusion is obvious; or if it provides an impenetrable exposition of all the possible conflicting interpretations of those facts without drawing any conclusion at all. In either case, the user is no better off than if he or she had saved time and expense and commissioned no tax due diligence at all.

2. The Principal Types of Due Diligence

Broadly, due diligence reviews may be sub-divided into the following principal types reflecting the different circumstances in which each is performed:

- Pre-acquisition or buy-side due diligence carried out by potential purchasers of a company, a group of companies (or, in some cases, a business – see Chapter 10).
- Vendor or sell-side due diligence carried out by sellers in relation to a company, a group of companies (or, in some cases, a business – see Chapter 10) for sale. A form of sell-side due diligence is also often carried out by a company or group seeking to refinance.
- 'Long form' due diligence required in connection with certain transactions typically involving listed companies, e.g. an Initial Public Offering ('IPO').

2.1. Pre-acquisition or buy-side tax due diligence

Pre-acquisition or buy-side tax due diligence is the tax due diligence carried out on behalf of a potential purchaser or lender prior to the acquisition of a company, a group of companies or, in some cases, the assets of a business or trade. Accordingly, the scope of a pre-acquisition tax due diligence review is determined by the purchaser, at least to the extent that commercial circumstances will allow.

The purpose of pre-acquisition tax due diligence is to identify the tax risks and/or benefits which the purchaser will inherit from the seller and to determine how best they might be addressed in the context of the transaction under consideration.

Specifically, pre-acquisition tax due diligence should assist the purchaser to answer the following fundamental questions:

- Whether to do the deal in its entirety or even at all?
- How to do the deal? What are the implications for the deal structure?
- At what price? What are the implications for the purchaser's valuation model?
- On what terms? What are the implications for the contract?
- Can the deal be financed?
- What are the implications for managing the target's tax affairs post-acquisition?

2.1.1. Whether to do the deal in its entirety or even at all?

Occasionally pre-acquisition tax due diligence will reveal tax risks or exposures which are so fundamental that, commercial circumstances permitting, the purchaser should either:

- carve out part of the target company or group and leave it with the seller; or
- walk away from the deal altogether. See Example 2.

Example 2

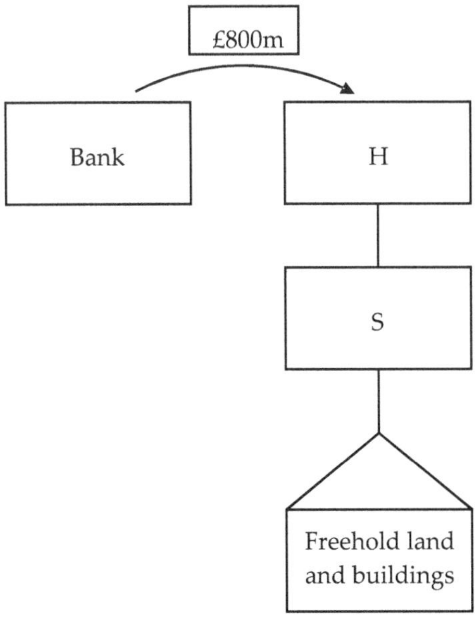

H approached Bank wishing to borrow £800 million.

As security, H offered the principal assets of S (freehold land and buildings), the disposal of which which H claimed would realise after-tax cash proceeds of £850 million.

Bank wished to carry out a tax due diligence review of the H group to ensure that none of the £850 million could be diverted to meet outstanding tax liabilities.

Before even proceeding with this due diligence, however, Bank commissioned due diligence on the proposed security itself.

This due diligence identified that the £850 million assumed that no tax would be payable on the substantial gain which would arise on disposal because of tax planning designed to shelter the gain with pre-entry capital losses.

Due diligence also concluded that the effectiveness of this tax planning was not sufficiently certain for the Bank to rely on a tax-free disposal of the land and buildings.

Bank did not proceed with the loan, thereby avoiding unnecessary risk and saving the costs of any further due diligence.

Even where the risk identified by tax due diligence does not merit walking away from the transaction in question, it may still justify carving out the piece of the target group in which the tax risk would crystallise. Occasionally, for example, part of a target group may have conducted its tax affairs so aggressively in the past that there is real risk of continuing reputational harm to the new owner. Where the associated tax risks can be confined to one or more discrete entities, it may be possible, to separate these from the group to be acquired, subject always to the commercial constraints of the transaction in question.

2.1.2. How to do the deal? Implications for the acquisition structure

The structure of an acquisition is often influenced, and is sometimes entirely driven, by the need to avoid the tax risks and/or to exploit the tax benefits inherent in the target company or group which have been identified through pre-acquisition tax due diligence.

At its simplest level, this can take the form of the purchaser's desire to buy assets rather than shares so as not to assume liability for the target's tax history. In consequence, transactions which would otherwise have been share purchases can become purchases of assets, or of a combination of assets and shares, as a result of tax due diligence findings.

But pre-acquisition tax due diligence can have other fundamental effects on acquisition structure as, for example, in the case of Example 13 (see 9.2.2).

2.1.3. At what price? Implications for value, price and purchase consideration

The findings of pre-acquisition tax due diligence may be such that they should be reflected in the purchaser's valuation model, the purchase price offered and the form of the purchase consideration. In this context, it should always be borne in mind that all decisions in relation to valuation, price and consideration are ultimately matters for the purchaser as principal. The due diligence adviser's role is to inform the purchaser about factors which might affect valuation and to provide advice and opinion on those factors.

Adjustment to valuation, price or consideration is usually the most immediate impact of pre-acquisition tax due diligence. If a particular tax exposure is high risk (see 6.2.2) and it can be quantified with a reasonable degree of accuracy, then consideration should be given to reducing the purchase price accordingly. See Examples 3 and 4.

Example 3

A UK target company had made a *Marks & Spencer* group relief claim to shelter £12.6 million of its profits with losses of a French company in the same group.

According to the *Marks & Spencer*[1] case, EU group relief claims can only be made where there is no other possible use for the losses in question. However, in this particular case, tax due diligence identified that the French company had continued to operate in France and to carry forward the same losses without restriction.

As a result, the purchaser was able to negotiate a price reduction of £3.8 million (i.e. £12.6 million @ 30%) plus interest.

Example 4

Tax due diligence identified that a UK target company (A) had previously made a share acquisition. Specifically, in July 2002, A had acquired the shares of another company (B). At the same time, A had purchased for £1 B's distressed debt with a par value of £75 million and repayable on demand.

Because of A's coincident purchase of B's shares and distressed debt, A and B were related parties when the distressed debt was acquired. Accordingly, under legislation applicable at the time but since amended (*Section 85(3)(c) Finance Act 1996*) A was required to assume that this related party debt would be repaid at par and should have recognised a taxable credit of £75 million.

HMRC recognised shortly after the enactment of *Finance Act 1996* that this was an unintended consequence of the legislation. To address the anomaly, HMRC published guidance to the effect that there may be circumstances when it would not be appropriate to recognise the taxable credit immediately even where the underlying loans were repayable on demand.

This guidance envisaged cases where the borrower was not sufficiently financially sound to be able to repay the debt on demand. In these situations, the taxable credit could be recognised over time on a basis acceptable to the borrower's auditors.

In the present case, A had assumed that the HMRC guidance would apply to its particular circumstances and had taken the view that B would have been unable to pay any of the £75 million between July 2002 and the present. Accordingly, A had recognised none of the £75 million as a taxable credit. However, A had not sought confirmation from HMRC that the guidance would apply and, apart from a note to the accounts, had made no separate disclosure of the facts to HMRC.

---

[1] *Marks & Spencer plc v Revenue and Customs Commissioners - [2008] STC 1408*

The negotiating strength of the purchaser was such that the purchase price was reduced by £22.5 million (i.e. £75 million @ 30%) plus interest to reflect the potential exposure.

In contrast, sellers will often encourage purchasers to reflect the target's tax assets (e.g. tax losses in particular) in the purchase price, especially in auction sales where a seller will invite bids for a target business from a number of competing bidders in a managed sale process. The competitive tension created by the auction often acts as an incentive to bidders to use the target's tax assets to support a higher bid. In this situation, pre-acquisition tax due diligence should focus on the likelihood of the purchaser realising value from these tax assets. See 9.1.

The price which a purchaser is prepared to offer will obviously reflect the purchaser's view of the target's value. In turn, value is usually driven by a valuation model which should reflect the findings of pre-acquisition tax due diligence. Specifically:

- Future tax exposures which are certain to crystallise post-completion should be reflected in the model as accurately as possible with regard to both amount and timing.
- Consideration should also be given to reflecting in the valuation model the future crystallisation of high risk tax exposures which can be quantified with a reasonable degree of accuracy.
- The future benefits of any high or medium risk tax planning might also be usefully discounted in the valuation model, in particular where such planning has been, or is required to be, disclosed to HMRC under the *Tax Avoidance Schemes (Prescribed Descriptions of Arrangements) Regulations 2006 (SI 2006/1543))*. See 9.1.2. Such disclosure would suggest that the benefits of the disclosed tax planning are likely to be short-lived.
- Consideration should also be given to the appropriateness of including in the valuation model the future benefits of pre-completion tax assets, in particular tax losses which in many jurisdictions are subject to change of ownership provisions and/or time-expiry.
- Pre-acquisition tax due diligence will often provide some general indication of the target's structural effective tax rate, i.e. the effective tax rate before factors such as tax relief for interest on acquisition debt are taken into account.

It is not, of course, always commercially possible for the purchaser to negotiate a permanent price reduction for a tax risk identified through due diligence. But in these circumstances it may still be possible to agree a temporary price adjustment, in the form of a retention of sale proceeds or payment into an escrow account, until the outcome of the particular tax risk is known. See 8.8.1.

2.1.4. On what terms? Implications for the contract

Tax issues or exposures indentified through pre-acquisition tax due diligence are most commonly managed contractually, principally by means of tax warranties and indemnities[2]. Indeed, most tax exposures which are not sufficiently fundamental to cause a transaction to fail or to justify an immediate adjustment to price are dealt with in this way. Such exposures tend to be those with a medium or low risk; or those which, although high risk, cannot be quantified with sufficient certainty for a price adjustment.

Chapter 8 provides further guidance on contractual remedies for risks identified by tax due diligence.

2.1.5. What are the implications for managing the target's tax affairs post-acquisition? Implications for future management of the target's tax affairs

Pre-acquisition tax due diligence will give the purchaser an early opportunity to consider how the target's tax affairs might best be managed in future and how its tax function can most effectively be integrated into that of the new owner. This will be of particular relevance to corporate, as opposed to financial, investors. Corporate purchasers tend to invest for long-term strategic reasons such that successful integration of the target is often critical to realising the value which the transaction is expected to create.

2.2. Vendor or sell-side tax due diligence

Vendor or sell-side tax due diligence is the independent tax due diligence commissioned by the seller of a target company, group of companies (or sometimes a business) in order to provide information about the target's tax position:

- to potential purchasers, of which there may be more than one (i.e. an auction); and sometimes also
- to the lending banks. Specifically, the seller's financial adviser may wish to use the vendor due diligence in relation to any stapled financing[3] to be offered to bidders; or bidders may wish to use the vendor due diligence to secure their own funding from other lending banks; or

---

[2] See Gibson, *The Tax Schedule*, Spiramus Press, 2009.

[3] Financing for an acquisition pre-arranged by the investment bank acting for the seller and offered to bidders in an auction of a target business as a potential means of funding the acquisition.

- to potential finance providers in connection with a refinancing.

Although vendor due diligence is commissioned by the seller, it is UK market practice that the due diligence provider accepts a legal duty of care to the eventual purchaser and lenders in relation to the vendor due diligence report. Specifically, the vendor due diligence provider:

- initially enters into a contractual engagement with the seller for the performance of the vendor due diligence review of the target; and
- subsequently enters into a contractual undertaking with the successful purchaser and lenders to enable them to rely on the vendor due diligence report.

The principal idea behind vendor due diligence is to enable the seller to facilitate and control an efficient, ordered and competitive auction process and to select the right type of purchaser for the particular commercial circumstances, thereby increasing or defending value.

With the volume of money invested in private equity funds and the perennial importance of strategic deals for corporate purchasers, the trend in the mergers and acquisitions market over recent years has been that the sales of many businesses have triggered fiercely contested auctions. Such auctions typically comprise two or more stages in which the number of bidders is whittled down each time until one successful bidder is selected as the purchaser. At each stage additional information may be shared with the remaining bidders so that they are in a position to refine their bids.

By commissioning and distributing to potential purchasers a vendor due diligence report, sellers are able to achieve the following objectives:

- provide information on the target to more than one bidder at the same time;
- avoid the need for extensive pre-acquisition due diligence by a large number of potential bidders and the consequent drain on management resources which this would entail. Any due diligence over and above the vendor due diligence provided to each bidder can then be restricted to the specific requirements of one (or sometimes more) selected bidders later in the auction process. Additional tax information, over and above a vendor tax due diligence report is still sometimes provided in the earlier stages of a sale process, but this usually takes the form of:

  selected documents in a data room to corroborate the vendor tax due diligence report; and/or

  a formal 'Question & Answer' process controlled by the seller and its advisers; and/or an opportunity for bidders to discuss the vendor tax due diligence report with the advisers who prepared it; and sometimes

an opportunity for bidders to discuss the target's tax position with its management;

- anticipate tax issues or exposures which are likely to be critical to potential purchasers generally and decide early in the sale process and with due consideration how they should be addressed. For example, any pre-sale reorganisation to package a target group for sale is likely to raise concerns in bidders' minds about the risk of resulting tax liabilities in the target companies themselves. Knowing this, the seller can decide in advance whether to allay bidders' concerns by making available full details of any such pre-sale reorganisation, including copies of related tax opinions and professional advice, or by offering comprehensive indemnification for any tax liabilities arising from the reorganisation, or a combination of the two. There may also be other contingent tax liabilities in relation to which a seller is willing to provide an indemnity to avoid the risk to value which the provision of extensive information and subsequent negotiation might cause. Anticipating tax issues or exposures which are likely to be critical to potential purchasers avoids the risk of rushed responses on the part of the seller to such issues or exposures raised by bidders later in the process; and it can demonstrate to bidders that the target's tax affairs are proactively managed. It also enables individual purchasers to concentrate their own due diligence time and resources on matters peculiar to their own individual circumstances;
- control the flow and presentation of information to bidders. By drip-feeding information to bidders at each stage of the auction and asking potential purchasers to bid on the basis of the information made available at that stage, competitive tension, and accordingly value and price, are maintained. Furthermore, information about tax issues or exposures of relevance to potential purchasers in formulating their bids can be presented to bidders early enough in the sale process and in sufficient detail for them to be factored into the size or terms of the bids. In other words, vendor tax due diligence will prevent such issues or exposures from emerging late in the sale process to surprise potential purchasers. Such nasty surprises can delay or de-rail a sale process or undermine potential purchasers' confidence in it; and they can raise doubts in the minds of potential purchasers about the seller's good faith or the target's ability to manage its tax affairs. Conversely, well managed and executed vendor due diligence can assist target management to demonstrate their knowledge and understanding of the target's tax affairs;

- reduce requests from bidders for tax warranties and/or indemnities in the contract, in particular for warranties with regard to matters which are disclosed in the vendor due diligence report;
- make direct comparisons between competing bids because each will have been made on the basis of the same information. (Due diligence tailored to the needs of individual bidders is generally delayed until a later stage of the auction – see above);
- raise important separation, completion and post-completion tax issues early on during the sale process to ensure that they do not emerge late in the process to become obstacles to completion or disruptions to management in the post-closing period;
- limit the number of questions from bidders;
- prepare for questions from bidders, enabling management to give robust responses which defend value; and
- manage the sale process and in particular to ensure that the timetable for the sale can be met.

In the European market, vendor due diligence originally tended only to be used for the largest transactions. Today, however, it has become the norm, given the competitive interest for most targets referred to above, and financial advisers will often advise sellers that it is a prerequisite of any sale process.

Vendor due diligence is less well established in the US market. In general, US purchasers, both trade and financial, tend not to be as familiar with it or as willing to rely on it. Accordingly, US purchasers will often still expect substantial additional information and access to target management and will tend to re-perform work already carried out as part of vendor due diligence in order to form their own due diligence conclusions.

The scope, depth and quality of a vendor tax due diligence review will determine the value which vendor tax due diligence will add to the sale process. Scope and depth are determined by the seller and the due diligence adviser. To achieve the principal commercial purpose of vendor tax due diligence, its scope and depth should be such that it answers all the main tax questions to which purchasers are likely to require answers in formulating their bids. If the scope is too narrowly defined in an attempt by the seller to minimise due diligence costs, it can fail to achieve its purpose altogether. If vendor tax due diligence does not address those matters which well-advised bidders would expect to be covered, then it will not prevent extensive questioning and requests for information and/or tax warranties from those bidders. In fact, if vendor tax due diligence is too limited in scope, it can erode value by shaking bidders' confidence with regard to the target's tax position; and it can cause friction with bidders who may have incurred time and expense reviewing a vendor tax due diligence report which does not progress their understanding of the target's tax affairs. In these circumstances, it is sometimes better to do no vendor tax due diligence at all and only to provide information about the target's tax position at a later stage of the auction to a limited number of bidders who may then perform their own buy-side tax due diligence.

Because sell-side tax due diligence is commissioned by the seller, potential purchasers might be expected to have less confidence in its scope and findings than in the scope and findings of tax due diligence which they had commissioned themselves. While to some extent this may be true, the following three factors compensate for this quite natural inclination for potential purchasers to be sceptical of sell-side tax due diligence.

- Vendor due diligence should always be carried out by a team of advisers comprising individual members without previous connections with, or knowledge of, the target company or group. In this way, potential purchasers should be confident that any risk of self-review by the due diligence provider has been avoided and that accordingly the vendor due diligence is balanced and credible.
- Potential purchasers may reasonably assume that the vendor due diligence team will have been given greater access to, and time with, target management than is usually provided in most buy-side due diligence processes.
- Although sell-side due diligence is commissioned by the seller before any bidder has been chosen as the successful purchaser, the due diligence provider accepts a legal duty of care to the ultimate purchaser and is aware of this when performing the due diligence review. The purchaser is then able to rely on the due diligence report. Where sell-side due diligence is commissioned by a company or group in relation to a refinancing, the due diligence provider accepts a legal duty of care to the ultimate provider of finance.

In a typical sale process, the vendor due diligence report is supplemented by an opportunity for each bidder to ask questions of the report's authors, either at a meeting or, where a meeting is impractical, by way of conference call. See 7.5. Occasionally, where the seller is anxious to maintain interest from one or more particular bidders, the seller will agree to commission further due diligence in relation to a specific matter of particular importance to those bidders.

2.2.1. Vendor assistance reports

As an alternative to a vendor tax due diligence report, a seller may sometimes provide potential purchasers with a vendor tax assistance report.

Like vendor tax due diligence, vendor tax assistance provides factual information about the tax position of a target company or group (e.g. the status of the target's tax compliance, details of any current tax litigation, the existence of tax losses carried forward at a particular date etc.). But it does not contain any conclusion or opinion on the potential implications of those facts or recommendations as to how they might be addressed by a purchaser (e.g. it would make no comment about any factors which might limit the purchaser's ability to make use of those tax losses post-acquisition). Bidders are expected to make their own assessment of the facts, taking their own separate advice where necessary. The purpose of vendor tax assistance is simply to provide information about the target's tax position which potential purchasers may take into account when formulating their bids. In this way, the bids should be directly comparable because they will have been prepared on the basis of the same information.

The most important distinctions between vendor due diligence and vendor assistance, however, are that:

- unlike vendor due diligence, vendor assistance is not necessarily provided by an independent adviser; and
- with vendor due diligence, the provider accepts a legal duty of care to the ultimate purchaser; whereas with vendor assistance, a duty of care is owed solely to the seller.

2.2.2. Exit readiness

The ultimate aim of any seller or company intending to float its shares will generally be to achieve:

- the best possible price;
- with the fewest conditions attached;
- in the shortest period of time;
- at the lowest cost consistent with the above objectives.

Among other things, this requires:

- a clear idea of how the sale or flotation is to be implemented;
- identification of any features of the target's tax profile which are likely to be particularly attractive to potential purchasers or investors;
- identification of any tax issues or exposures which are likely to require remedial action before sale or flotation; and

- a smooth sale or flotation process with the minimum of obstacles and consequent delays. So sellers will wish to avoid anything which might hold up the sale or flotation process or cause friction in negotiations with potential purchasers.

In particular, the target business may not already be neatly packaged for sale or flotation. Furthermore, its tax affairs are unlikely to have been subjected to the same level of scrutiny and analysis as that required by a potential purchaser, sponsor (see 2.3.2), or nominated adviser (see 2.3.3); and the demands which this would place on the seller and target management should not be underestimated.

Before embarking on the sale or flotation process (in particular before embarking on any sell-side or long form tax due diligence), a seller should therefore consider an exit readiness tax review. This is a review of the target's tax position, carried out for the benefit of the seller or target rather than for any third party, to assess how readily the target's sale or flotation could be achieved. It can be performed either by the seller's or the target's existing tax adviser or by an independent adviser appointed specially for the purpose.

An exit readiness tax review is intended to identify those tax matters which will need to be addressed before a sale or flotation can be completed successfully and the action necessary to address them. From a tax perspective, there are four main areas to consider.

- How to structure the disposal or flotation and any tax liabilities for either seller or purchaser which the disposal or flotation structure might trigger. In particular, what is the most attractive way to sell or float the business from the seller's perspective? What is the most attractive way to sell or float the business from the purchaser's or investor's perspective? If these do not coincide, which is most likely to enhance the value derived? What are the relative costs of each? Is any pre-sale or pre-flotation restructuring required? For example, where a business can be sold by means of a sale of shares which would qualify for the substantial shareholdings exemption, then a seller would normally prefer this route; however, a purchaser might be prepared to pay more for business assets which are eligible for tax relief. If the incremental purchase price were to exceed the seller's additional tax burden in the case of an asset sale, then a seller's preferred disposal route might switch to an asset sale.
- What tax matters are likely to enhance or erode value? Are there any tax matters which might cause potential purchasers, investors or a financial adviser to revise their opinion of the target's value either positively or negatively? In particular:

Does the target business have any tax assets which could or should be enhanced, preserved and/or marketed to potential purchasers and investors?

Are there any tax risks or exposures within the target business which are likely to require remedial action before sale or flotation and what would be required to achieve this?

- Is the target business up to date with its tax compliance obligations? Are potential purchasers, investors, a sponsor or a nominated adviser likely to place confidence in the target business' ability to manage its tax affairs effectively? If not, what must be done to remedy the situation?
- Is there anything which might prevent the target business from providing information which potential purchasers, investors, a sponsor or a nominated adviser might reasonably be expected to request?

Guidance on the timing of any action required to address the above areas is crucial. This enables the seller to avoid incurring sale or flotation costs unless and until it is necessary to do so. For example, a target business might be carried on by a number of companies in a group, some of which may also have other business activities which are to be retained or excluded from a sale or flotation. In this situation, some pre-sale/pre-flotation reorganisation is likely to be required in order to separate and package the business for sale or flotation. Until a plan for this reorganisation is established, it will not be certain which corporate entities and which business assets will need to be sold or floated in order to achieve the overall commercial objective. There is little point incurring the cost of sell-side or long form tax due diligence until this is known.

An exit readiness review is best performed as soon as possible after any strategic decision is made to sell or float. It should obviously precede vendor or long form due diligence and the preparation by an investment bank of any information memorandum. But vendor or long form due diligence can follow on immediately afterwards such that exit readiness due diligence can form the first phase of any subsequent due diligence.

The following template, completed by way of illustration as Example 5, is recommended for reporting on a target's readiness for sale or flotation.

Example 5
PROJECT X

Key tax findings from an exit readiness tax review of Company X

Tax area/ issue	**Assessment**	**Comment**	**Recommendation**
Tax planning for the disposal	Minimal further work required before commencement of sale process	A sale of the shares of Company X is expected to qualify for the Substantial Shareholdings Exemption and could therefore be effected tax-free. Accordingly, purely from a tax perspective, it would generally be the seller's preferred exit route. If the divisions within Company X are to be sold separately as sales of their respective businesses and assets, there could be a tax cost for the seller depending on the precise circumstances of the separate disposals. However, a number of options exist to minimise this tax cost and in certain situations to reduce it to a very material extent. The choice of option would be determined by the value attributed to the individual assets in each business and negotiation with specific purchasers. Separate sales of the business and assets of the divisions within Company X might be tax advantageous for purchasers and the seller might therefore be able to extract more value by agreeing to sell the businesses in this way. This will be worthwhile if the additional value exceeds the tax cost. This is only possible to calculate once the terms of a specific transaction and the circumstances of a particular purchaser are known.	There is little further action required until the commercial terms of specific bids for one or more of the businesses are known, other than an exercise to apportion on some just and reasonable basis the net book values and tax written down values of Company X's assets among its constituent businesses.

Tax area/ issue	Assessment	Comment	Recommendation
		Any gains on disposals of capital assets, including land and buildings, are expected to be sheltered by capital losses elsewhere in the seller's group. It should be possible to extract from Company X without material tax cost the divisions and subsidiaries to be retained by the seller's group.	
Tax compliance	Minimal further work required before commencement of sale process	We understand that Company X's tax compliance is up to date and that there are currently no HMRC enquiries into its tax affairs. Accordingly, purchasers' due diligence should not identify any tax matters which might erode value. The seller requires access to the books and records of Company X in order to respond to an HMRC enquiry into another group company, Company Y. Accordingly, the seller is taking steps to resolve this enquiry before the Company X sale process commences and access to Company X's books and records becomes more limited.	The seller is already taking steps to resolve the enquiry into Company Y while it still has unrestricted access to Company X's books and records which would be our recommendation.

2.3. Long form due diligence

2.3.1. When is long form due diligence commissioned

'Long form' due diligence is the due diligence commissioned:

- when a company lists its shares for the first time on either the Main Market or the Alternative Investment Market ('AIM') of the London Stock Exchange (an Initial Public Offering or 'IPO'); or
- in connection with certain transactions involving a company the shares of which are already listed on either the Main Market or AIM of the London Stock Exchange.

Such transactions will require a sponsor (see 2.3.2) or nominated adviser (see 2.3.3) who will wish:

- to demonstrate that they have fulfilled their obligations under the *United Kingdom Listing Authority Listing Rules* or the *AIM Rules for Nominated Advisers, February 2007,* as the case may be, including the related declarations which they are required to make; and
- to manage their risk of potential claims arising from their association with a prospectus or admission document being used to raise capital on a stock exchange.

Accordingly, a sponsor or nominated adviser will require that due diligence is commissioned of which tax due diligence is an important part.

2.3.2. Main Market of the London Stock Exchange

Where any of the transactions described at 2.3.1 involves the Main Market, the company is required to appoint a sponsor.

Specifically, the *United Kingdom Listing Authority Listing Rules*[4] stipulate at reference *LR 8.2* those circumstances when a company is required to appoint a sponsor or to obtain a sponsor's assistance.

Broadly, a company with a primary listing of its equity securities[5] on the Main Market, or applying for such a listing, must appoint a sponsor whenever it:

- applies for admission of its equity securities to the official list of the London Stock Exchange (this generally involves the issue of a prospectus[6]);
- is required to produce a circular[7] in connection with a Class 1 transaction[8];

---

[4]The *United Kingdom Listing Authority Listing Rules* are contained within the *Financial Services Authority Handbook* (*www.fsa.gov.uk/pages/handbook*).

[5]Equity securities are defined for these purposes as equity shares and securities convertible into equity shares.

[6]A prospectus is a document which a company is required to publish under the Prospectus Directive (*Directive of the European Parliament and of the Council of 4 November 2003 No 2003/71/EC*) whenever its securities are offered to the public or admitted to trading.

[7]A circular is any document issued to holders of listed securities, excluding prospectuses, listing particulars, annual reports and accounts, interim reports, proxy cards and dividend or interest vouchers.

[8]Broadly, a Class 1 transaction is a transaction which represents at least 25% of the gross assets, profits, consideration or gross capital of the listed company proposing to enter

- produces a circular in connection with a non-Class 1 reconstruction or refinancing;
- produces a circular requiring a working capital statement under *LR 13.7.1R(2)* in connection with a non-Class 1 purchase of its own shares; or
- is otherwise required to do so by the FSA under *LR 8.2.1(5)*.

A company listed on the Main Market must obtain a sponsor's assistance if it is proposing to enter into a transaction:

- which could amount to a Class 1 transaction or a reverse takeover (*LR 8.2.2*); or
- which is or may be a related party transaction (*LR 8.2.3*).

Under the *United Kingdom Listing Authority Listing Rules* (at *LR 8.4*) a sponsor has certain obligations, and must make certain related declarations, to the FSA in relation to transactions entered into by a company to which it has been appointed sponsor. In order to satisfy these obligations, and to support the related declarations, the sponsor will, as a matter of market practice, require the company to commission due diligence from a reporting accountant.

2.3.3. The Alternative Investment Market ('AIM') of the London Stock Exchange

Companies admitted to AIM must have a nominated adviser (a term often abbreviated to 'nomad'). Specifically, the *AIM Rules for Companies, February 2007* require, as a condition of eligibility for AIM:

- that all companies applying to list shares on AIM must appoint a nominated adviser; and
- that all AIM companies must retain a nominated adviser at all times.

In accordance with both the *AIM Rules for Companies, February 2007* and the *AIM Rules for Nominated Advisers, February 2007* a 'nominated adviser is responsible to the [London Stock] Exchange for assessing the appropriateness of an applicant for AIM, or an existing AIM company when appointed its nominated adviser, and for advising and guiding an AIM company on its responsibilities' under the AIM rules.

This responsibility to the London Stock Exchange essentially comprises compliance with the *AIM Rules for Nominated Advisers, February 2007* and with

---

into it (see *United Kingdom Listing Authority Listing Rules* at *LR 10.2* and the class tests set out at *LR 10 Annex 1 G* as modified by *LR 10.7*).

undertakings provided to the Exchange in a nominated adviser's declaration[9]. In order to meet this responsibility, and to support the declaration, the nominated adviser will, as a matter of market practice and a requirement of the *AIM Rules for Nominated Advisers, February 2007*[10], require the AIM company to which it has been appointed to commission due diligence from a reporting accountant in relation to its financial position (including tax).

2.3.4. Long form tax due diligence

The scope of a long form tax due diligence review is ultimately determined by the sponsor or nominated adviser. However, the sponsor or nominated adviser will often consult the party engaged to perform the tax due diligence on an appropriate scope for the particular circumstances.

In this regard, the sponsor or nominated adviser will often resist attempts to limit the long form due diligence provider's liability. Long form tax due diligence is therefore generally the most thorough type of tax due diligence. Areas of potential tax risk tend only to be excluded, with the agreement of the sponsor or nominated adviser, where it is appropriate to do so in the professional judgement of the party engaged to perform the tax due diligence, e.g. because such areas are unlikely in the circumstances to be the cause of a tax risk of sufficient materiality for the purposes of the transaction in question.

Although it is the sponsor or nominated adviser who ultimately needs to be satisfied with the scope of the long form tax due diligence review, it is the listed or listing company which ultimately bears the cost. This fact can often give rise to tension where the company may be confident of its tax position without the extent and depth of due diligence required by the sponsor or nominated adviser. In the final analysis, long form due diligence is simply a cost of gaining access to the public capital markets.

Long form tax due diligence is often therefore regarded by the target company or group as an unavoidable cost standing in the way of the successful completion of the transaction in question. As a result, the additional value which long form tax due diligence is capable of delivering over and above its primary purpose is often overlooked at the time of the transaction.

Such additional value principally arises from:

---

[9]See *AIM Rules for Nominated Advisers, February 2007 - Part 2, Continuing Obligations of a Nominated Adviser; Schedule 2, Nominated Adviser's Declaration*; and *Schedule 3, Nominated Adviser Responsibilities*.

[10]See *AIM Rules for Nominated Advisers, February 2007 - Schedule 3, Nominated Adviser Responsibilities*.

- the benefit of an independent review of a company's tax position to non-executive directors joining the board at the time of an Initial Public Offering; and
- the opportunity provided by the long form tax due diligence exercise to review the overall tax position of what is often a large, complex and cross-border group. In practice, this type of review is rarely possible in the normal course of events. A long form tax due diligence exercise is often the first time such a thorough review of an entire group is carried out and often discloses tax benefits and/or risks of which management may not previously have been aware. The exploitation of these benefits or the avoidance of these risks can sometimes substantially mitigate the costs of the long form tax due diligence review.

The ideal outcome of a long form tax due diligence review would be a short report which identifies no tax issues or exposures of sufficient magnitude to derail, or even delay, the transaction in question. It follows, therefore, that companies seeking a listing for the first time should give careful consideration to their tax affairs before embarking on the long form due diligence process. An exit readiness tax review (see 2.2.2) may be helpful in this regard. Specifically, to the extent that it is within their control to do so, they would be well advised to ensure:

- that all outstanding tax returns have been filed;
- that all tax liabilities due have been paid;
- that all matters outstanding with any tax authority are concluded;
- that advice, opinions and evidence exists to support all filing positions, especially those which might be considered contentious;
- that, in short, there are as few matters as possible on which the tax due diligence could focus.

Not only will this approach smooth the path of the IPO etc., but it should also keep tax due diligence costs to a minimum.

More often than should be the case in practice, known tax issues or exposures are not managed or mitigated in advance of a long form due diligence review of a company's or group's tax affairs. Instead, they are left as an unpleasant surprise for the sponsor or nominated adviser, to be discovered by whoever carries out the tax due diligence review. IPOs can often be stalled in these circumstances, especially where the tax issue concerned relates to aggressive tax planning the benefits of which are still being recognised at the expected date of the IPO. Such situations are often aggravated where the firm carrying out the tax due diligence takes a different view of the risk from the company's or group's auditors or tax advisers. It is clearly much better if such planning is unwound or fully provided for in advance of the IPO. It is otherwise likely to require disclosure which could discourage potential investors and in extreme cases can result in the IPO being stopped at the insistence of the sponsor or nominated adviser until the planning is unwound or the matter is otherwise resolved.

It may not always be possible to anticipate or resolve tax issues or exposures in advance of long form due diligence, especially where they arise from uncertainty in connection with tax positions in emerging markets. Having identified such issues or exposures, long form tax due diligence should provide a proper understanding and explanation of the issue or exposure in order to facilitate disclosure of the risk in the prospectus or admission document if appropriate.

To avoid the risk of self-review by the due diligence provider, long form due diligence should always be carried out by a team of advisers comprising individual members without previous connections with, or knowledge of, the target company or group.

2.4. 'Twin track' exits

Occasionally, shareholders seeking to exit from an investment may employ a tactic known as a 'twin track' exit in which the processes of both an auction sale and an IPO of the target take place concurrently. Only at a late stage in both processes will a decision between the two finally be made by the selling shareholders, i.e. whether to continue with the auction and sell the target to one of the bidders, or to abandon the auction and sell to the market via an IPO.

A 'twin track' exit keeps the seller's options open for as long as commercially possible and is designed to maintain price. Specifically, the possibility of an IPO introduces a further degree of competitive tension into the auction; and the IPO process sets an indicative price which acts as a benchmark for the bids of potential purchasers.

Against these advantages of a 'twin track' exit must be weighed the additional costs of running the two processes concurrently. Furthermore, the risk that an auction could be abandoned in favour of an IPO may discourage the participation of some potential bidders.

A 'twin track' exit requires tax due diligence which serves the purposes of both a sale (vendor due diligence) and an IPO (long form due diligence). In practice, therefore, its fieldwork tends to be sufficiently thorough in scope to satisfy the requirements of a sponsor or nominated adviser in an IPO. However, the emphasis of the final tax due diligence report will depend on the exit route eventually chosen:

- in the case of an auction sale, details of those aspects of the target's tax position which are likely to be relevant to potential purchasers in the formulation of their bids (see 6.3.2); and
- in the case of an IPO, details of unprovided tax exposures which are sufficiently material to bring to the sponsor's or nominated adviser's attention (see 6.3.3).

2.5. Buy-side tax due diligence where the seller provides a vendor tax due diligence report

See Chapter 7.

3. The Tax Due Diligence Process

A tax due diligence engagement rarely proceeds exactly as envisaged at its outset; and no two tax due diligence exercises are identical. Flexibility of approach is essential. However, depending on their type (see Chapter 2), tax due diligence exercises will have similarities. They will tend to follow a similar pattern and comprise similar phases and processes. This brief chapter outlines these phases and processes before later chapters describe in more detail the issues associated with each.

3.1. Instruction

Sometimes a client (i.e. a potential purchaser, seller, quoted company, sponsor or nominated adviser, depending of the type of due diligence involved) will commission tax due diligence directly and will instruct the chosen provider to carry out a tax-only due diligence review of a target. This is often the case where the client has decided to carry out non-tax due diligence itself or to divide the overall due diligence exercise among two or more separate providers, each of which is responsible for a different area of due diligence, e.g. financial, pensions, IT, commercial, environmental etc.

More usually, tax due diligence is commissioned from a single provider as part of a combined due diligence engagement together with financial (and often pensions, IT and sometimes commercial) due diligence. In this situation, the instruction to carry out tax due diligence may come via:

- another part of the firm chosen to carry out the combined due diligence engagement, e.g. the corporate finance or transaction advisory department of a firm of accountants;
- the client's financial adviser, sponsor or nominated adviser; or
- another of the client's advisers, e.g. its lawyers.

Where the client is based in a different jurisdiction from the target and the chosen due diligence provider is an international firm, the client may choose to instruct its local office of the international firm. This office will often then sub-contract the due diligence to an office of the same firm in the jurisdiction of the target.

Whatever the route by which instructions are received, the due diligence provider should establish precisely who is the client for the purposes of the tax due diligence review, whether this is a potential purchaser, seller etc. or whether it is an office of the due diligence provider in another jurisdiction. Once identified, appropriate engagement terms should be entered into, and instructions clarified, with that client.

3.2. Scope

Once a formal engagement exists and instructions have been clarified, the next step is to agree the scope. Chapter 4 describes the process by which a potential purchaser's, seller's etc. tax due diligence objectives are translated into a formal scope of work based on the knowledge and experience of the tax due diligence provider.

Sometimes, the scope of a tax due diligence review needs to be agreed, at least in draft, within a very short period of time and/or with little or no information about the target and its tax position. Occasionally, not even the number and jurisdiction of the entities comprising the target will be known. In such circumstances, the initial scope can only be a general or standard one based on the experience of the tax due diligence provider of similar transactions, although it may be possible to make reasonable assumptions about the target, supported where possible by publicly available information (see Chapter 5).

In any event, it is important that scope should be revised as and when information becomes available to suggest that such revision is necessary. In practice, such information is often received throughout the course of a tax due diligence review such that agreeing scope tends to be a continuous process reflecting changing circumstances. For this reason, the document recording the formal scope of the due diligence engagement should necessarily be a living document. This should avoid any discrepancy between the tax due diligence report ultimately delivered and the client's expectations of it.

3.3. Fieldwork

Fieldwork comprises the review and analysis of information about the target's tax position necessary to fulfil the agreed scope of tax due diligence. This includes:

- review of publicly available information (see Chapter 5);
- review of any information memorandum, vendor due diligence report or vendor assistance report prepared in connection with the transaction and an interview with the authors of any vendor due diligence or assistance report (see 2.2, and Chapter 7);
- review of information requested and provided through a formal written 'Question & Answer' process. Such 'Q&A' processes are typically operated by sellers in auction situations (and are managed by their advisers) to control the provision of information to bidders and to ensure that consistent information is provided to each (see 2.2);
- interviews with those members of target management responsible for the tax matters within the agreed scope. This can be particularly helpful if

access to management is made available at an early stage of the fieldwork because it can be used to verify scope and to indentify areas on which subsequent fieldwork should focus (see 4.2.10);

- interviews with any professional advisers who have provided advice to the target in relation to tax matters within the agreed scope and/or access to their files;
- review of the files of the target's auditors (see 4.2.6);
- review of documents (see 4.4, 4.5 and 4.6 for generic/proforma information requests);
- review of non-tax due diligence materials and reports, e.g. financial and legal due diligence; and
- analysis of information obtained from the above sources.

Access to the above sources of information may not be possible initially, either in full or even at all. In particular:

- access to the target's auditors and professional advisers and their files will generally be subject to agreement of 'hold harmless'[11] terms with the auditors or advisers and may not be possible at all; and
- sellers disposing of a target company or group by means of an auction process may limit potential purchasers' access to some or all of the above in the early stages of the auction and may only make tax information available once one or two preferred bidders have been identified (see 2.2).

Information for the purposes of tax due diligence is often provided via a 'data room', a physical or virtual repository of information, the contents of which are controlled by the seller and usually listed in a data room index. The seller will grant access to the data room to selected interested parties subject to terms and conditions intended to protect the confidentiality of the data room's contents. Virtual data rooms are often made available by third party providers of such services and the management of their contents for any particular transaction is often delegated by the seller to its advisers. Physical data rooms often take the

---

[11] i.e. agreement that a person (usually a potential purchaser or its advisers) may have access to certain documents, information and related explanations on condition that that person may not rely on those documents etc. and is owed no duty of care in relation to them. 'Hold harmless' agreements generally apply to documents etc. which were not prepared for the purposes of the transaction in relation to which access to them is granted. Rather they were prepared for some other purpose and could not have had in contemplation the interests of the person now seeking access to them, e.g. the contents of audit files or work papers in relation to completion, submission and agreement of tax returns.

form of office space at a neutral site away from the seller's premises so as to minimise disruption to the seller's business and to preserve the confidentiality of the transaction within the seller's organisation for as long as commercially necessary.

3.4. Reporting tax due diligence findings

See Chapter 6.

3.5. Review of the contract for the sale/purchase of the target

Tax issues and exposures identified by due diligence are commonly addressed by means of contractual protection in the agreement for the sale and purchase of the target's shares. Accordingly, review of this agreement is often part of the tax due diligence process. See Chapter 8.

3.6. Timing

The time required by each of the above phases, fieldwork in particular, will vary widely from transaction to transaction. Among other things, it will depend on the extent of the agreed scope and the extent and timing of access to the information, documents and people necessary to fulfil that scope. As a general rule, it is difficult to complete any meaningful full scope tax due diligence review of a single company in less than a week; and a substantial tax due diligence review of a complex cross-border group may take several months. However, limited scope tax due diligence, or due diligence focused on one or more discrete tax issues or exposures, can often be achieved in a few days, especially when based extensively on interviews with management with only limited review of documents. See 4.2.10.

4. Defining the Scope of a Tax Due Diligence Review

4.1. Introduction

In many ways, tax due diligence is the most important of all the tax workstreams for any transaction. It informs all the crucial tax decisions which arise between the origination of a deal and its completion; and it provides the framework and support for:

- tax-efficient structuring and funding of the transaction;
- tax aspects of the share or asset purchase agreement (including in particular warranties and indemnities); and
- the tax assumptions on which the purchaser's valuation model or hypothesis is based.

In short, without the factual underpinnings which tax due diligence provides, it is simply not possible to structure or fund a transaction tax-efficiently, nor to model its tax effects or to negotiate a favourable contract for its completion.

So tax due diligence should receive careful attention at the planning stage to ensure that it is exploited thoroughly and that its full value can be realised. It should never be regarded as a commodity and the temptation to treat it as such should be resisted when commissioning a tax due diligence exercise and agreeing its scope. The full benefits of a tax due diligence review are rarely realised when its scope has been defined imprecisely, for example as 'high level', 'standard' or 'full' scope or even, like catalogue shopping, as 'small-', 'medium-' or 'large-scale'. Money is also often wasted on tax due diligence where its scope is defined by a limit on its cost, as in 'as much tax due diligence as can be achieved for £20,000'.

This is not to say that tax due diligence should always be comprehensive and correspondingly expensive. Rather, it should be focused on the specific tax matters which are capable of affecting the value which the transaction in question is expected to generate. And it can be layered such that time and money is expended on investigating a tax issue or exposure only to the precise extent necessary to enable a particular transaction decision to be made. There is little point in analysing tax matters which, while interesting, will have no bearing on:

- the decision whether or not to proceed with a transaction;
- the transaction structure;
- price or value; or
- the terms of the contract.

4.2. Defining scope

Tax due diligence should be focused on the specific tax matters which are capable of affecting, positively or negatively, the value which the transaction in question is expected to generate. So the first step in defining the scope of tax due diligence is to understand what these matters are.

4.2.1. Type of due diligence

First and foremost, this will depend on the type of due diligence involved. See Chapter 2 for a description of the three principal types. In summary, the scope of:

- pre-acquisition or buy-side tax due diligence should be defined so as to provide the purchaser with sufficient information to address the matters which will affect the decision to buy;
- vendor or sell-side tax due diligence should be defined so as to provide potential purchasers with sufficient information to make reasonable bids without extensive due diligence of their own and without a heavily marked-up draft contract to accompany their bids; and
- long form tax due diligence should be defined so as to provide sufficient comfort to the company, sponsor or nominated adviser that there are no tax issues or exposures which could materially and adversely affect the progress of the transaction in question, and to provide a proper understanding and explanation of tax issues or exposures which require disclosure in the prospectus, admission document etc. As a matter of normal market practice, there is generally no limitation of the due diligence provider's liability in relation to long form due diligence. In consequence, long form tax due diligence tends to be particularly thorough and its scope is rarely limited.

4.2.2. Value

In light of the above, the party commissioning tax due diligence should articulate the factors driving the value expected to be derived from the contemplated transaction. This in turn will help to identify the tax matters which are pertinent to those value drivers. See Examples 6, 7 and 8.

Example 6

For example, the future utilisation of tax losses to shelter post-acquisition profits from tax may be fundamental to a purchaser's investment decision. Where this is the case, the scope of tax due diligence should focus on these losses before any more general tax due diligence is performed, specifically to answer the following key questions.

- What sort of losses are they?
- Are they capable of sheltering the future profits as expected?

- In what years or periods did the losses arise?
- Have any claims already been made to use similar losses?
- Have such claims been agreed by the relevant tax authorities?
- Is there any other evidence to suggest that the tax authorities are unlikely to challenge the losses?
- To what extent are the losses likely to be required to cover pre-completion tax exposures?
- Are there any time limits on the period for which the losses may be carried forward?
- Is there any risk that the post-acquisition availability of the losses could be challenged or denied on the basis of change of ownership or other anti-avoidance provisions?

Correspondingly, the scope of vendor tax due diligence should be defined so as to provide potential purchasers with as much reassurance on the above questions as possible in order:

- to encourage them to reflect the tax losses in their bids; or
- at least to take the tax losses into account when marking up the draft contract to provide protection for pre-completion tax liabilities.

Example 7

Sometimes, within the historical period potentially open to audit or adjustment by the tax authorities, a target group will have entered into material transactions designed to reorganise its corporate structure. Such transactions are often effected without adverse tax consequences. This may be because of the circumstances of the particular transaction (e.g. high tax base costs, low market valuations or the existence of tax losses) or because legislation permits them to be effected on a tax-free or tax-neutral basis. In either case, claims or elections may be necessary or clearances may be desirable. If, however, the tax-free or tax-neutral basis for such transactions is not sustainable, the consequences for a purchaser could be disastrous. In such situations, the scope of a purchaser's tax due diligence should focus on these historical transactions before anything else.

Correspondingly, the scope of vendor tax due diligence should be defined so as to provide potential purchasers with as much information as is needed to support the tax-free or tax-neutral basis of the transaction in question.

Example 8

A purchaser may wish to reorganise a target group post-acquisition so as to integrate it within the purchaser's existing group structure more efficiently. In this case, it may be sensible to focus the scope of tax due diligence on the information needed to confirm whether or not such a reorganisation can be effected tax efficiently, specifically on:

- the tax base costs of any shareholdings or assets to be reorganised; and
- the existence of tax losses or any other reliefs which could be used to shelter any tax charges which might arise.

Once the specific tax matters capable of affecting value have been established, the following factors will influence the scope of tax due diligence.

4.2.3. The existence and extent of reliable tax warranties and indemnities

Before including a particular matter within the scope of a purchaser's tax due diligence review or deciding in how much depth to investigate an issue, it is worthwhile first considering whether any tax liabilities to which such matter could give rise are likely to be for the seller's account under the terms of the contract. In particular, will they be covered by tax warranties and indemnities? If a purchaser is confident that reliable contractual protection will be available in connection with a particular matter, then:

- that matter may often be excluded from the scope of tax due diligence; or
- the depth to which it is to be investigated in accordance with that scope may be much reduced.

The seller may have indicated from an early stage whether or not contractual protection will be offered. For example, this may be stated specifically in a vendor tax due diligence report or process letter from the investment bank acting for the seller; or a draft contract may be provided to bidders in an auction sale (see 2.2 and 8.3.5). If the seller has not given early indication of the level of contractual protection to be offered, it may be sensible, depending on the commercial circumstances, to broach the subject with the seller before defining the scope of the purchaser's tax due diligence.

Equally, when defining the scope of vendor tax due diligence, sellers should consider the extent to which they may be prepared to offer contractual protection to potential purchasers for any tax matters which might otherwise become contentious. It may be expedient, for example, for the seller to offer potential purchasers an indemnity if this will avoid protracted negotiations over price, contractual terms or the need for further due diligence, in particular where the seller is confident that the risk of doing so is low. The tax implications of pre-sale reorganisations (see Example 7), in advance of which advice and opinions are usually obtained, are often dealt with in this way. Tax warranties and indemnities are also often provided with regard to dormant target group companies. This usually avoids the need for a due diligence review of these companies to confirm their dormant status.

The above, of course, assumes that any contractual protection can be relied upon. Before excluding any matter from the scope of tax due diligence, a purchaser will need to be satisfied:

- that the party giving any tax warranty or indemnity will be financially sound and accessible; and
- that any contractual limitations or restrictions on claims under the tax warranties and indemnities will not materially undermine the protection which they might otherwise afford.

Even where the purchaser is satisfied in relation to both of the above, it may still be unwise to exclude a matter from the scope of tax due diligence altogether. A purchaser will still want to be aware of the historical tax exposures which might arise once the target business has been acquired and of any inappropriate practices or procedures in relation to tax which might lead to material tax exposures in the future. The purchaser will also want to understand the general tax philosophy of the target from a reputational perspective. But the existence of reliable tax warranties and indemnities is likely to reduce the depth of tax due diligence required.

Contractual protection given to the seller by a previous owner of the target, the assignability of such protection to the purchaser and the consequent effects on scope are considered at 8.4.

4.2.4. The existence and extent of any vendor due diligence or vendor assistance report provided by the seller

Once confined to only the largest sale processes, vendor due diligence is now commonplace. See 2.2. The successful bidder should normally be able to rely on any vendor tax due diligence report provided by the seller. See 2.2. Where this is the case, the scope of a purchaser's pre-acquisition tax due diligence review should avoid duplication of matters adequately covered by vendor due diligence.

Instead, the scope of the purchaser's tax due diligence should generally focus on the following matters (see Chapter 7):

- review of the scope and conduct of the vendor tax due diligence report to identify any limitations or restrictions which detract from its quality and which may need to be supplemented by additional pre-acquisition tax due diligence;

- review of the vendor tax due diligence report to identify any differences of opinion;
- explanation of how the issues and exposures identified in the vendor tax due diligence report might affect a specific purchaser and recommendations as to how that purchaser should address them in the context of the transaction;
- request for information on, or explanations of, matters omitted from or inadequately covered by the vendor tax due diligence report.

4.2.5. The existence and extent of any tax losses or other tax assets within the target company or group

The target company or group may have tax losses or other tax assets which may be available to shelter pre-completion tax liabilities. Where the existence of these is not relied on by the purchaser or reflected in the purchase price, they are essentially a cushion for historical tax exposures, reducing the extent of the purchaser's risk. Accordingly, the existence of such tax losses or other tax assets may reduce the scope of the purchaser's pre-acquisition tax due diligence (see 8.3.4 and 9.1) and/or raise the level of materiality applied to it; although it is also likely to shift the emphasis of due diligence to investigation of the validity of the losses or assets.

4.2.6. Audit file review

The auditors of the target company or group may be willing, on a hold harmless basis, to provide a potential purchaser with access to the audit files in relation to the last audited financial statements. From the perspective of tax due diligence, the audit files may be of limited value to a potential purchaser in that:

- they will have been prepared for a different purpose and to a different level of materiality;
- they are unlikely to contain detailed information on the target's tax position; and
- the purchaser will not be able to rely directly on information contained within them.

However, any offer to review the target's audit files should generally always be accepted by a potential purchaser because, notwithstanding the above limitations, the files may:

- disclose analysis of the tax balances, both current and deferred, in the audited balance sheet; and
- indicate potential tax exposures or areas of tax risk on which the purchaser's other due diligence procedures might usefully focus.

4.2.7. Materiality

Materiality will clearly influence the scope of tax due diligence. Nevertheless, it is surprising how often tax due diligence commences without a clear agreement on the appropriate level of materiality to be applied.

Purchasers should always have some idea of the scale of exposures (both individually and in aggregate) which would begin to concern them and potentially affect their investment decision.

Equally, sellers should have some idea of the degree of materiality which strikes a balance between:

- providing potential purchasers with the material information necessary to form a view of the value of the business for sale; and
- providing them with too much immaterial detail which is unlikely to be relevant to their valuations.

The latter can actually detract from the sale process by confusing the key messages about a target's tax position which the sell-side due diligence should be conveying. And by disclosing a large number of immaterial tax issues or exposures, a sell-side tax due diligence report can give the impression that there may be failures or weaknesses in the management of the target's tax position.

Reporting immaterial issues or exposures identified during the course of a tax due diligence review can also increase the risk of the due diligence provider. Specifically, it implies that the scope of the tax due diligence review has been designed to identify all exposures of similar or greater magnitude. In practice, tax due diligence reports tend to include immaterial items simply because such items have been identified and the report writer is reluctant to leave them out. In the rare circumstances where there are good commercial reasons to report immaterial tax issues or exposures, suitable caveats should be included. See Example 9.

Example 9

In performing our tax due diligence procedures and identifying potential tax exposures, an [annual/aggregate] threshold materiality level of an additional [£/€/$ X] of [cash taxes/taxable income] was used [per jurisdiction/per entity/per issue]. However, we report certain tax exposures which fall below this materiality threshold where we have become aware of them during the course of our work; but it cannot be inferred from their inclusion that all exposures which fall below the above materiality threshold have been identified by our tax due diligence procedures.

For the link between materiality and the financial limits on claims in the contract for the sale and purchase of the target's shares, see 8.6.4.

4.2.8. Jurisdictions to be included within scope

A target may be a multinational business with operations in a number of jurisdictions. To include all of these jurisdictions within scope can add considerably to the cost of a tax due diligence review. This is largely because most tax matters, compliance in particular, tend generally to be managed at the level of the target's local operations in each jurisdiction rather than centrally at holding company or head office level. A tax due diligence review which includes within its scope more than one jurisdiction requires tax due diligence advisers for each with knowledge and experience of the local tax regime. This contrasts with financial due diligence much of which can be performed from the centre without the need for local advisers.

Accordingly, once matters 4.2.1 to 4.2.7 have been taken into account, the next matter to consider should be which jurisdictions will need to be included within the scope of the tax due diligence review and which may be excluded without increasing risk beyond a commercially acceptable level.

Materiality will clearly be important in this context. It is often the case that, while a target may operate in a large number of jurisdictions, its principal activities may be confined to a more limited number. It is often therefore possible and appropriate to limit the scope of a tax due diligence review to those jurisdictions which provide sufficient coverage of the business as a whole, i.e. those jurisdictions which represent, say, 80% of:

- turnover;
- profit before tax;
- number of employees; or
- some other measure appropriate for the particular circumstances, e.g. the existence of material tax losses.

Additional jurisdictions may then be added to the scope to address specific concerns which may not strictly be material but which may be important to the transaction, e.g. to test the tax compliance in a jurisdiction where operations have historically been small but which are forecast to grow rapidly in the foreseeable future.

4.2.9. Legal entities to be included within scope

An approach similar to that described in 4.2.8 can be used to decide which legal entities should be included within the scope of a tax due diligence review.

In any particular jurisdiction, the target business often comprises more than one legal entity. Not all legal entities within a jurisdiction will need to be included within scope. Some may be holding companies requiring only limited review while others may be dormant. So in any given jurisdiction it may be possible to limit the scope of a tax due diligence review to those legal entities which provide sufficient coverage of the jurisdiction as a whole, i.e. those jurisdictions which represent, say, 80 % of:

- turnover;
- profit before tax;
- number of employees; or
- some other measure appropriate for the particular circumstances, e.g. the existence of material tax losses.

4.2.10. Tiered approach

The approach described in 4.2.8 and 4.2.9 will inevitably lead to the exclusion from scope of one or more jurisdictions or legal entities. This may be wholly appropriate to the circumstances of the particular transaction.

However, as an alternative to complete exclusion, it may be sensible instead to identify those jurisdictions or legal entities which, whilst not sufficiently material for a full scope tax due diligence review, nevertheless still merit some level of due diligence. This is commonly the case where the materiality of jurisdictions or legal entities declines in clearly defined steps as in Example 10.

Example 10

A target group comprises 15 operating companies in 10 jurisdictions with the following sales, gross profit, EBITDA and total assets for the year ended 31 December 200X:

	Sales	*Gross Profit*	*EBITDA*	*Total Assets*
	€'000	*€'000*	*€'000*	*€'000*
Sweden				
Company A	26,086	12,451	8,875	45,345
Company B	5,441	1,510	668	4,617
Italy				
Company C	32,307	9,342	3,825	64,792
Netherlands				
Company D	39,951	7,934	3,758	39,576
Company E	2,747	(244)	(679)	1,223

	Sales	*Gross Profit*	*EBITDA*	*Total Assets*
Norway				
Company F	6,629	1,368	648	4,420
India				
Company G	676	294	144	1,460
Company H	5,657	1,037	455	9,862
China				
Company I	7,809	1,981	1,171	6,624
Company J	490	121	(89)	2,002
Australia				
Company K	5,132	830	(25)	5,872
Brazil				
Company L	4,707	944	235	2,818
US				
Company M	6,848	2,065	46	7,154
Uruguay				
Company N	58	1	(44)	1,104
Company O	2,347	428	119	2,108
	-------------	-------------	-------------	-------------
Total	146,885	40,062	19,107	198,977
	=======	=======	=======	=======

Companies A, B, I, J and K have tax losses carried forward as at 31 December 2007 as follows (in €'000):

A	25,442
B	1,129
I	432

J	176
K	366

Companies A, C and D are the largest three companies and represent between them 67.0% of sales, 74.2% of gross profit, 86.1% of EBITDA and 75.2% of total assets. The scope of the tax due diligence review of the target group should therefore include A, C and D as a minimum; and full scope tax due diligence is recommended for these three.

A, C and D operate in Sweden, Italy and The Netherlands respectively. B also operates in Sweden and E in The Netherlands. It may therefore be appropriate to extend the scope in these two jurisdictions to include B and E, especially because B has tax losses carried forward and E is likely to be part of a tax consolidated group.

Of the remaining target group companies, a clear distinction of materiality can be drawn between F, H, I, K, L, M and O on the one hand and G, J and N on the other.

Consideration should be given to including F, H, I, K, L, M and O within the scope of tax due diligence in order to extend the coverage of the target group. However, these companies need not necessarily be the subject of full scope tax due diligence but may be reviewed to a more limited extent. A proforma scope for such a limited tax due diligence review is suggested at 4.5 below.

It is likely to be possible to exclude G, J and N from scope without materially undermining the integrity of the review.

It would also be possible to exclude O from scope on the basis that on some measures of materiality it falls below F, H, I, K, L and M and there appear to be no other tax-specific reasons for including it.

In any event, as a precursor to any level of substantive tax due diligence, it may be appropriate to commence with an initial meeting with the management of the target company or group (and possibly also its tax advisers) to explore what tax issues or exposures could exist in the target and which areas of its tax affairs might require detailed investigation subsequently.

Where the target management is receptive to this approach and is prepared to participate in full and frank discussion, such meetings alone can often enable the tax due diligence adviser quickly to achieve a number of objectives early in the transaction process:

- to form a preliminary view of the material tax issues or exposures identified by management as currently affecting the target company or group;

- to form a preliminary view of the material tax issues or exposures which, although not yet identified by management as currently affecting the target company or group, are suggested by the facts disclosed to the purchaser's tax due diligence adviser at the meeting;
- to enable an initial key issues status report to be provided to the purchaser at an early stage of the transaction; and
- to scope and plan the subsequent phases of tax due diligence fieldwork required:

  to substantiate the principal conclusions drawn from the meeting by the tax due diligence adviser;

  to substantiate the material facts, representations and assurances provided by management at the meeting; and

  to investigate those matters which, for whatever reason, were not addressed at the meeting.

If and to the extent that the material facts, representations and assurances provided by management at the meeting cannot be substantiated by subsequent fieldwork, it may be appropriate for a purchaser to seek warranties to support them. See 8.5.

To derive maximum value from the meeting, the agenda and questions should be carefully planned in advance and the meeting itself should be managed effectively by the tax due diligence adviser.

Notwithstanding the benefits of the above phased approach to scoping a tax due diligence exercise, purchasers should be made aware of the limitations of initial meetings with management. Appropriate wording to describe these limitations is set out below for suggested inclusion in any document recording the scope of such an exercise. See Example 11.

Example 11

As [agreed/instructed/requested] by you, we have discussed the tax position of [target company] with its management [names of specific target company representatives] at a meeting on [date]. Our discussion covered [corporation tax, VAT, employment taxes etc.].

On the basis only of this discussion, we report to you below those tax matters raised by management which may be material to your assessment of the proposed acquisition.

Please note that our work does not on its own constitute a tax due diligence review and cannot be relied upon as such. In particular, we have relied exclusively on representations made to us by management at the meeting without any independent testing or verification on our part. Accordingly, our work may not have identified all tax matters relevant to your assessment of the proposed acquisition; and there may be additional tax matters which were not raised by management but which would materially affect your assessment had they been disclosed to us.

4.2.11. Taxes to be included

Having determined which jurisdictions and legal entities should be included within the scope of tax due diligence (see 4.2.8 and 4.2.9), consideration should next be given to the types of tax which will need to included in order to address the questions of value identified at 4.2.2 above.

Broadly, what is referred to as 'full scope' tax due diligence will typically include corporate income taxes, sales-based taxes and employment or payroll taxes.

For the UK this translates as corporation tax, Value Added Tax ('VAT') and Pay-As-You-Earn ('PAYE') and National Insurance contributions ('NIC').

It should be noted, however, that normal market practice in this respect can differ from jurisdiction to jurisdiction. Anyone commissioning tax due diligence covering more than one country should not generally assume that a similar scope will be employed in each but should seek specific confirmation that this will be the case. To discover that, say, employment taxes have not been reviewed as part of a 'full scope' tax due diligence exercise in a particular territory may be hard to recify late in a transaction.

Where a cross-border tax due diligence exercise is project-managed and co-ordinated centrally, as will usually be the case, it is the responsibility of the project manager to ensure consistency of scope in all the countries covered.

4.2.12. The period(s) to be reviewed

Generally, market practice is to review tax returns for all tax periods which are still potentially open to audit or adjustment by the tax authorities assuming:

- that sufficient disclosure has been made to those tax authorities to prevent them from reopening returns for periods which would otherwise be closed; and
- the absence of negligence or fraud.

As with the types of tax included in the scope of a standard tax due diligence review, normal market practice can vary from jurisdiction to jurisdiction. For example, in some jurisdictions it is market practice to review a set number of complete fiscal years regardless of the statute of limitations. Years further back than this will only be investigated if the review of the years originally within scope suggests a need to do so (e.g. in Finland it is normal market practice to review three years and only to go back further if these three years suggest that it is necessary, e.g. if there are concerns about the amount or quality of tax losses brought forward). For cross-border tax due diligence exercises, careful project management is therefore essential to ensure consistency of scope in all the countries covered.

4.2.13. How much tax due diligence will actually be possible?

4.2.1 to 4.2.12 above describe factors which can determine how much tax due diligence is desirable with regard to any given transaction. In practice, however, the circumstances of a particular transaction may prevent the completion of the desired scope which may need to be modified accordingly.

For example, the level of access to information and/or target management may be restricted by the seller, especially in auctions (see 2.2) or bids for listed companies.

Time constraints may also limit the extent of possible tax due diligence.

In these circumstances, recourse will be necessary to publicly available information (see Chapter 5) and, where commercially appropriate, to contractual means of protection against historical tax risks and forcing disclosure of information (see Chapter 8).

4.3. A Generic/Proforma Scope for a Full Scope Tax Due Diligence Review

The scope of any particular tax due diligence review will clearly be determined by the factors described at 4.2 above. Set out below at 4.3.1 and 4.3.2 are generic/proforma scopes for both pre-acquisition and vendor tax due diligence reviews. Set out below at 4.4.1 and 4.4.2 are the corresponding generic/pro forma information requests. These have a bias towards UK tax due diligence but are sufficiently general in nature to be regarded as the starting point for scope and corresponding information request for due diligence in any jurisdiction before revision to reflect the particular circumstances of a specific transaction.

4.3.1. Pre-acquisition or buy-side tax due diligence

- Review the status of the corporation tax returns for the material entities within the target group for all years/periods still potentially open to audit or adjustment by the tax authorities.
- Review open correspondence with the tax authorities in connection with

the returns for all years/periods still potentially open to audit or adjustment by the tax authorities.

- Review and comment on any anticipated tax losses carried forward and any other tax reliefs or assets (including in particular closing tax depreciation pools) as at the last balance sheet date.
- Review and comment on whether the proposed transaction (including any pre-sale reorganisation) will crystallise any corporation tax liabilities or will have any other adverse tax effects, including:

  de-grouping or exit charges;
  any other crystallisation of deferred gains;
  impact on any tax losses carried forward or any other tax reliefs or assets; and/or
  impact on any deferred tax assets or liabilities.
- Review and comment on the profit & loss account tax charges and balance sheet tax balances, including both current and deferred, in the latest consolidated financial statements of the target group/company.
- Review the VAT/sales tax compliance of the target group/company, typically by means of a detailed VAT/sales tax due diligence questionnaire to be completed by the target's management. In the UK, any such questionnaire should include, but should not be limited to, the following matters:

  the target's VAT compliance history;
  the main types of supply made and received by the target and the VAT-status of each;
  whether the target is partially exempt for VAT purposes, including details of any partial exemption method applicable;
  any capital goods scheme adjustments applicable to the target;
  the target's property portfolio;
  any supplies of goods and services made by the target outside the UK;
  the target's Customs Duty position;
  any VAT planning implemented by the target; and
  the most recent HMRC visit to inspect the target's VAT position, including details of its findings.
- Review the employment tax compliance of the target group/company, typically by means of a detailed employment tax due diligence questionnaire to be completed by the target's management. In the UK, any such questionnaire should include, but should not be limited to, the following matters:

  the target's PAYE procedures and compliance history;

the most recent HMRC Employer Compliance Review;
expense and authorisation procedures;
business and staff entertainment;
travel and subsistence;
benefits-in-kind, including cars, telephones, living accommodation, relocation packages, vouchers and incentives, beneficial loans etc.;
employees sent to work abroad;
foreign nationals assigned to the UK;
the PAYE and NIC status/treatment of contractors;
the construction industry scheme;
the PAYE and NIC treatment of termination payments;
any remuneration planning; and
details of any share schemes or awards.

- Describe and quantify any material potential tax exposures and report on:

  whether they represent permanent or timing adjustments to the filed tax returns;
  whether they are likely to be sheltered by tax losses carried forward or any other tax reliefs or assets; and/or
  the extent to which provision has been made for them in the target's financial statements.

- Comment at a high level on the thin capitalisation and transfer pricing position of the target group/company. Note that, for reasons of cost and timing, a detailed review or benchmarking of the position is not normally included within the scope of a tax due diligence review unless specifically required.
- Review the draft contract for the purchase of the target's shares (as tax advisers, not lawyers) and comment on the contractual protection offered in light of items identified in due diligence.

4.3.2. Vendor or sell-side tax due diligence

- Review the status of the corporation tax returns for the material entities within the target group for all years/periods still potentially open to audit or adjustment by the tax authorities.
- Review open correspondence with the tax authorities in connection with the returns for all years/periods still potentially open to audit or adjustment by the tax authorities.
- Review and comment on any anticipated tax losses carried forward and any other tax reliefs or assets (including in particular closing tax depreciation pools) as at the last balance sheet date.
- Review and comment on whether the proposed transaction (including any

pre-sale reorganisation) will crystallise any corporation tax liabilities or will have any other adverse tax effects, including:

de-grouping or exit charges;
any other crystallisation of deferred gains;
impact on any tax losses carried forward or any other tax reliefs or assets; and/or
impact on any deferred tax assets or liabilities.

- Review and comment on the profit & loss account tax charges and balance sheet tax balances, including both current and deferred, in the latest consolidated financial statements of the target group/company.
- Review the VAT/sales tax compliance of the target group/company, typically by means of a detailed VAT/sales tax due diligence questionnaire to be completed by the target's management. In the UK, any such questionnaire should include, but should not be limited to, the following matters:

the target's VAT compliance history;
the main types of supply made and received by the target and the VAT status of each;
whether the target is partially exempt for VAT purposes, including details of any partial exemption method applicable;
any capital goods scheme adjustments applicable to the target;
the target's property portfolio;
any supplies of goods and services made by the target outside the UK;
the target's Customs Duty position;
any VAT planning implemented by the target; and
the most recent HMRC visit to inspect the target's VAT position, including details of its findings.

- Review the employment tax compliance of the target group/company, typically by means of a detailed employment tax due diligence questionnaire to be completed by the target's management. In the UK, any such questionnaire should include, but should not be limited to, the following matters:

the target's PAYE procedures and compliance history;
the most recent HMRC Employer Compliance Review;
expense and authorisation procedures;
business and staff entertainment;
travel and subsistence;
benefits-in-kind, including cars, telephones, living accommodation, relocation packages, vouchers and incentives, beneficial loans etc.;

employees sent to work abroad;
foreign nationals assigned to the UK;
the PAYE and NIC status/treatment of contractors;
the construction industry scheme;
the PAYE and NIC treatment of termination payments;
any remuneration planning; and
details of any share schemes or awards.

- Describe and quantify any material potential tax exposures and report on:

  whether they represent permanent or timing adjustments to the filed tax returns;
  whether they are likely to be sheltered by tax losses carried forward or any other tax reliefs or assets; and
  the extent to which provision has been made for them in the financial statements of the target group/company.

- Comment at a high level on the thin capitalisation and transfer pricing position of the target group/company. Note that, for reasons of cost and timing, a detailed review or benchmarking of the position is not normally included within the scope of a tax due diligence review unless specifically required.
- Review the assumptions in respect of corporation tax used in the earnings and cash flow forecasts/projections and comment in light of applicable tax law and the historical tax position of the target group/company.

4.4. A Generic/Proforma Information Request for a Tax Due Diligence Review

4.4.1. Pre-acquisition or buy-side tax due diligence

- A diagram of the corporate structure of the target group, together with a summary of the status and activities of each target entity, i.e. trading, investment, holding, dormant etc.
- Copies of corporation tax, VAT/sales tax and employment tax returns and supporting caculations and schedules for all years/periods still potentially open to audit or adjustment by the tax authorities.
- Copies of any open correspondence with any tax authorities.
- Details of all historical or pre-sale restructuring undertaken, including copies of any advice or opinions sought.
- Copies of the calculations and schedules supporting the profit & loss account tax charges and balance sheet tax balances, including both current and deferred, in the latest consolidated financial statements of the target group/company.

- Access to management and/or advisers who deal with the corporation tax, VAT/sales tax and employment tax affairs of the target group/company.
- Details of the findings of the most recent tax authority audits or inspections for all taxes[12] .
- Draft contract for the purchase of the target's shares, including any tax indemnity and warranties.
- Access to legal advisers responsible for negotiating/agreeing the draft contract for the purchase of the target's shares on behalf of the purchaser.

4.4.2. Vendor or sell-side tax due diligence

- A diagram of the corporate structure of the target group, together with a summary of the status and activities of each target entity, i.e. trading, investment, holding, dormant etc.
- Copies of corporation tax, VAT/sales tax and employment tax returns and supporting caculations and schedules for all years/periods still potentially open to audit or adjustment by the tax authorities.
- Copies of any open correspondence with any tax authorities.
- Details of all historical or pre-sale restructuring undertaken, including copies of any advice or opinions sought.
- Copies of the calculations and schedules supporting the profit & loss account tax charges and balance sheet tax balances, including both current and deferred, in the latest consolidated financial statements of the target group/company.
- Access to management and/or advisers who deal with the corporation tax, VAT/sales tax and employment tax affairs of the target group/company.
- Details of the findings of the most recent tax authority audits or inspections for all taxes[13] .
- Details of the tax assumptions made in the earnings and cash flow forecasts/projections.
- Access to management and/or advisers responsible for the preparation of the earnings and cash flow forecasts/projections.

---

[12]In the UK, this could usefully be extended to include the outcome of any HMRC Risk Review of the target, including the Risk Rating and Risk Review Summary Template.

[13]See footnote 12 above.

4.5. A Generic/Proforma Scope/Information Request for a Limited Scope Tax Due Diligence Review

This more limited scope/information request may be appropriate where less material entities within a target group are to be included within the scope of a tax due diligence review to extend its coverage but not to the same depth as the more material entities. See Example 10. Because it takes the form of a questionnaire, it will not necessarily be supported by independently reviewed documents. However, it assumes greater authority if it can be completed by the relevant target company's auditors rather than its management. In any event, a purchaser is likely to require its salient points to be warranted. See Chapter 8.

4.5.1. Corporate income tax

- What is the status of the company's tax compliance? i.e.:

  Have all returns been filed by their due dates?

  Have all tax liabilities declared in those returns been paid?

  Are there any outstanding issues or enquiries in connection with those returns?

- Are there any material contentious issues or areas of risk (whether or not already under enquiry by any tax authority) which might give rise to tax liabilities over and above those referred to above? Has any provision for these been made in the latest financial statements?
- When were the last audits by the tax authorities; did any significant problems arise; and, if so, have these been resolved?
- If there are losses or other tax assets carried forward as at the latest accounting date please provide details of the relevant amounts. Are these recognised in the latest financial statements?

4.5.2. Employment taxes and Value Added Tax/sales tax

- What is the status of the company's tax compliance? i.e.:

  Have all returns been filed by their due dates?

  Have all tax liabilities declared in those returns been paid?

  Are there any outstanding issues or enquiries in connection with those returns?

- Are there any known problems or potential liabilities in respect of the company's compliance with the relevant regulations?
- When were the last audits by the tax authorities; did any significant problems arise; and, if so, have these been resolved?

4.5.3. Tax in accounts

- Are all outstanding tax liabilities fully provided for in the company's latest balance sheet?

- Does the effective tax rate in the company's profit and loss account for the last three years differ materially from the statutory tax rate applicable to the company? If so, please reconcile the two rates.
- Are all deferred tax liabilities fully provided for and/or are all deferred tax assets fully recognised in the company's latest balance sheet? Please provide details.

4.6. A Generic/Proforma Information Request for a Stamp Taxes Due Diligence Review

A tax due diligence review does not generally include stamp taxes as a matter of course but its scope is sometimes extended specifically to include them. Where stamp taxes are included within the scope of a tax due diligence review, the following generic/proforma information request may be helpful. See 9.16 and 10.1.8.

4.6.1. General

- A diagram of the corporate structure of the target group.
- Details of any target group companies holding charitable status.

4.6.2. Stamp Duty/SDLT on UK real estate

- Details of any UK property held either directly or indirectly (e.g. through partnerships) where the market value or consideration on acquisition would have exceeded £500,000, including:

  the full address and postcode; and
  the nature of the interest held (e.g. freehold, leasehold or other tenure).
- Where any of the above property is a lease or other tenure, full details of that lease or other tenure.
- Where legal title is held by another entity, details of the entity holding legal title and how the split title structure arose.
- Details of any relief claimed on acquisition.
- Details of any planning used on acquisition.
- Has the acquisition been registered at the Land Registry?
- Has any property been transferred within the target group since acquisition? If so, when?
- Was any relief claimed on transfer within the target group or was stamp duty/SDLT paid?
- Details of any intra-group leases granted or varied, including the dates of such grant or variation and whether any relief was claimed.

- Details of any contingent or uncertain consideration.
- Details of any disposals of property acquired by the target company or group since 1 December 2003.

4.6.3. SDRT/Stamp Duty on securities

- Confirmation that the name of the beneficial owner of all UK shares held by the target company or group (including any subsidiary companies) appears on the register of members.

4.6.4. Other property

- Did the target company or group acquire the trade and assets of another company prior to 1 December 2003? If so, details of any assets still held, including:

  the date of acquisition;
  whether stamp duty was paid; and
  whether any reliefs were claimed.

- Details of any other significant assets (e.g. loans) held by the target company or group and acquired prior to 1 December 2003 including:

  the date of acquisition;
  whether stamp duty was paid; and
  whether any reliefs were claimed.

4.6.5. Partnerships

- Details of any partnership of which any of the target group companies is a member, including in particular any UK property (or other partnership interests) held by the partnership.
- Details of any land transferred from one or more partners, or a person connected with them, on or after 19 October 2004, including:

  any SDLT paid; and
  any reliefs claimed.

4.6.6. Sundry

- Copies of land register extracts for all land interests held.
- Copies of SDLT returns.
- In relation to previous company reorganisations:

  evidence that all Stamp Duty and SDRT has been paid, and/or
  details of any relief claimed.

5. Publicly Available Information

Full scope tax due diligence is only possible with the co-operation of the seller and/or target. Generally, it assumes unrestricted access to:

- the target's books and records insofar as they are relevant to tax;
- those members of the target's management responsible for tax matters; and sometimes also
- the target's tax advisers.

Inevitably, however, there will be occasions when such access is limited or even denied altogether.

Access limitations may only be temporary, e.g. until a particular phase of an auction process has been reached (see 2.2) or until a particular member of target management is made aware of what, up to that point, may have been a confidential transaction.

However, access limitations may also be permanent. This will obviously be the case with regard to hostile bids for public companies; but even where a takeover bid for a public company is recommended to shareholders by the board, the company will be keen to limit the information made available to the bidder because of the obligation imposed by *Rule 20.2 of The City Code on Takeovers and Mergers*. Specifically, *Rule 20.2* requires that 'Any information, including particulars of shareholders, given to one offeror or potential offeror, whether named or unnamed, must, on request, be given equally and promptly to another offeror or bona fide potential offeror even if that other offeror is less welcome…'

In any event, whether or not access to information is to be restricted, some level of information about a target's tax position is always helpful prior to the formal commencement of due diligence fieldwork. In particular, even a basic level of information can often provide an initial indication of the target's corporate structure and possible areas of tax risk. This in turn can help the tax due diligence adviser to scope, plan and focus subsequent due diligence and to refine what would otherwise be generic information requests.

In most jurisdictions, private and/or public companies are obliged to make publicly available a certain level of information about their financial position, e.g. annual financial statements (or summaries of them). Furthermore, many companies make available on their websites more information than is strictly required by law. The detail and extent of this publicly available information will vary from jurisdiction to jurisdiction and in some cases it may be of only limited value for the purposes of tax due diligence. However, at the very least it may indicate the areas of the world in which a target operates, the extent of its transactions with related parties, whether it is taxpaying, whether it has tax losses or other tax assets, whether it has subsidiaries, its effective tax rate, whether it has share schemes etc. Accordingly, such publicly available information should always be the starting point of any tax due diligence exercise; and sellers and purchasers alike will expect their advisers to have made use of it.

A general guide to the minimum information publicly available in a sample of jurisdictions is set out at 5.1 to 5.29.

5.1. UK

A very substantial amount of information about a UK company (e.g. news items, broker reports, share price and trading data etc.) can be obtained by a search of the internet, including the company's own website. Some of this information may only be accessible via one of a large number of web-based company research services available for a subscription.

In the UK, the principal source of publicly available company information is Companies House[14] at which certain information is required to be filed by the following entities:

- companies incorporated in Great Britain under the *Companies Acts*;
- companies incorporated outside Great Britain with a branch or place of business in Great Britain;
- limited partnerships;
- limited liability partnerships (LLPs);
- European Economic Interest Groupings (EEIGs);
- open-ended investment companies (OIECs); and
- proprietors of certain newspapers published in England, Wales or Northern Ireland (*Newspaper Libel and Registration Act 1881*).

With certain exceptions (e.g. in relation to small or unlimited companies) companies are required to file within set time limits the following information at Companies House which is then available for public inspection:

- the company's memorandum and articles of association together with any subsequent amendments;
- details (including changes) of the company's directors and company secretary;
- an annual return;

---

[14] www.companieshouse.gov.uk

- accounts, generally including a directors' report, an auditors' report, a profit and loss account, a balance sheet, accompanying notes and, where applicable, group accounts. Listed companies must also include a directors' remuneration report.[15] For financial years beginning before 6 April 2008, private companies must file accounts within ten months of their accounting reference date and public companies must file accounts within seven months of their accounting reference date. For financial years beginning on or after 6 April 2008, these filing periods are reduced to nine months and six months respectively by *Section 442 Companies Act 2006;*
- details of any changes to the company's accounting reference date and registered office;
- details of allotments of shares;
- details of mortgages and charges created by the company;
- details of certain notifiable events; and
- certain members' and directors' resolutions.

For financial years beginning on or after 6 April 2008, quoted companies must make their annual accounts and reports available on a website until the annual accounts and reports for the next financial year are made available on the website (*Section 430(1) Companies Act 2006*). The website must be maintained by or on behalf of, and must identify, the quoted company (*Section 430(2) Companies Act 2006*). Access to the annual accounts and reports on the website, and the ability to obtain a hard copy of them from the website, must be free of charge or any other restriction (*Section 430(3) Companies Act 2006*).

Companies listed on the Main Market of the London Stock Exchange are subject to additional information disclosure requirements imposed by the *United Kingdom Listing Authority Disclosure Rules and Transparency Rules*[16]. Certain of these rules also apply to companies listed on the Alternative Investment Market of the London Stock Exchange. For companies listed on the Main Market, the rules include requirements:

- to publish an annual financial report, including audited financial statements, within four months of the end of each financial year and to ensure that this annual financial report remains publicly available for at least five years;

---

[15]The precise requirements in any particular case will depend on whether the company in question is small, medium-sized, unquoted or quoted.

[16]The *United Kingdom Listing Authority Disclosure Rules and Tansparency Rules* are contained within the *Financial Services Authority Handbook* (www.fsa.gov.uk/pages/handbook).

- to publish a half-yearly financial report, including condensed financial statements, within two months of the end of the first six months of each financial year and to ensure that this half-yearly financial report remains publicly available for at least five years;
- to publish interim management statements during the first and second six-month periods of each financial year. These should include an explanation of material events and transactions during the relevant period and their impact on the financial position of the listed company together with a general description of the company's financial position and performance during the period.

The *Financial Services and Markets Act 2000* generally requires that a company must make available to the public an FSA-approved prospectus[17]:

- before transferable securities are offered to the public in the UK (*Section 85(1)*); or
- before a request is made to admit transferable securities to trading on a regulated market in the UK (*Section 85(2)*).

Such publicly-available prospectuses must contain the information referred to in the *United Kingdom Listing Authority Prospectus Rules* at *PR 2*[18].

Companies listed on the Main Market of the London Stock Exchange may from time to time be required to issue circulars[19] to their shareholders. These are often publicly available and should contain a substantial amount of financial and other information about the company and the transaction which is the subject matter of the circular. Specifically, such circulars must contain the information required by the *United Kingdom Listing Authority Listing Rules* at *LR 13*[20].

A company listed on the Alternative Investment Market of the London Stock Exchange is required by *Rule* 26 of the *AIM Rules for Companies, February 2007*

[17] A prospectus is a document which a company is required to publish under the Prospectus Directive (*Directive of the European Parliament and of the Council of 4 November 2003 No 2003/71/EC*) whenever its securities are offered to the public or admitted to trading.

[18] The *United Kingdom Listing Authority Prospectus Rules* are contained within the *Financial Services Authority Handbook* (*www.fsa.gov.uk/pages/handbook*).

[19] A circular is any document issued to holders of listed securities, excluding prospectuses, listing particulars, annual reports and accounts, interim reports, proxy cards and dividend or interest vouchers.

[20] The *United Kingdom Listing Authority Listing Rules* are contained within the *Financial Services Authority Handbook* (*www.fsa.gov.uk/pages/handbook*).

to maintain a website on which to make available, free of charge, certain information in relation to:

- its business and investing strategy;
- its directors;
- its country of incorporation and main country of operation;
- the rights of its shareholders;
- its current constitutional documents;
- its AIM-listed securities, including any restrictions on their transfer, the number in issue, the percentage not publicly held, significant shareholders and any other exchanges or trading platforms on which any of its securities are admitted or traded;
- its most recent annual report;
- all interim reports published since its last annual report;
- all notifications which it has made in the last 12 months;
- its most recent admission document (which must include the information listed in Schedule 2, AIM Rules for Companies, February 2007);
- any circulars etc. sent to shareholders within the past 12 months; and
- its advisers, including its nominated adviser.

It is sometimes possible from publicly available accounts to make a reasonable estimate of a company's tax written down value of expenditure available for future capital allowances (i.e. tax depreciation).

- The notes to a company's accounts may provide an analysis of any deferred tax provision or asset as at the balance sheet date.
- In particular, this may disclose the amount of such provision or asset attributable to accelerated or decelerated capital allowances.
- Broadly, this figure will have been derived by applying the UK corporation tax rate to the difference between:

  the Net Book Value of the company's assets qualifying for capital allowances; and

  the Tax Written Down Value of those same assets.
- By making some broad assumptions about which classes of fixed assets might qualify for capital allowances (e.g. plant & machinery), the Net Book Value of the company's assets qualifying for capital allowances can be estimated from the fixed asset note in the company's accounts.
- The Tax Written Down Value of those same assets can then be estimated by:

grossing up at the UK corporation tax rate the deferred tax provision or asset in relation to accelerated/decelerated capital allowances; and

subtracting the result from the estimate of the Net Book Value of the company's assets qualifying for capital allowances.

5.2. Australia

Financial	Broadly, companies which are disclosing entities (e.g. public companies and their subsidiaries, foreign held private companies, private companies with external debt) are required to lodge an annual return and financial statements with ASIC, the Australian corporate regulator. A small fee is payable to obtain copies of these annual returns and financial statements. Annual returns disclose changes in the details of the company, its officers and shareholders and rights attaching to its shares. If a parent company has provided a cross guarantee to a subsidiary, that subsidiary may be relieved from the requirement to lodge financial statements where the parent has lodged consolidated financial statements.
Tax	All tax filings are private except for class rulings. For example, a class ruling can be applied for by a company on behalf of its shareholders. These are available from the Australian Tax Office website. Typically, a private ruling, which is anonymised and published on the ATO website, accompanies a class ruling and deals with the tax consequences for the corporate taxpayer.

5.3. Austria

Financial	A company's financial statements can be viewed in the commercial register. However, depending on the size of the company, these may be a shortened version of the full financial statements.
Tax	Generally, the only publicly available tax information is that which can be derived from the financial statements described above.

5.4. Belgium

Financial	A company's published financial statements can be obtained from the National Bank of Belgium or from a number of private databases.
Tax	Generally, no tax-specific filings or information are publicly available. The only publicly available tax information is that which can be derived from the financial statements described above.

5.5. China

Financial	For listed companies, financial statements, prospectuses and company announcements are publicly available. Currently, unlisted domestic companies are not required to have audited financial statements.
Tax	Tax returns are not in the public record. The only publicly available tax information is that which can be derived from the financial information described above.

5.6. Czech Republic

Financial	In theory, company statutory financial statements are publicly available, although in practice many companies do not file these.
Tax	Generally, the only publicly available tax information is that which can be derived from the statutory financial statements described above. Recently the Supreme Administrative Court (the highest court for taxes) started to publish its judgments in a non-anonymous form where the taxpayer is a company. It should now therefore be possible to find out whether a target company has been in dispute with the tax authorities to the level of the Supreme Administrative Court.

5.7. Denmark

Financial	Financial statements of Danish companies are published by the Danish Commerce & Companies Agency. The Articles and Memorandum of Association of Danish companies can be ordered from the Danish Commerce & Companies Agency.
Tax	Tax returns are not publicly available. Generally, the only publicly available tax information is that which can be derived from the financial statements described above.

5.8. Finland

Financial	Company financial statements and bylaws are usually available through the Trade Register. Some other basic information can also be obtained through the Trade Register, e.g. board members, date of formation etc.
Tax	In addition to any tax information which can be derived from the financial information described above, the following information about a company's tax position is publicly available from the tax authorities: • name; • place of domicile; • business ID; • taxable income; • amount of tax payable; • amount of advance taxes paid; and • amount of tax refund.

5.9. France

Financial	A company's financial statements are publicly available. However, the latest such financial statements available will be those for the financial year ended before the last complete financial year. For example, in 2008 financial statements are only available for the financial year ended in 2006.
Tax	Generally, the only publicly available tax information is that which can be derived from the financial statements described above.

5.10. Germany

Financial	Corporations and large partnerships are legally bound to disclose the following financial information: • balance sheet; and • profit & loss statement. In practice, such information is rarely made publicly available because there is no penalty for failure to do so. The rules in this regard are currently under review and penalties for non-compliance may be introduced in future.

Tax	Generally, the only publicly available tax information is that which can be derived from the financial information described above.

5.11. Greece

Financial	For companies which are obliged, or which have opted, to adopt IFRS: • balance sheet; • income statement; • cash flow statement; • statement of changes in equity; and • notes to the financial statements. For companies adhering to Greek GAAP: • balance sheet; • income statement; • profit appropriation table; and • notes to the accounts.
Tax	Generally, the only publicly available tax information is that which can be derived from the financial information described above.

5.12. Hong Kong

Financial	For companies listed in Hong Kong: • the annual report; • interim report; and • Hong Kong Stock Exchange filings. Financial statements of unlisted companies are not publicly available.
Tax	Tax filing information is not publicly available in Hong Kong. Generally, the only publicly available tax information is that which can be derived from the financial information described above for listed companies.

5.13. Hungary

Financial	Company financial statements are publicly available. The Company Law Registry will also provide certain other basic corporate information, although this will not extend to tax matters.

Tax	Generally, the only publicly available tax information is that which can be derived from the financial information described above.

5.14. India

Financial	The financial statements and annual reports of Indian companies are filed with the Registrar of Companies and the Stock Exchange and are publicly available.
Tax	Generally, the only publicly available tax information is that which can be derived from the financial information described above.

5.15. Ireland

Financial	An Irish company is obliged to file financial statements (either full financial statements or abridged financial statements) on an annual basis with the Irish Companies Office. The filed financial statements are made publicly available. The extent to which a company must disclose either full or abridged financial statements depends on the company's size. A company is classified as a small company if it meets two or more of the following three tests: • turnover less than €3.81m; • balance sheet total less than €1.9m; and • less than 50 employees. A small company is only required to file *abridged* accounts (balance sheet with limited supporting notes). If the company is classified as other than small it must file complete accounts with the Companies Office. The financial statements of Irish listed companies are publicly available from various sources (e.g. the Irish Stock Exchange website, the listed company's own website etc.).

Tax	There are a number of publicly available sources of information in connection with a company's tax position as follows: • tax-related information disclosed in a company's financial statements as filed with the Irish Companies Office/Stock Exchange (see above); • where a company has taken advantage of certain tax reliefs, its name may be disclosed on the Irish Revenue's website, e.g. list of eligible charities; • the name of any company found to have evaded tax over a certain limit will be published on the Irish Revenue's tax defaulters list; • court cases taken by a company against the Irish Revenue and vice versa may lead to information regarding a company's tax position being made publicly available; and • Tribunals of Enquiry or Special Oireachtas Investigations can lead to disclosure of tax information about a company.

5.16. Italy

Financial	For SPAs (i.e. stock companies) and SRLs (i.e. quotaholder companies), financial statements, Board of Directors reports, Board of Auditors (Collegio Sindacale) reports and audit reports are generally publicly available from the Chamber of Commerce and other public sources.
Tax	No information related to income tax returns is publicly available. Some limited tax information is included in the Board of Directors report enclosed with the financial statements.

5.17. Japan

Financial	For listed companies, financial statements, annual security reports, business reports and brief summaries of reorganisations and other transactions should be publicly available. Generally, no financial information is publicly available for unlisted companies.
Tax	Generally, the only publicly available tax information is that which can be derived from the financial information described above in relation to listed companies.

5.18. Luxembourg

Financial	Financial statements and articles of association are publicly available.
Tax	Generally, the only publicly available tax information is that which can be derived from the financial information described above.

5.19. Mexico

Financial	The financial statements of publicly traded companies are publicly available.
Tax	Generally, the only publicly available tax information is that which can be derived from the financial statements described above.

5.20. Netherlands

Financial	Company balance sheets (and in most cases also profit & loss accounts) are publicly available through the Dutch Chamber of Commerce ('Kamer van Koophandel').
Tax	Generally, the only publicly available tax information is that which can be derived from the financial information described above.

5.21. Norway

Financial	Financial statements are publicly available.
Tax	In addition to any tax information which can be derived from the financial information described above, a register of taxpayers is made available by the tax authorities each year for a three-week period after the tax assessment for that year is finalised. The actual start date for this three-week period is published on the website of the Norwegian tax authorities (*www.skatteetaten.no*). From this date, the register is published on the website and a paper copy is available for inspection at tax offices throughout Norway. From income year 2006 onwards, the press is able to order a copy of the complete register and several Norwegian newspapers take advantage of this facility. The press sometimes publishes information about a Norwegian taxpayer after the three-week period has ended. The register contains the following information for each taxpayer: • name; • postal code; • for individual taxpayers: date and year of birth; for all other taxpaying entities: business number; • net wealth; • net income (i.e. ordinary income before special tax allowances); • total tax charge.

5.22. Poland

Financial	Entities governed by the *Accounting Act* are obliged to prepare financial statements (and, if applicable, consolidated financial statements). Financial statements (together with certain other related company documents) must be filed with the registration court. This information is publicly available. Entities which are required to be audited publish elements of their financial statements in the Commercial Bulletin (*Monitor Polski B*) which is also publicly available. Polish listed entities submit financial statements (including

	interim quarterly and half-year reports) as Stock Exchange reports. These, too, are publicly available.
Tax	Tax returns are not publicly available in Poland. Generally, the only publicly available tax information is that which can be derived from the financial information described above.

5.23. Portugal

Financial	The financial statements of Portugese companies should be publicly available, although delays are often experienced in obtaining them.
Tax	Generally, the only publicly available tax information is that which can be derived from the financial statements described above.

5.24. Russia

Financial	Company financial information is not generally publicly available, although open joint stock companies are required to publish their annual financial statements prepared under Russian GAAP.
Tax	Generally, the only publicly available tax information is that which can be derived from the financial statements described above.

5.25. Slovak Republic

Financial	All companies are required to file a copy of their financial statements with the Slovak Commercial Register. Copies are available from the Commercial Register on request and for a fee. Certain entities defined by law are required to publish their financial statements on the internet and in the Commercial Journal. Consolidated financial statements must also be published in the Commercial Journal.
Tax	Generally, the only publicly available tax information is that which can be derived from the financial statements described above.

5.26. Spain

Financial	Spanish companies are required to file their financial statements with the Commercial Registry which will provide copies on application by any party.

Tax	Generally, the only publicly available tax information is that which can be derived from the financial statements described above.

5.27. Sweden

Financial	The annual reports of Swedish companies are available from the Swedish Companies Registration Office.
Tax	In addition to any tax information which can be derived from the financial information described above, the following information in relation to a Swedish company's tax position is publicly available: • the company's final notice of assessment (available from the Swedish Tax Agency) containing details of taxable income, tax losses carried forward, real estate tax paid, yield tax and tax payable on pensions; and • the amount payable/receivable by the company according to its VAT return.

5.28. Turkey

Financial	The Trade Registry makes publicly available certain company financial information.
Tax	Generally, the only publicly available tax information is that which can be derived from the financial information described above.

5.29. United States

Financial	Financial information contained in public filings or offering documents of certain publicly traded companies or companies with certain publicly issued or traded securities can be retrieved from the Securities & Exchange Commission's ('SEC') EDGAR database (*www.sec.gov/edgar.shtml*). This financial information is usually audited by an independent auditor. Such financial information can be reviewed in SEC Forms 10-Q or Forms 10-K or in certain offering documents. Similar financial information can also sometimes be obtained from the investor relations pages of certain public and non-public companies' websites (e.g. the company's annual report).
Tax	Limited tax information may be derived from the footnotes to financial statements contained in public filings or offering documents which certain publicly traded companies or

	companies with certain publicly issued or traded securities file with the SEC. This tax information is typically restricted in detail and provides only limited insight into the companies' tax affairs or positions (e.g. Fin 48 disclosures).

6. Reporting Tax Due Diligence Findings

6.1. Reporting language

As has already been stressed, tax due diligence is as much commercial advice as it is tax advice. To the greatest extent possible, therefore, the language of due diligence reports should reflect this.

In particular, tax due diligence reports should be drafted with a non-tax specialist reader in mind. Although the principal user of tax due diligence is often the Tax Director or Manager of a corporate purchaser, it is equally important to ensure that those other parties responsible for decision-making and execution of a transaction fully understand the commercial implications of a tax issue or exposure for that transaction. These other parties will include Chief Financial Officers ('CFOs') or Corporate Development Officers ('CDOs') or their equivalents of corporate purchasers, partners or directors of private equity houses and the purchaser's other advisers and debt providers. As none of these will necessarily have specialist tax knowledge, a detailed understanding of the tax analysis behind tax issues or exposures identified by due diligence will be of secondary importance to them.

It is therefore desirable to draft tax due diligence reports as clearly and succinctly as possible. Tax jargon, statutory references etc. are better relegated to footnotes or appendices (unless they are brief and self-explantory) together with any other material which would not readily be understood by a non-specialist reader. In certain instances, technical analysis supporting a due diligence conclusion may even be omitted from the report altogether. This may be appropriate where only the conclusion is likely to be of immediate relevance to the transaction and where the detailed analysis is unlikely to assist the reader with his or her investment decision. However, the full analysis supporting the conclusion should always be retained on the tax due diligence provider's files for future reference.

Clarity and brevity should automatically result if the guidelines set out below are followed for each tax issue or exposure to be included in the tax due diligence report.

- Which facts does the reader need to know in order to understand the tax issue or exposure? – Only these facts should be included in the main body of the report. Anything else which may be useful but is not essential to answering this question should be included in footnotes or appendices.
- How does the the tax issue or exposure arise from these facts? - Only a brief explanation of the basis for the issue or exposure should be included

in the main body of the report. Anything else which may be useful but is not essential to answering this question should be included in footnotes or appendices.

- So what? What is the implication and what should the reader do about the issue or exposure in the context of the particular transaction under consideration? A recommendation for addressing the issue or exposure should be included in the main body of the report. See 6.3 below for further guidance.

Recommendations should be carefully drafted to ensure that they comprise advice and guidance for the client's consideration. Advisers can advise but principals must ultimately decide. In other words, the due diligence adviser should not make an investment decision on a client's behalf.

All conclusions, opinions advice and recommendations should be as precise and as objective as possible and should be grounded in factual evidence derived from the tax due diligence findings. Vague words and expressions should be avoided. They are unhelpful to the reader and can imply a greater degree of assurance than may be appropriate in the circumstances. To say, for example that a particular tax balance in a target company's balance sheet at a particular date is 'reasonable' does not articulate with sufficient precision the outcome of the due diligence procedures applied to that balance. What is usually meant in this context is something along the lines of 'The unpaid tax liabilities in the company's tax returns together with other potential tax exposures identified by due diligence do not exceed the tax creditor or provision in the company's balance sheet as at a particular date.'

All assumptions and representations should be attributed to their source.

6.2. Classification of tax risks

Clearly, in order to make the appropriate commercial decisions, it is important for the user of tax due diligence to understand the degree of risk attached to each tax exposure identified. Some consistent method of classifying risk is therefore required.

Risk, in this context, should refer to the likelihood or probability that a particular tax exposure will actually crystallise; rather than to the likelihood or probability of the exposure being raised during an audit by the relevant tax authorities.

Some tax due diligence expresses the likelihood of the crystallisation of each tax exposure as a percentage. The danger of this approach is principally twofold:

- it implies a degree of precision; and

- suggests a direct link with provisioning for the purposes of financial statements;

neither of which can be provided by due diligence.

Tax due diligence is not after all an exact science. It is essentially a form of transaction advice and opinion. Just like any other tax advice or opinion, it deals with uncertainties and has to strike a balance between two or more possible and often mutually exclusive outcomes.

It is therefore better to classify risk in some way which does not suggest an inappropriate or unsupportable degree of accuracy. Any classification of risk chosen should be directly aligned to the commercial decisions which have to be made in the context of a transaction. The following risk classifications are suggested:

- 'certain, 'high', 'medium' and 'low'; or
- 'certain', 'probable', 'possible' and 'remote'.

On balance, the former is to be preferred on grounds of clarity; but whichever classification is chosen should be defined in the tax due diligence report.

6.2.1. Certain exposures

Certain exposures are tax liabilities which have already crystallised or which will certainly crystallise upon some future event where no mitigating action is possible.

Typically, these are liabilities which have simply been missed by the seller in error and which will need to be disclosed to the tax authorities.

6.2.2. High risk

There is a strong likelihood that the tax authorities, if provided with all of the known facts, would successfully challenge the issue or exposure based on its merits.

High risk exposures would indicate a need for the purchaser strongly to consider a price reduction and, in any event, some form of specific indemnification in the contract.

6.2.3. Medium risk

If provided with all of the known facts, the outcome of a challenge by the tax authorities is uncertain.

Medium risk exposures are generally best dealt with by means of general tax indemnities and warranties.

6.2.4. Low risk

It is unlikely that the tax authorities, if provided with all of the known facts, would successfully challenge the issue or exposure based on its merits.

Low risk exposures are generally best dealt with by means of the general tax indemnities and warranties. In some cases, purchasers may decide that they may be addressed with remedial action post-acquisition.

6.3. Reporting emphasis for each type of due diligence

The type of due diligence review may have an impact on its scope (see Chapters 2 and 4) but it will not generally affect the fundamental nature of the review procedures adopted to fulfil that scope. However, the type of due diligence will influence the way in which tax due diligence findings are reported.

6.3.1. Pre-acquisition or buy-side tax due diligence

As a general guide, in relation to each issue or exposure identified, pre-acquisition or buy-side tax due diligence should:

- report those facts, and only those facts, which the purchaser needs to know in order to understand the tax issue or exposure;
- explain how the tax issue or exposure arises from the facts described above;
- quantify the exposure to the extent possible with the available information, making clear whether such quantification includes or excludes interest and penalties. The basis of any quantification should always be stated, including its underlying assumptions. If there is insufficient information available to provide any meaningful quantification, or if quantification would be outside the scope of the tax due diligence review (as might be the case in relation to transfer pricing, for example), then some indication of potential scale should be given (e.g. in relation to transfer pricing, it might be possible to provide the total amount of related party transactions by transaction type);
- indicate the degree of risk associated with the exposure;
- indicate the timing of any cash tax payments to which the issue or exposure is likely to give rise;
- answer the question, 'so what?' in the context of the acquisition;
- explain:

  whether the issue or exposure is likely to be sheltered by tax losses or other tax attributes, and, if so, the consequent impact on the tax losses or other tax attributes; or whether it is a timing issue or exposure (e.g. assuming that a capital asset is fully depreciable for tax purposes, even if a tax audit were to result in a reduction in the amount of depreciation available in any specific year or years, the overall depreciation available over the asset's life should not be affected); or

the extent to which it is already provided for in the latest balance sheet of the specific entity in which the issue or exposure arises or in the latest consolidated balance sheet which includes such entity;

etc.;

- explain any mitigating factors and include an estimate of the exposure if these mitigating factors were to apply;
- if known, describe any action which the seller intends to take to address the issue or exposure;
- where applicable, explain what contractual protection the seller is prepared to offer the successful purchaser;
- provide the potential purchaser with a recommendation for addressing the tax issue or exposure. Typically, this might include:

  consideration of the issue or exposure by the purchaser when formulating the valuation or bid; and/or

  appropriate contractual protection, e.g. a warranty or indemnity (see Chapter 8); and/or

  insurance (see 8.8.2); and/or

  further specific tax due diligence; and/or

  pre-acquisition disclosure to the tax authorities for a ruling (provided that the seller agrees); and/or

  post-acquisition remedial action, including post-acquisition disclosure to the tax authorities for a ruling (provided that such action would not invalidate other protection afforded by the seller, e.g. contractual protection).

6.3.2. Vendor or sell-side tax due diligence

As a general guide, in relation to each issue or exposure identified, vendor or sell-side tax due diligence should:

- report those facts, and only those facts, which a range of potential purchasers might be expected to need to know in order to understand how the tax issue or exposure might arise from those facts, depending on the circumstances of a particular potential purchaser;

- quantify the exposure to the extent possible with the available information, making clear whether such quantification includes or excludes interest and penalties. The basis of any quantification should always be stated, including its underlying assumptions. If there is insufficient information available to provide any meaningful quantification, or if quantification would be outside the scope of the tax due diligence review (as might be the case in relation to transfer pricing, for example), then some indication of potential scale should be given (e.g. in relation to transfer pricing, it might be possible to provide the total amount of related party transactions by transaction type);
- indicate the degree of risk associated with the exposure;
- indicate the timing of any cash tax payments to which the issue or exposure is likely to give rise;
- answer the question, 'so what?' in the context of the acquisition;
- explain:

  whether the issue or exposure is likely to be sheltered by tax losses or other tax attributes, and, if so, the consequent impact on the tax losses or other tax attributes; or

  whether it is a timing issue or exposure (e.g. assuming that a capital asset is fully depreciable for tax purposes, even if a tax audit were to result in a reduction in the amount of depreciation available in any specific year or years, the overall depreciation available over the asset's life should not be affected); or

  the extent to which it is already provided for in the latest balance sheet of the specific entity in which the issue or exposure arises or in the latest consolidated balance sheet which includes such entity;

  etc.;
- explain any mitigating factors and include an estimate of the exposure if these mitigating factors were to apply;
- describe any action which the seller intends to take to address the issue or exposure;
- where applicable, explain what contractual protection the seller is prepared to offer the successful purchaser;
- address the implications of the issue or exposure for potential purchasers without providing advice or recommending any particular solution. It is not appropriate for vendor or sell-side tax due diligence to recommend specific action to address the tax issue or exposure because it is carried out at a time before the nature or circumstances of the purchaser are known.

6.3.3. Long form tax due diligence

As a general guide, in relation to each issue or exposure identified, long form tax due diligence should:

- report those facts, and only those facts, which the company and the sponsor or nominated adviser need to know in order to understand the tax issue or exposure;
- explain how the tax issue or exposure arises from the facts described above;
- quantify the exposure to the extent possible with the available information, making clear whether such quantification includes or excludes interest and penalties. The basis of any quantification should always be stated, including its underlying assumptions. If there is insufficient information available to provide any meaningful quantification, or if quantification would be outside the scope of the tax due diligence review (as might be the case in relation to transfer pricing, for example), then some indication of potential scale should be given (e.g. in relation to transfer pricing, it might be possible to provide the total amount of related party transactions by transaction type);
- indicate the degree of risk associated with the exposure;
- indicate the timing of any cash tax payments to which the issue or exposure is likely to give rise;
- answer the question, 'so what?' in the context of the IPO or other public transaction;
- explain:

  whether the issue or exposure is likely to be sheltered by tax losses or other tax attributes, and, if so, the consequent impact on the tax losses or other tax attributes; or

  whether it is a timing issue or exposure (e.g. assuming that a capital asset is fully depreciable for tax purposes, even if a tax audit were to result in a reduction in the amount of depreciation available in any specific year or years, the overall depreciation available over the asset's life should not be affected); or

  the extent to which it is already provided for in the latest balance sheet of the specific entity in which the issue or exposure arises or in the latest consolidated balance sheet which includes such entity;

  etc.;
- explain any mitigating factors and include an estimate of the exposure if these mitigating factors were to apply;

- describe any action which the company intends to take to address the issue or exposure;
- suggest any other options for addressing the issue or exposure pre-transaction.

7. Buy-side Tax Due Diligence where the Seller Provides a Vendor Tax Due Diligence Report

Where a seller provides a vendor tax due diligence report, the pre-acquisition tax due diligence performed by potential purchasers will differ from the approach described at 2.1, Chapter 4 and Chapter 6 above. Specifically, bidders are likely to have very little access to tax information in the early stages of an auction and accordingly will be able to do very little pre-acquisition tax due diligence of their own. Responding to bidders' information requests is likely to be deferred until a later phase of the auction process; and any data room (physical or virtual) is likely to contain information which only confirms the contents of the vendor due diligence report but which does not add to them.

Accordingly, in these circumstances tax due diligence for a potential purchaser should comprise the following matters.

7.1. Review of the scope, independence and quality of the vendor tax due diligence report to identify any limitations or restrictions which detract from its quality and which may need to be supplemented by additional pre-acquisition tax due diligence

Specifically, the report should be scrutinised for over-reliance on representations from management which have not been verified independently and which might therefore suggest that the vendor due diligence has been heavily influenced by management. This will usually be evidenced by:

- extensive use throughout the report of expressions such as 'We understand that…', 'According to management…', etc.;
- a paucity of independent conclusions drawn by the provider of the vendor tax due diligence report; and
- a heavily caveated scope section to the report.

Any materiality level applicable to the vendor tax due diligence should also be carefully reviewed, in particular to understand how it was arrived at and to consider whether it is appropriate for a particular purchaser's needs. If the materiality level has been determined or influenced by the seller, it may be too high and might have excluded tax risks which individually may not be significant but which cumulatively could be of concern.

The basis for excluding any particular jurisdictions and/or companies should be considered to determine whether these are appropriate for a particular purchaser's circumstances. Such exclusions are normally based on turnover or profit before tax but these measures are not always helpful for determining materiality for tax purposes. They could, for example, lead to the exclusion from scope of:

- companies with trading losses;
- dormant or near-dormant companies, the activities of which have been material at some point within the period covered by tax returns which are potentially open to audit or adjustment by the tax authorities; and
- companies with minimal activity themselves but which are, or have been, party to tax planning within the period covered by tax returns which are potentially open to audit or adjustment by the tax authorities.

Where the vendor tax due diligence is deficient in relation to scope, independence or quality, it may be possible to supplement or corroborate it with information from other sources such as:

- financial statements and other publicly available information (see Chapter 5.);
- any information memorandum provided to potential purchasers;
- the contents of any data room provided for the use of potential purchasers;
- any formal 'Question & Answer' process provided to assist potential purchasers;
- interviews with management;
- other due diligence reports commissioned by the seller and made available to potential purchasers, e.g. any legal due diligence report; and
- site visits which can occasionally provide useful insights into tax matters. For example, a site visit to a target's warehouse may reveal large amounts of stock delivered from a related party which would indicate that transfer pricing may be a risk area. Equally, substantial new equipment at a target's factory might corroborate a seller's claims about the extent of future tax depreciation available to shelter the target's otherwise taxable profits.

Making the most of such limited and disparate sources of information generally involves comparing and reconciling them to identify:

- inconsistencies; and
- information which is supported by more than one source.

7.2. Review of the vendor tax due diligence report to identify any differences of opinion

A purchaser's tax due diligence advisers may take a different view of matters raised in the vendor tax due diligence report from the seller's advisers. On the basis of the same facts, a purchaser's advisers may reach different conclusions with regard to the quantification of, or more usually the degree of risk associated with, a particular tax exposure. Such differences are likely to influence a purchaser's view of value and/or the level of tax warranties and indemnities required in the draft contract. Such differences can also detract from the confidence which a purchaser feels able to place on a vendor tax due diligence report if that purchaser's advisers consistently take a more pessimistic view of risk than that articulated in the report.

7.3. Explanation of how the issues and exposures identified in the vendor tax due diligence report might affect a specific purchaser and recommendations as to how that purchaser should address them in the context of the transaction

The vendor tax due diligence report clearly cannot have been drafted with the circumstances of any particular purchaser in mind. Rather its purpose will have been to provide a range of potential purchasers with the information necessary to enable them to formulate bids for the target which reflect the target's tax profile. The role of a potential purchaser's tax due diligence advisers should therefore be to interpret this information and apply it to the circumstances of their client.

Accordingly, for each tax issue or exposure identified in the vendor tax due diligence report, the bidder's advisers should explain the implications for their client's bid and recommend how it should be addressed in the context of the transaction in question, e.g. by means of a price adjustment or contractual protection etc. See 2.1.3, 2.1.4, 6.3.1 and Chapter 8.

7.4. Request for further information

Given the purpose of vendor due diligence (see 2.2), the vendor tax due diligence report is unlikely on its own to provide potential purchasers with all the tax information needed to arrive at a final bid. Additional tax information is usually provided in later stages of the auction to enable bidders to refine their bids at each stage. Finally, the successful bidder is usually given more extensive access to the target's management, advisers and tax records to arrive at a final offer.

Part of the role of the bidder's tax due diligence advisers should therefore be to identify and request:

- whatever clarifications are required to enable their client to understand the basis for, and implications of, matters raised in the vendor tax due diligence report; and

- the further information which the report does not provide and which their client will require in order to understand how tax should be reflected in its bid.

This will involve preparation and submission to the seller of a list of questions and requests for further information. While these may not be answered until a later stage of the auction, they are an important step in establishing those matters to which a bid at any particular stage is subject. For example, bids can be expressed as subject to further tax due diligence generally; or to the provision of further specific information with regard to tax.

Depending on the formality of the auction process, there is often a set procedure mandated by the seller for requesting further information. This is to ensure that control is maintained over the flow of information to all competing bidders and that the information provided to each is consistent.

7.5. Interrogation of the advisers who prepared the vendor tax due diligence report (the 'bidder meeting')

A meeting or conference call to discuss the contents of the vendor tax due diligence report with its authors is normally part of the procedure by which further tax due diligence information is obtained. See 2.2. This helps to reduce the time which target management needs to spend with each bidder.

Among other things, such a meeting or call provides an opportunity for potential purchasers and their tax due diligence advisers to understand the scope and independence of the vendor tax due diligence. Specifically, the authors of the vendor tax due diligence report are commonly asked one or more of the following illustrative questions:

- Who determined the scope, you, the seller or management?
- How was the scope determined?
- Were any matters excluded from the scope by the seller or management which you would otherwise have included?
- Describe the team which performed the vendor tax due diligence review, i.e. was the review adequately staffed and carried out by a team of advisers comprising individual members without previous connections with, or knowledge of, the target?
- What period of time was available to you for your review?
- What fee did you receive for your review? Is any part of your fee conditional or contingent?
- What level of materiality was applied for the purposes of your review?
- Was your scope restricted by the seller or management?

- Were there any limitations on the information available to you or on access to target staff?
- To what extent has the vendor tax due diligence report been reviewed by the seller and/or target management?
- Did either the seller or target management request or require amendments to, or deletions from, the vendor tax due diligence report?
- Was the scope or content of your final vendor tax due diligence report influenced by comments from the seller or management on earlier drafts; and, if so, in what way?
- Describe the size and capability of the target's tax function.
- With the benefit of hindsight, are there any additional matters which you would have included within the scope of your review or matters already included which you would have approached differently?
- As a potential adviser to the purchaser, what areas would you recommend should be the focus of further tax due diligence?

7.6. Format of report to a potential purchaser on a vendor tax due diligence report

The successful bidder will usually be able to rely on the seller's vendor tax due diligence report. See 2.2. Accordingly, there is little point in the bidder's advisers repeating in a separate report anything already adequately covered in the vendor tax due diligence report.

Instead, the bidder's advisers should generally confine their buy-side tax due diligence report to the matters identified by means of 7.1 to 7.5 above. A template similar to the following is recommended for this purpose.

Tax issue or exposure	**Reference in VDD report**	**Seller's advisers' view of quantification and risk**	**Bidder's advisers' view of quantification and risk**	**Implications for bidder**	**Recommendation for addressing the issue or exposure in the context of the transaction**

The following example (Example 12) illustrates the use of a template of a similar type in practice.

Example 12
PROJECT X:

Key tax findings from a review of the vendor tax due diligence ('VDD') report

Prepared by Y

Dated Z

Item		Maximum exposure £m	Why important to client, Bidder A	Proposed action
1	**Scope of tax VDD** The scope of the tax review is limited, and the report makes a number of references to comprehensive tax warranties and indemnities being provided by the Seller to cover pre-completion tax liabilities.	Unknown	The draft share purchase agreement ('SPA') does not currently provide comprehensive protection in relation to tax (see below). There is a risk that not all potential pre-completion tax exposures have been identified, given the limited scope of the review, and that those which have been identified would not count towards the warranty/indemnity thresholds of £250,000 and 3% of purchase price.	• Discuss scope and implications with the VDD report's authors. • Consider removing tax from warranty/indemnity claim thresholds to ensure appropriate protection for all pre-completion tax exposures. • Consider feasibility of further tax due diligence if full SPA protection is not available.

Item		Maximum exposure £m	Why important to client, Bidder A	Proposed action
2	**Transfer pricing** The target group has a significant number of intra-group arrangements to which transfer pricing rules will apply to require that they take place on arm's length terms. While the VDD report has a specific section on transfer pricing, it does not appear to be comprehensive and mentions (in overview only) a number of areas currently being addressed by the seller which could indicate potential exposures.	Unknown	While pre-completion transfer pricing exposures should be capable of being protected against via the SPA (assuming that it is properly amended), Bidder A will need to ensure that all transfer pricing arrangements are understood, documented, justified and appropriate for the combined group post acquisition.	• This area is likely to merit (potentially significant) further work pre-completion. Bidder A should consider the extent to which this can or should be done as part of the due diligence process.
3	**Structure** The structure was established in 2001/02 since when various group entities have operated as contract manufacturers for Company B. The VDD report does not comment on whether the tax treatment of the transfers of businesses to Company B has been agreed by all relevant tax authorities but does identify that certain areas still need to be addressed in	Unknown	As with transfer pricing, pre-completion tax exposures should be capable of being protected against via the SPA (again assuming it is properly amended). However, Bidder A will need to understand precisely what further steps are required to support the structure going forward; and any cost in relation to this should be borne by the Seller, arguably regardless of when the steps take place.	• This area is also likely to merit (potentially significant) further work pre-completion. Again, Bidder A should consider the extent to which this can or should be done as part of the due diligence process.

Item		Maximum exposure £m	Why important to client, Bidder A	Proposed action
	relation to the structure, including transferring intellectual property to Company B, completing documentation, addressing technical issues of substance and economic relationships etc.			
4	**Tax assets** The VDD report discloses tax assets in Country C of €120m (gross) in relation to goodwill amortisation over the next 6 years and €60m (gross) in relation to losses which may be available (possibly with an x year limit from when they were incurred). There is insufficient detail in the report to conclude on their availability and value to Bidder A, particularly in relation to the losses, the allocation of which would need to be agreed with the Country C tax authorities.	N/A - potential value item	Bidder A is being asked to value the tax assets as part of the final offer.	• Specific questions for the VDD report's authors. • Bidder A should consider the extent to which the likely profit profile in Country C going forward will affect the value of the tax assets.

Item		Maximum exposure £m	Why important to client, Bidder A	Proposed action
5	**Tax compliance and reporting** The target group has numerous tax compliance and filing requirements.	N/A	Bidder A will need to establish suitable tax compliance arrangements for post completion periods.	• Specific questions for the Seller and the VDD report's authors on the target's current tax function. • Ensure appropriate treatment in transitional services agreement.
6	**Seller's disposal structure** Some aspects of the Seller's disposal structure appear yet to be resolved (e.g. whether there will be a disposal of assets or shares in Country D). Pre-sale reorganisations are stated to be required in Country E and Country F, although precise details have not been provided. In addition, exit and transfer tax charges etc. are expected to arise in Country G, Country H and Country I.	Unknown	The precise disposal structure and the Seller's steps to arrive at it will impact on Bidder A's own acquisition and financing structure. Any tax liabilities in relation to pre-sale reorganisations and exit charges triggered by the transaction need to be borne by the Seller (this is not currently the position in the draft SPA).	• Confirm the precise disposal structure. • Mark up the SPA.
7	**Detailed potential pre-completion tax exposures** A summary of the potential pre-completion tax exposures identified in the VDD report is attached as Appendix 1 (*not reproduced here*).			See Appendix 1 (*not reproduced here*).
8	**SPA** Our tax comments on the SPA are attached as Appendix 2 (*not reproduced here*). We would be happy to discuss these			See Appendix 2 (*not reproduced here*) for

Item		Maximum exposure £m	Why important to client, Bidder A	Proposed action
	with your in-house and external lawyers. It will, of course, be important to ensure that mark-ups to the SPA do not unnecessarily disadvantage your bid. As well as the detailed mark-ups, there are three overriding points on the SPA. The thresholds for claims in Schedule y of the SPA (£250,000 per claim, 3% of total consideration in aggregate) make the tax indemnities largely redundant. This is unlikely to be acceptable given our comments above on the scope of the VDD. There is currently no protection for tax liabilities which arise on or as a result of completion itself, or in relation to any pre-sale reorganisations undertaken by the Seller. These should be borne by the Seller. Generally, the tax deed is 'seller friendly' and in a number of respects does not represent normal market practice.			detailed comments and suggested mark-ups.

8. Tax Due Diligence: Implications for the Contract

This chapter provides general guidance on the link between tax due diligence and the contract for the sale and purchase of the target shares or business, referred to variously as the Sale & Purchase Agreement, Share Purchase Agreement ('SPA'), Business Purchase Agreement ('BPA') etc. The chapter is largely, although not exclusively:

- relevant to acquisitions of shares (as opposed to acquisitions of business assets) on the basis that historical tax risks generally only pass from seller to purchaser on a sale of shares (see 1.2 and Chapter 10);
- written from the perspective of a purchaser, although the seller's perspective can be inferred from the purchaser's; and
- focused on UK law and market practice, although many of the principles described are of wider application.

8.1. Is a review of the contract part of tax due diligence?

8.1.1. Pre-acquisition or buy-side tax due diligence

One of the principal ways of addressing tax risks identified by pre-acquisition due diligence is through the contract for the purchase of the target shares or business. See 2.1.4. Accordingly, there is a direct link between pre-acquisition tax due diligence and the contract. Given that, in the UK at least, a purchaser of business assets does not generally assume tax liabilities of the business' previous owner[21], the link between pre-acquisition tax due diligence and the contract is more fundamental in relation to share acquisitions.

It follows that whoever has carried out the tax due diligence review of the target is in the best position to advise on whether the contract adequately addresses the tax risks identified; and, if it does not, how the contract might be amended to ensure that it does.

Notwithstanding this obvious connection between tax due diligence and review of the contract, the two are often regarded as distinct and separate exercises. The scope of the engagement for the tax due diligence does not always include review of the contract. Where it is not included, there is a risk that the full benefits of the due diligence will not be realised and that some tax risks may slip through the net of protection for the purchaser which the contract is intended to provide.

---

[21]See footnote 36 with regard to VAT and Chapter 10 with regard to the general principle.

Often the scope of the due diligence engagement is silent on the question of contract review simply because the purchaser will have assumed that the link between the two will be made by the client's advisers generally as a matter of course. But the danger of such an assumption will be obvious.

It is clearly better for the purchaser and tax due diligence provider to agree in advance, when defining the scope and setting the fee for a tax due diligence review:

- whether contract review is to be included or excluded; and
- if excluded, how tax due diligence findings will be taken into consideration in the contract negotiations. (Usually this is achieved by the due diligence provider making available the due diligence report to the purchaser's legal advisers who will negotiate a contract which takes into account its findings.)

The above approach should ensure that the purchaser is not, through oversight, left avoidably exposed in the contract to tax risks.

It should also address any concern on the part of the purchaser, quite common in practice, that review of the contract by the tax due diligence provider is unnecessary duplication of the work of the lawyers responsible for drafting and/or negotiating the contract.

The distinct roles of the purchaser's tax due diligence provider and lawyers responsible for drafting and/or negotiating the contract

The purchaser's lawyers are responsible for drafting and/or negotiating a contract which protects their client's interests in the transaction in question. In doing so they will require guidance from the tax due diligence provider with regard to the specific tax risks which the drafting and negotiation need to take into account.

Only the purchaser's lawyers should draft, amend or negotiate the contract. However, there is nothing to prevent the due diligence provider (who will generally not be lawyers) from suggesting appropriate wording for inclusion in the contract (e.g. the wording of a particular tax warranty or indemnity), provided that the lawyers decide independently whether or not it should be incorporated into the contract and assume responsibility for its legal effectiveness.

8.1.2. Vendor or sell-side tax due diligence

The position of the provider of vendor or sell-side due diligence is rather more complicated.

Although vendor due diligence is commissioned by the seller, it is UK market practice that the due diligence provider accepts a legal duty of care to the eventual purchaser and lenders in relation to the vendor due diligence report (see 2.2). Specifically, the vendor due diligence provider:

- initially enters into a contractual engagement with the seller for the performance of the vendor due diligence review of the target; and
- subsequently enters into a contractual undertaking with the successful purchaser and lenders to enable them to rely on the vendor due diligence report.

The due diligence provider therefore owes a duty of care to both parties in a sell-side due diligence engagement. This makes it difficult to provide advice on the contract to either party without potentially prejudicing the interests of the other.

Accordingly, the provider of sell-side tax due diligence should generally avoid reviewing the contract for either seller or purchaser.

8.2. Brief outline of the key contract provisions relevant to tax due diligence

There are four principal parts of a contract[22] for the purchase of the shares of the target company or group which are of direct relevance to tax due diligence:

- the tax warranties (see 8.2.1, 8.3.3 and 8.11);
- the tax indemnity, sometimes referred to as the tax covenant or deed (see 8.2.2 and 8.3.2);
- the disclosures against the tax warranties (see 8.6.2 and 8.7); and
- the price adjustment mechanism based on completion accounts or a 'locked box' balance sheet (see 8.10 and 9.14).

8.2.1. Tax warranties

A warranty is a contractual representation by the seller that certain particular circumstances do or do not exist or that certain particular facts are or are not true. See 8.11 for example tax warranties.

If a warranty is breached (which a purchaser must prove), the purchaser is potentially able to make a claim against the seller, but only if and to the extent that the purchaser can also prove that he or she has suffered a loss as a result of the breach and has taken reasonable measures to mitigate it.

In relation to a breach of a tax warranty, the loss suffered by the purchaser is not necessarily the same amount as the tax which becomes due as a result of the breach. Rather, the loss for which the purchaser may claim is the reduction

---

[22] For detailed guidance on this area see Gibson, *The Tax Schedule*, Spiramus Press, 2009.

in the value of the purchaser's investment (i.e. the shares of the target company or group) as a result of the breach. In some cases there may be no loss at all in this sense even where a warranty is breached. In others, it may be a multiple of the tax cost if the tax relates to a recurring item and has been taken into account in the valuation of the target.

The burden of tax warranties to the seller (and their corresponding benefit to the purchaser) may be reduced by means of the formal process of disclosure against the warranties. See 8.7. Disclosure may also be used by the purchaser to force the provision by the seller of information about the tax position of the target company or group. See 8.7.5.

If the purchaser is able to prove breach of warranty and consequent loss, the seller is required to pay compensation. *Section 49(1)(c) and (2) Taxation of Chargeable Gains Act 1992* provide that such warranty payments are treated for tax purposes as adjustments to the purchase price. They are not therefore immediately taxable in the hands of the recipient (unless and to the extent that they exceed the purchase price which is unlikely and in most cases prevented by the cap on all claims usually imposed by the contract). If the disposal of the target's shares qualifies for the Substantial Shareholdings Exemption from tax on capital gains, the the fact that a warranty payment will be treated as a reduction in the purchase price received may not be relevant to the seller unless its taxability in the hands of the purchaser gives rise to an obligation to gross-up the payment. See 8.3.2.

The warranties, including the tax warranties, are usually to be found in a schedule to the contract. Accordingly, without specific drafting to the contrary, they are subject to all the same limitations as are imposed on all warranty claims by the contract generally. This is in contrast to the tax indemnity which usually takes the form of a separate document (often referred to as 'the tax deed of covenant') which can more easily be excluded from limitations on claims imposed by the main contract itself.

See 8.11 for a list of examples of tax matters which are commonly the subject of warranty protection in a typical UK contract for the sale/purchase of the shares of a target company or group. If the review of the contract by the purchaser's tax due diligence adviser identifies the need for further specific tax warranties, these should be suggested to the purchaser's lawyers and drafted by them. However, as noted at 8.1.1 above, the due diligence provider may suggest appropriate wording for inclusion in the contract provided that the purchaser's lawyers assume responsibility for its legal effectiveness.

In any event, tax warranties should be as precise and focused on a specific risk as possible. If they are too broad, not only is the seller likely to reject them, but they may also be too vague to enable the purchaser to prove breach and/or loss.

8.2.2. The tax indemnity

An indemnity is an undertaking by the seller to meet on a £ for £ basis a particular defined pre-completion liability of the target if and when it falls due. There is no need for the purchaser to prove or to mitigate loss. A tax indemnity is therefore a mechanism by which the risk of pre-completion tax exposures is divided between seller and purchaser on the basis of which the purchase price is struck. See below for an example tax indemnity.

In the UK, a payment under a tax indemnity is potentially taxable in the hands of its recipient under *Section 22 Taxation of Chargeable Gains Act 1992*. This is because, on the basis of *Zim Properties Ltd v Procter (Inspector of Taxes) [1985] STC 90*:

- the right to receive the payment is treated as an asset for capital gains purposes; and
- the payment itself is treated as a capital sum derived from that asset.

This result can generally be avoided, however, by the application of *Extra Statutory Concession D33 (ESC D33)*. Where it applies, *ESC D33* treats the payment under the tax indemnity as an adjustment to the purchase price.

According to *ESC D33*, 'A person who receives a capital sum derived from an asset is treated for the purposes of capital gains tax as disposing of that asset. The case of *Zim Properties Ltd v Procter 58 TC 371* has established that the right to take court action for compensation or damages is an asset for capital gains tax purposes. It follows that a person who receives compensation or damages, whether by court order or arbitration or by negotiated settlement as a result of a cause of action may be regarded as disposing of the right of action. A capital gain may accrue as a result.'

However, *Paragraph 13 of ESC D33* provides [*with added emphasis*] that 'The principle in *Zim Properties Ltd* is not regarded as applicable to payments made **by the vendor to the purchaser of an asset under a warranty or indemnity included as one of the terms of a contract of purchase and sale.**'

'Where such a contractual payment is made, then the cost of the asset to the person acquiring it will, on the occasion of a further disposal be reduced by the sum received. The sale proceeds of the person who makes (or is treated by *TCGA 1992 s 171A* as making) the disposal of the asset are adjusted under *TCGA 1992 s 49* in respect of the sum received. **Where a warranty or indemnity payment is not made in accordance with the terms of the contract, the principle in *Zim Properties* may apply and the sums received by the vendor**

or purchaser as appropriate may be identified as capital sums derived from the asset, or from the right of action, depending on the facts of the case.'

The highlighted text of the Extra Statutory Concession makes clear that payments under a tax indemnity will only be protected from tax by *ESC D33* in the hands of its recipient if:

- the payment is made by the seller to the purchaser;
- under a warranty or indemnity included as one of the terms of a contract of purchase and sale. A tax indemnity will usually satisfy this condition even where it is drafted as a separate document from the main contract of purchase and sale provided that it is legally incorporated into the contract.

It therefore follows that indemnity payments which do not meet the above conditions are in principle taxable. These might include:

- payments from the seller to the target company or to a party to whom the benefit of the indemnity was assigned (see 8.4 below);
- payments outside the terms of a contract of purchase and sale, or where there is no contract of purchase and sale, as for example where the shares of a company are acquired by means of an offer to shareholders; and
- possibly, payments from the purchaser to the seller under a purchaser's covenant. See below.

Because *ESC D33* treats a payment under the tax indemnity as an adjustment to the purchase price, such a payment will be taxable in the recipient's hands as a capital sum derived from an asset if and to the extent that it exceeds the purchase price. However, this remote possibility is invariably prevented by the terms of the contract which usually cap the total amount of all claims at the purchase price or some commercially reasonable percentage of it.

If the disposal of the target's shares qualifies for the Substantial Shareholdings Exemption from tax on capital gains, the fact that an indemnity payment will be treated as a reduction in the purchase price received may not be relevant to the seller unless its taxability in the hands of the purchaser gives rise to an obligation to gross-up the payment. See 8.3.2.

For further guidance on this topic generally, see *Inland Revenue Capital Gains Manual* at *13040 to 13048*.

In the UK, the tax indemnity may be included as a series of clauses in, or schedule to, the main contract. More usually, however, it comprises a separate document (a tax deed of covenant). Whichever is the case, a standard English law tax indemnity follows broadly the same pattern as follows[23]:

A definitions clause

This is usually the first clause of any tax deed of covenant, although it is sometimes relegated to an appendix. It defines the words and terms which are pertinent to the operation of the tax indemnity.

The indemnity or covenant itself

This is the principal clause of any tax deed of covenant and contains the contractual undertaking by the seller to meet defined tax liabilities of the target if and when they fall due. Generally, these comprise all tax liabilities of the target relating to the period up to, and including, a defined effective date which, depending on the terms of the particular transaction agreed between the parties, could be:

- the date of completion;
- the date of the last financial statements; or
- the date of a 'locked box' balance sheet.

The indemnity or covenant usually follows immediately after the definitions as Clause 2 and commonly comprises a general indemnity for the target's pre-effective date tax liabilities to which specific tax indemnities may be added by the purchaser following tax due diligence.

The principal basic operative provision of the general tax indemnity or covenant typically takes a form similar to the following example.

This example is intended only as a guide to the terms of the general tax indemnity. It is not drafted in terms which are necessarily legally effective in any particular case and legal advice should always be sought in relation to the drafting of any particular contract.

The example general indemnity assumes that the target of a particular acquisition comprises two or more legal entities. However, the example is equally applicable, *mutatis mutandis,* if the target comprises a single legal entity.

---

[23]For further guidance, see *Inland Revenue Manual 13040 to 13048.*

Example of the principal basic operative provision of a general tax indemnity or covenant under English law

The **seller** covenants with the **purchaser** to pay to the **purchaser** an amount equal to:

- any tax liability of any of the **defined target companies** which arises directly or indirectly, and whether before, on, or after the effective date, as a consequence of, in connection with, in respect of, or by reference to:

  one or more *events* which occurred, or which are deemed for any tax purpose to have occurred, on or before **the effective date**;

  any *transaction* effected, or deemed for any tax purpose to have been effected, on or before **the effective date**;

  any income, profits or gains earned, accrued or received, or deemed for any tax purpose to have been earned, accrued or received, on or before **the effective date**;

  any income, profits or gains earned, accrued or received, or deemed for any tax purpose to have been earned, accrued or received in relation to a period ended on or before, **the effective date**; or

  any payments made by the **seller,** or any member of the seller's group, to employees, directors or officers, or former employees, directors or officers, of any of the **defined target companies**;
- any tax liability of any of the **defined target companies** which would have arisen, and for which the **seller** would have been liable to reimburse the **purchaser**, but for the setting off of a **purchaser's relief** against that tax liability, or against the income, profits or gains which would have given rise to that tax liability;
- the amount of any **purchaser's relief** which is denied, forfeited or lost or, where that **purchaser's relief** was a deduction from or set-off against income, profits or gains, the tax which would have been saved but for the denial, forfeiture or loss of that **purchaser's relief**;
- any payment of tax by any of the **defined target companies** the liability for which arises as a result of the failure of another person, other than another of the **defined target companies** or a member of the **purchaser's group**, to make a payment of tax for which that other person is primarily liable;
- any liability of any of the **defined target companies** to pay or repay an amount in relation to tax under a warranty, indemnity or covenant entered into on or before **the effective date**;
- any tax liability of any of the **defined target companies** or the

purchaser in respect of inheritance tax which:

as a result of the death of any person within seven years after a transfer of value, or deemed transfer of value, on or before **the effective date**, is or becomes at or after **the effective date** a charge on any of the shares or assets of any of the **defined target companies**, or gives rise to a power to charge, mortgage or sell any such shares or assets; or

arises as a result of a transfer of value occurring, or deemed to occur, on or before **the effective date**, whether or not in conjunction with the death of any person at any time, where such transfer of value changed the value of the estate of any of the **defined target companies**;

- any and all costs and expenses properly and reasonably incurred by the **purchaser** and/or any of the **defined target companies** in relation to a liability of any of the **defined target companies** to make any payment of tax for which the **seller** is liable under any of the provisions of the tax indemnity or covenant; or
- any and all costs and expenses properly and reasonably incurred by the **purchaser** and/or any of the **defined target companies** in relation to the taking of any action at the request or direction of the **seller**.

The terms in bold are typically given precise definitions for the purposes of the tax indemnity or covenant to the extent that they are not already defined elsewhere in the contract. In particular:

- **event** and **transaction** should be sufficiently widely defined to cover any circumstances which could give rise to a tax liability (other than the normal earning, accrual or receipt of profits or income in the ordinary course of business - always provided, of course, that such earning, accrual or receipt of profits or income in the ordinary course of business is covered by a separate limb of the general tax indemnity); and
- a **purchaser's relief** is generally taken to mean:

  any tax relief or asset to which any of the defined target companies was entitled at the effective date and for which the purchaser has paid or which the purchaser has otherwise taken into account when agreeing the purchase price; and

  any tax relief or asset available to the purchaser or any member of the purchaser's group other than any of the defined target companies.

To this general tax indemnity or covenant specific tax indemnities may be added by the purchaser following tax due diligence. Common areas for such specific indemnification often include pre-effective date tax liabilities arising as a result of:

- transfer pricing or thin capitalisation adjustments;
- any corporate reorganisation or restructuring activity carried out by the seller before the effective date;
- the application of any anti-avoidance provisions to transactions or arrangements to which any of the defined target companies was a party before the effective date; and
- any of the defined target companies being tax resident for any period before the effective date in any jurisdiction other than a jurisdiction in which they are already acknowledged to be tax resident.

Exclusions or 'carve-outs' from the indemnity

The exclusions clause limits the indemnity by setting out the circumstances in which a pre-effective date tax liability will not be met by the seller. It usually follows immediately after the indemnity or covenant as Clause 3. See 8.3.2.

Other clauses in the tax deed of covenant

Subsequent clauses of the tax deed of covenant will generally include provisions:

- to allow the seller to settle claims for which it is liable under the tax covenant by means of:

  a payment to the purchaser in cash; or

  a surrender of group relief for no payment from a member of the seller's group to a target company;

  a reallocation for no payment of a de-grouping charge under *Section 179A Taxation of Chargeable Gains Act 1992* such that the de-grouping charge is treated as a gain of another member of the seller's group to which current year trading losses, capital losses, group relief , rollover relief *(Section 179B Taxation of Chargeable Gains Act 1992)* etc. may be available; or

  a reallocation for no payment of a de-grouping charge under *Paragraph 66 Schedule 29 Finance Act 2002*; or

  an election for no payment under *Section 171A Taxation of Chargeable Gains Act 1992* to treat a pre-effective date disposal of a chargeable asset to a third party by a target company as having been made by another member of the seller's group; or

  a transfer pricing balancing payment under *Paragraphs 7A to 7D Schedule 28AA Income and Corporation Taxes Act 1988*;

- to prevent claims where the tax liability to which they relate is sheltered by some pre-effective date tax asset or relief for which the purchaser has not paid or which has not otherwise been reflected in the purchase price;
- to determine when payments under the tax indemnity become due and the consequences with regard to interest etc. if they are made late;
- to take into account when determining the liability of the seller:

  additional tax benefits which arise to the purchaser as a result of successful claims under the tax indemnity;

  the purchaser's ability to recover the potential tax indemnity claim from a third party or under an insurance policy;

  over-provisions for tax at the effective date from which the purchaser will benefit;

  any other similar benefits available to the purchaser which ought reasonably to be reflected to the seller's advantage so as to prevent the purchaser from recovering more than the actual economic loss suffered;
- setting out the procedure for making and conducting tax claims and for dealing with disputed tax claims. The seller will normally require control of disputed claims. This is generally reasonable provided that the purchaser is:

  indemnified for the costs of any action required by the seller to defend the tax claim; and

  not required to take any action which might prejudice its post-completion tax position or its future relationship with the tax authorities.
- setting out the procedure for filing and agreeing (including the conduct of any appeal) the tax returns of the target company or group for:

  accounting periods ending on or before completion (the right to manage these periods is usually granted to the seller, at the seller's expense, with appropriate safeguards for the purchaser); and

  the accounting period which begins before and ends after the completion date (generally referred to as the 'straddle period'), the right to manage which is usually granted to the purchaser, at the purchaser's expense, with appropriate safeguards for the seller;
- to protect the seller against tax liabilities which are commercially and economically liabilities of the purchaser but which in certain circumstances can be recovered from the seller (the 'purchaser's covenant'

or 'counter-indemnity' provided by the purchaser). In the UK, these may include:

secondary tax liabilities arising under

Sections 767A and 767AA Income and Corporation Taxes Act 1988 (see Secondary Liabilities at 8.3.2 below);

Section 190 Taxation of Chargeable Gains Act 1992 (see Secondary Liabilities at 8.3.2 below);

Schedule 28 Finance Act 2000 (see Secondary Liabilities at 8.3.2 below);

Paragraph 68 Schedule 29 Finance Act 2002 (see Secondary Liabilities at 8.3.2 below);

Paragraph 75A Schedule 18 Finance Act 1998 (see Secondary Liabilities at 8.3.2 below);

Section 132 Finance Act 1988 (see Secondary Liabilities at 8.3.2 below);

post-completion VAT liabilities of a target company which are potentially recoverable from the seller's VAT group under *Section 43 Value Added Tax Act 1994* if that target company does not leave the seller's VAT group immediately on completion;

tax liabilities resulting from amendments after completion under the purchaser's ownership to claims and elections made before completion under the seller's ownership in repect of pre-completion accounting periods;

tax liabilities resulting from cessation of a target company's business or trade, or its winding up etc. after completion under the purchaser's ownership; and/or

tax liabilities resulting from certain special types of payment after completion under the purchaser's ownership, e.g. chargeable payments following a pre-completion tax-free demerger or the payment of an abnormal dividend;

- to gross-up tax indemnity payments where they are subject to withholding or are taxable in the hands of the recipient. See 8.3.2.

For an example of a standard tax indemnity, see above.

8.3. What should such contract review comprise?

8.3.1. The scope of the contract review by the tax due diligence provider

The scope of a review of the contract by whoever has carried out tax due diligence will depend on the precise scope of that tax due diligence. See Chapter 4 and 8.1.

Broadly, however, where contract review is to be included within the scope of a tax due diligence review (see 8.1), best practice tax due diligence should as a minimum:

- determine the extent to which:

    indemnities and warranties protect the purchaser against tax exposures identified by due diligence; and

    key representations made by the seller, or key assumptions made by the purchaser, with regard to tax are supported by warranties;
- suggest alternative means of protection where indemnities and warranties are inadequate and cannot appropriately be extended;
- ensure that disclosures against the warranties and other limitations on indemnity or warranty protection are reasonable and acceptable; and
- review and comment on tax aspects of any price adjustment mechanism provided for in the contract based on completion accounts or a 'locked box' balance sheet (see 8.10 and 9.14).

The contract review by the tax due diligence provider should therefore also include a check of any provision in the contract which seeks to define, exclude or limit claims under either the tax indemnities or warranties for exposures identified by tax due diligence. In addition to the disclosures, these can include matters such as:

- the definitions of terms which are fundamental to the ability to make such claims, e.g. 'tax', 'relief', 'event' etc.;
- whether interest and/or penalties are included within the definition of what can be claimed under the tax indemnities or warranties (as a general principle, they should be);
- whether claims can be made for tax exposures in whichever jurisdiction they arise;
- whether the circumstances in which claims can be excluded by the seller are reasonable and/or commercially acceptable;
- whether the time limits within which valid tax claims must be made are reasonable and/or commercially acceptable;
- whether the financial limits on claims under the tax indemnities or warranties are reasonable and/or commercially acceptable; and
- other specific limitations, e.g. the carve-outs from the scope of the tax indemnity. See 8.3.2.

The provider of tax due diligence reviewing the contract should be aware of the status of the particular draft of the contract on which comment is required.

It is usually the seller's lawyers who issue the first draft of the contract, the terms of which, as might be expected, will tend to favour the seller. The purchaser's lawyers, in consultation with the purchaser and the purchaser's other advisers, will then mark up the seller's draft with the amendments required by the purchaser. In response, the seller's lawyers, in consultation with the seller and the seller's other advisers, will then agree the purchaser's amendments, propose further revisions to them or reject them altogether. And so on until the final contract is negotiated.

Before commenting on any particular draft of the contract, the purchaser's tax due diligence adviser should therefore be clear on two things:

- whether the draft contract has last come from the seller's or the purchaser's lawyers; and
- whether the amendments marked up in the draft are agreed or are merely proposals by one side which have not yet been agreed by the other.

Without clarity on these two questions, the purchaser's tax due diligence adviser might otherwise decide not to comment on a particular provision of the contract relevant to a due diligence finding, as marked up by the purchaser's lawyers, on the basis that the mark-up already covers the finding in question. However, the purchaser's mark-up may be rejected by the seller leaving the purchaser exposed. In these circumstances, the purchaser's tax due diligence adviser should always raise a tax exposure of material concern to emphasise its importance and to stress that it is covered only by the purchaser's mark-up. In this way, the purchaser and its advisers will be aware of the significance if the mark-up is subsequently rejected or further revised by the seller.

8.3.2. Review of the tax indemnity or covenant by the tax due diligence provider

The purpose of the review of the tax indemnity by the tax due diligence provider is essentially to compare the protection which the indemnity affords with the tax exposures identified by due diligence.

In most cases where a market practice tax indemnity is being offered by the seller, tax exposures identified by due diligence will be covered by the general tax indemnity. If there is any doubt about whether this is the case, that doubt should be referred to the purchaser's legal advisers on the purchaser's behalf.

Even where the general indemnity does cover a particular tax exposure, the tax due diligence provider should consider whether exclusions and/or limitations imposed on the general indemnity elsewhere in the contract or tax deed of covenant render this protection ineffective. For example, the general indemnity may cover a particular exposure but may be subject to a de minimis amount or claim threshold which exceeds the amount of any potential claim. Where this is the case, it may be appropriate to recommend a specific indemnity for the particular exposure which may then be specifically excluded from the exclusion or limitation in question.

Tax liabilities which arise on or as a result of the act of completion itself

As a matter of normal UK market practice, the tax indemnity should oblige the seller to meet not only all tax liabilities which arise pre-completion (or pre-effective date - see 8.2.2), but also those tax liabilities which arise on or as a result of the act of completion itself. This is important to protect the purchaser against tax charges or claw-backs which are triggered on exit from a selling group. In the UK, these may include:

- de-grouping charges which arise where a company leaves a capital gains group holding an asset transferred to it within the preceding six years by way of a tax neutral intra-group transfer from a group company to be retained by the seller *(Section 179 Taxation of Chargeable Gains Act 1992)*. See 9.2. A market practice tax indemnity will usually reserve the right for the seller to meet *Section 179* de-grouping charges by means of:

  a payment to the purchaser in cash; or

  a reallocation for no payment of the de-grouping charge under *Section 179A Taxation of Chargeable Gains Act 1992* such that the de-grouping charge is treated as a gain of another member of the seller's group to which current year trading losses, capital losses, group relief, rollover relief *(Section 179B Taxation of Chargeable Gains Act 1992)* etc. may be available; or

  a surrender of group relief for no payment;

- the equivalent de-grouping charge under *Paragraph 58 Schedule 29 Finance Act 2002* where the asset in question is an intangible fixed asset created or acquired on or after 1 April 2002 in the circumstances described in *Paragraph 118 Schedule 29 Finance Act 2002;*
- claw-back of relief from Stamp Duty Land Tax under *Paragraphs 3 and 4A Schedule 7 Finance Act 2003.*

Also potentially within the category of tax liabilities which arise on or as a result of the act of completion itself are certain PAYE and NIC liabilities on the exercise of share options and the award of shares which vest on completion. Technically, however, these are often triggered immediately prior to completion. PAYE and employee's NIC should be recoverable from the employees benefiting from the options or awards where the seller has obtained appropriate indemnities from the employees (typically, the rules of the relevant share scheme should allow for such recovery). In any event, as a due diligence matter, the purchaser will want to know whether such indemnities are in place without which the PAYE and employee's NIC become a liability of the target company or group. Where a PAYE and NIC charge is triggered, the employer's NIC will be a charge to the target company.

Secondary liabilities

It will also be important for the purchaser to ensure that the tax indemnity will provide protection against tax liabilities which may become recoverable from a target company even though they are primarily liabilities of an entity either retained or formerly owned by the seller's group, i.e. so-called 'secondary liabilities.' In the UK, these may include secondary liabilities arising under the following provisions.

Section 767A Income and Corporation Taxes Act 1988

Section 767A was introduced in 1994 to counter tax avoidance of the type described in *Revenue Interpretation 90 (October 1994) Corporation Tax – company purchase scheme.* The section applies where there has been a change in the ownership of a company and where corporation tax which has been assessed on that company before the change in ownership remains unpaid for six months. In certain circumstances, *Section 767A* permits the recovery of the unpaid corporation tax from any person who previously controlled the company, or from any company which was under the control of that person within the period of three years before the change in ownership.

Accordingly, a target company could become secondarily liable under *Section 767A* for corporation tax primarily assessed on another company which was formerly owned by the seller but which has changed ownership.

Specifically, *Section 767A* provides that where:

- there has been a change in ownership of a company (*Section 767A(1)(a)*); and
- corporation tax relating to an accounting period beginning before the change in ownership remains unpaid for more than six months (*Section 767A(1)(b)*); and
- one of the conditions in *Sections 767A(4), (5) or (6)* is satisfied (*Section 767A(1)(c)*);

then the unpaid tax can be recovered from:

- any person who at any time during either the three years before the change of ownership of the company, or, if shorter, the period since a previous change of ownership, controlled the company (*Section 767A(2)(a)*); or

- any company which that person controlled at any time during the three years before the change of ownership (*Section 767A(2)(b)*). In *Revenue Interpretation 90,* HMRC acknowledge that such companies as are envisaged by *Section 767A(2)(b)* 'may have been sold before the sale of the company which has failed to meet its tax liability. Anyone buying a company will want to consider seeking an indemnity from the vendor in case the company purchased is faced with a liability under' *Section 767A. Revenue Interpretation 90* goes on to say that 'if the Revenue does have to apply the legislation, it will seek to obtain the outstanding tax from those who previously controlled the company and from any companies which can be charged and which are still controlled by the vendor before looking to companies which are no longer under the vendor's control. It is unlikely that the Revenue will have to look to a company which has been sold…' *Revenue Interpretation 90* also suggests that 'it would clearly be unwise for warranties and indemnities not to be sought in respect of all disposals of companies.'

Control, for these purposes, is based on the definition in *Section 416 Income and Corporation Taxes Act 1988* as modified by *Section 767B (5) and (6) Income and Corporation Taxes Act 1988.*

Section 767AA Income and Corporation Taxes Act 1988

Section 767AA was introduced by *Finance Act 1998* to counter tax avoidance schemes which attempted to circumvent *Section 767A* as described in *Inland Revenue Company Taxation Manual* at *6505.*

Like *Section 767A, Section 767AA* also addresses unpaid corporation tax and requires a change in the ownership of a company. However, before *Section 767AA* can apply, it must be reasonable to infer that a potential corporation tax liability would be unlikely to be met.

Under *Section 767AA,* a target company could become secondarily liable for corporation tax primarily assessed on a company (or a company associated with it) which was formerly owned by the seller but which has changed ownership.

Specifically, *Section 767AA* provides that where:

- there has been a change in ownership of a company (*Section 767AA(1)(a)*); and

- corporation tax relating to an accounting period ending on or after the change in ownership has been assessed on that company (or on a company associated with it) (*Section 767AA(1)(b)*); and
- the tax assessed remains unpaid for more than six months (*Section 767AA(1)(c)*); and
- it would be reasonable to infer from the terms of the transactions entered into in connection with the change in ownership (and/or other circumstances of the change or transactions) that at least one of the transactions was entered into by one or more of the parties to it on the assumption that a potential tax liability would be unlikely to be met (*Section 767AA(2)*);

then the unpaid tax can be recovered from:

- any person who at any time during either the three years before the change of ownership of the company, or, if shorter, the period since a previous change of ownership, controlled the company; or
- any company which that person controlled at any time during the three years before the change of ownership.

As for *Section 767A*, control is based on the definition in *Section 416* as modified by *Section 767B (5) and (6)*.

Section 190 Taxation of Chargeable Gains Act 1992

Under *Section 190 Taxation of Chargeable Gains Act 1992*, a target company could become secondarily liable for corporation tax primarily due from a company retained by the seller for an accounting period in which a chargeable gain accrues to that retained company. Under *Section 190*, where the whole or part of that corporation tax remains unpaid at the end of the period of six months after it becomes payable, it may be recovered from:

- a company which was the principal company of the seller's group at the time when the gain accrued *(Section 190(3)(a)(i))*; or
- any other company which for any part of the 12 months ending with the time when the gain accrued was a member of the seller's group and owned, in whole or in part, the asset disposed of. (Where the asset disposed of comprises an interest in, or right over, another asset, ownership of either asset will be enough to fall within this provision) *(Section 190(3)(a)(ii))*.

Schedule 28 Finance Act 2000

Under *Schedule 28 Finance Act 2000*, a target company could become secondarily liable for corporation tax primarily assessed on a non-resident company retained or formerly owned by the seller.

Where such tax remains unpaid after six months, *Paragraph 2 Schedule 28* provides that it may be recovered from any company which at any time beginning twelve months before the start of the accounting period for which the tax was assessed and ending when the unpaid tax first became payable:

- was a member of the same group of companies as the non-resident company (*Paragraph 2(1)(a)*);
- was a member of a consortium which at the time referred to above owned the non-resident company (*Paragraph 2(1)(b)*); or
- was a member of the same group of companies as a company which at the time referred to above was a member of a consortium owning the non-resident company (*Paragraph 2(1)(c)*).

Section 282 Taxaxtion of Chargeable Gains Act 1992

Where a chargeable gain accrues to any company on the disposal of an asset by way of gift (or any other transaction otherwise than by way of a bargain made at arm's length) and any corporation tax on chargeable gains remains unpaid for more than 12 months, then under *Section 282(1) Taxation of Chargeable Gains Act 1992* the donee may be assessed and charged to corporation tax in the name of the donor. However, any secondary tax liability paid under *Section 282(1)* can be recovered from the donor under *Section 282(2).*

Paragraph 68 Schedule 29 Finance Act 2002

Where a tax-neutral intra-group transfer of an intangible fixed asset has taken place and the transferee leaves the transferor's group within six years of the transfer, a de-grouping charge may arise in the transferee company.

Under *Paragraph 68 Schedule 29 Finance Act 2002,* a target company could become secondarily liable for corporation tax primarily due from a company retained by the seller in relation to such a de-grouping charge.

If the corporation tax in relation to the de-grouping charge has been assessed on the transferee company and remains unpaid at the end of the period of six months after it becomes payable, it may be recovered from:

- a company which was the principal company of the group at the time when the de-grouping charge accrued *(Paragraph 68(2)(a)(i))*; or
- any other company which at any time in the 12 months ending with the time when the de-grouping charge accrued was a member of the group and owned, in whole or in part, the intangible fixed asset in relation to which the de-grouping charge arises *(Paragraph 68(2)(a)(ii)).*

Paragraph 75A Schedule 18 Finance Act 1998

Paragraph 75A Schedule 18 Finance Act 1998 can create a secondary liability where a company has claimed group relief from another group member but subsequently becomes liable to tax as a result of the withdrawal or cancellation of the surrender of that group relief under *Paragraph 75 Schedule 18 Finance Act 1998*.

If any of this tax remains unpaid six months after the chargeable company's time limit for group relief claims, then the tax may be recovered from any other company which obtained group relief as part of the same surrender.

Accordingly, a target company acquired by a purchaser could become secondarily liable in relation to a pre-acquisition withdrawal of group relief from a company retained by the seller.

Section 132 Finance Act 1988

Section 132 Finance Act 1988 can create a secondary liability where a company ceases to be resident in the UK without having settled tax liabilities for periods before its migration. If such liabilities have not been paid within six months from the date on which they became due, HMRC can recover the unpaid tax from any company which was a member of the same group as the migrating company within the twelve months before the migration.

Section 43 Value Added Tax Act 1994

A member of a VAT group is jointly and severally liable for the group's VAT liabilities in relation to the period during which it was a member. This liability continues even after membership of the VAT group has ceased. Accordingly, if before its acquisition a target company has been a member of a VAT group, it will remain jointly and severally liable for that group's VAT liabilities in relation to the period during which it was a member even after it has been acquired by a purchaser.

Liabilities other than actual tax liabilities

Care should be taken to ensure that the tax indemnity covers not only actual tax liabilities but also:

- liabilities which are not strictly tax themselves but which are clearly tax-related such that they could reasonably be expected to be met by the seller. These will include penalties and interest for late payment of tax and the gross-up charge under *Section 222 Income Tax (Earnings and Pensions) Act 2003* which applies where PAYE has not been recovered from employees within 90 days;
- liabilities which may become due from the target company or group

under any pre-existing tax indemnity which the target may have given to a third party, for example in connection with a previous share disposal of its own;

- liabilities to make payments for group relief surrendered to the target company from a company in the seller's retained group;
- liabilities to make repayments to a company in the seller's retained group in respect of group relief which was surrendered by the target to that company for payment but which is no longer available;
- liabilities to make payments in connection with a group payment arrangement under *Section 36 Finance Act 1998* with regard to pre-completion accounting periods;
- liabilities to make other intra-group payments or repayments in relation to tax;
- tax liabilities where no actual tax becomes payable because the liability is sheltered either:

  by a tax asset or relief arising pre-completion for which the purchaser has paid or which is reflected in the purchase price; or

  by the carry back of a tax asset or relief arising post-completion.

Carve-outs

Having established the extent to which the indemnity protects the purchaser against tax exposures identified by due diligence, it will next be necessary to ensure that the carve-outs from the scope of the indemnity do not unreasonably detract from this indemnification. The carve-outs which are generally accepted as normal market practice in the UK (in the absence of specific reasons to the contrary) include the following.

Carve-outs referable to acts or defaults of the purchaser

- Tax liabilities which would not have arisen but for, or are increased by, some voluntary act or omission on the part of the purchaser or a target company after completion. Such voluntary acts or omissions are sometimes defined specifically to include the making by the purchaser or a target company after completion of any claim, disclaimer, election etc.; although this latter more often takes the form of a separate exclusion. The carve-out for post-completion voluntary acts is usually qualified to exclude:

  post-completion acts or omissions by the purchaser or a target company which are required by law;

  post-completion acts or omissions by the purchaser or a target company which are required by the terms of the agreement between seller and purchaser or by some other legally binding obligation incurred before completion;

post-completion acts or omissions by the purchaser or a target company which are otherwise agreed or approved by the seller;

post-completion acts or omissions in the ordinary course of the target's business as carried on at completion;

the post-completion stamping, or bringing into the UK, of any document executed prior to completion; or

any other act or omission by the purchaser or a target company which is not strictly 'voluntary'.

- Tax liabilities which would not have arisen but for, or are increased by, a failure on the part of the purchaser or a group company to make any claim, disclaimer, election etc. which has been taken into account in the computation of the provision for tax in a specified set of financial statements agreed between the parties (e.g. the last audited financial statements or any completion accounts). In these circumstances, the purchaser's tax due diligence will therefore need to provide a full understanding of the basis on which this tax provision has been calculated. Additionally or alternatively, the seller should be required to disclose this information.
- Tax liabilities recovered by the purchaser by means other than a claim under the tax indemnity, for example:

  by some other mechanism provided for in the contract, e.g. a warranty claim. In this context, the seller will want to prevent double recovery by the purchaser, while the purchaser will want the right to decide under which particular contractual provision the claim will be made;

  from a third party; or

  under a policy of insurance.
- Tax liabilities which would not have arisen but for, or are increased by, a post-completion change in the accounting bases, methods, policies or practices of a target company, including a change in the accounting reference date. Purchasers will wish to qualify this carve-out to exclude such changes where they are necessary to correct an accounting policy or practice which did not previously comply with the appropriate GAAP.
- Tax liabilities which would not have arisen but for, or are increased by, some post-completion failure on the part of the purchaser or a target company to meet some tax compliance obligation with regard to a pre-completion accounting period.

- Tax liabilities which would not have arisen but for, or are increased by, some failure on the part of the purchaser or a target company to fulfil the obligations imposed by the contract with the seller, in particular with regard to notification of potential claims to the seller.
- VAT liabilities which arise:

  from a post-completion annual adjustment to the amount of input VAT provisionally recovered by a partially exempt business during the previous periods of the tax year (*Regulation 107 VAT Regulations 1995*); or

  where there is a post-completion change in an intention to use goods or services for the purposes of making taxable supplies. Specifically, before completion goods or services may have been acquired by the target business with the intention of using them to make taxable supplies and input VAT may have been recovered accordingly. If within six years, and before the goods or services are actually brought into use, there is a post-completion change in this intention, then there may be an adjustment to the input VAT originally recovered (*Regulation 108 VAT Regulations 1995*).

Carve-outs referable to matters beyond the purchaser's control and to other matters

- Tax liabilities for which provision or reserve has been made in a specified set of financial statements agreed between the parties. These may be the last audited financial statements or any completion accounts prepared for the purposes of the transaction in question; but the intention is to exclude from the indemnity any tax liability which will already have been provided for in the financial statements on the basis of which the purchaser has agreed the purchase price.
- Where there is to be no price adjustment based on completion accounts, it is normal UK market practice for the purchaser to be responsible for tax liabilities in respect of profits arising in the ordinary course of the target company's business between:

  the date of the accounts on the basis of which the purchaser has agreed the purchase price; and

  completion;

  so such liabilities are generally excluded from the scope of the tax indemnity which in relation to the above period will cover only tax liabilities arising outside the ordinary course of the target company's business.
- The target company or group may already have paid a particular tax liability before completion; or it may be required to pay its corporation tax

liability under the instalment payments regime. In a transaction where there are to be no completion accounts, any such payments or instalment payments which a target company or group may have made on account of the tax liability for the period from the date of the last audited balance sheet up to completion will not be recognised in any price adjustment. The seller will therefore be keen to ensure that any such payments on account are excluded from claims under the tax indemnity (including where they may have been greater than actually required); while the purchaser will be equally keen to ensure that inadequate instalment payments can be recovered, together with any consequent interest and penalties. The purchaser's due diligence provider should:

identify the amount of any instalment payments made by the target company or group between the date of the last audited balance sheet and the date of the tax due diligence review; and

identify the dates on which the above payments were made; and

form a view, in light of available forecasts and projections for the period, on whether the instalment payments were adequate.

- Income may have been received by a target company before completion which is not recognised as income for tax and accounting purposes until a later post-completion period. The seller will argue that any tax liability arising in connection with this income should be for the purchaser's account on the basis that the purchaser will have had the benefit of the income in the intervening period.
- Tax liabilities which are economically offset by a corresponding relief or saving. For example, a tax return for a pre-completion accounting period may be adjusted following HMRC enquiry to disallow certain expenditure on the basis that it is capital rather than revenue in nature. This could have the effect of increasing the tax liability in connection with that particular pre-completion accounting period and prima facie thereby give rise to a potential claim by the purchaser under the tax indemnity. However, if the disallowed capital expenditure qualifies for capital allowances, the target company in question may still obtain tax relief for it, albeit over a period of time rather than in one year. Where this is the case, it would not be reasonable to require the seller to reimburse the purchaser for the increased pre-completion tax liability, only for the purchaser to obtain tax relief for the same expenditure in subsequent accounting periods.
- Tax liabilities which are economically offset by an overprovision for tax in a specified set of financial statements agreed between the parties (e.g. the last audited financial statements or any completion accounts).

- Tax liabilities which are sheltered by some pre-completion tax asset or relief for which the purchaser has not paid or which has not otherwise been reflected in the purchase price.
- Tax liabilities which would not have arisen but for, or are increased by, a change in the rates of taxation or in tax law or practice or procedure occurring after completion but with retrospective effect.

Timing of indemnity payments

The tax deed of covenant will include clauses stipulating when payments under the tax indemnity become due and the consequences with regard to interest etc. if they are made late. Broadly, interest which is added to a successful claim to compensate the recipient for its payment after the date stipulated in the contract will be taxed as such (e.g. under *Section 100 Finance Act 1996*). It will not generally be treated as an adjustment to the purchase price. However, if the parties agree, it can sometimes be subject to a gross-up obligation. These are ultimately matters for commercial negotiation between the parties.

However, the tax due diligence provider should review these provisions to ensure that they are reasonable in the context of the specific tax liabilities identified by due diligence. Specifically, provided that a claim is notified to the seller in good time, they should be such as to enable the purchaser or the relevant target company to meet the pre-completion tax liability to which the claim relates without incurring interest or penalties.

This will depend on the nature of the tax liability for which an indemnity claim has been made:

- where the claim relates to an actual tax liability, the tax due diligence provider may be required to determine its due date and recommend an appropriate earlier date by which the tax indemnity claim should be settled by the seller;
- similarly, where the claim relates to the loss of a tax repayment due to a target company in connection with a pre-completion accounting period, the tax due diligence provider may be required to estimate the likely date when such repayment would otherwise have been received;
- where, however, the claim relates to a loss of a pre-completion tax relief, the tax due diligence provider may be required to comment, based on projections etc., on when an actual tax liability may become due in the future as a result of the loss of that pre-completion tax relief.

Grossing up tax indemnity claims

Contracts for the sale of a target company's shares will usually include a gross-up clause, the purpose of which is to gross-up tax indemnity payments where they are subject to withholding or are taxable in the hands of the recipient.

Specifically, where a payment under the tax indemnity is taxable in the hands of its recipient, the gross-up clause requires the payer to increase the sum payable to an amount which after such taxation would leave the recipient in the same position as if no tax had been payable.

A seller might resist a gross-up clause, arguing that it is unnecessary on the basis that *ESC D33* should apply to payments under the tax indemnity such that they should be treated as non-taxable adjustments to the purchase price.

However, as explained at 8.2.2 above, there are situations in which *ESC D33* will not apply and a gross-up clause will protect the purchaser in these circumstances. Where *ESC D33* does not apply and accordingly an indemnity payment is potentially taxable, the payer would therefore be required to gross up the indemnity payment.

In any event, where *ESC D33* does apply a gross-up clause should not harm the seller; and it will provide corresponding protection for the seller itself where payments are made by the purchaser to the seller under a purchaser's covenant.

A gross-up clause is not generally necessary with regard to tax warranty payments because *Section 49(1)(c) and (2) Taxation of Chargeable Gains Act 1992* provide that warranty payments are treated for tax purposes as adjustments to the purchase price. See 8.2.1 above.

8.3.3. Review of the tax warranties by the tax due diligence provider

The purpose of the review of the tax warranties by the tax due diligence provider is essentially to compare the protection which the warranties afford with the tax exposures identified by due diligence. Specifically the purchaser's tax due diligence provider should determine the extent to which:

- the tax warranties protect the purchaser against tax exposures identified by due diligence; and
- key representations by the seller, or assumptions by the purchaser, with regard to tax are supported by warranties.

Generally, the tax indemnity is the principal means by which the purchaser is protected against historical tax exposures and tax warranties tend to be of secondary importance in this regard. However, tax warranties are important in the following respects:

- in contrast to the tax indemnity, tax warranties are capable of providing the purchaser with a measure of contractual protection beyond completion. In particular, they are capable of forming the basis of a claim by the purchaser where there is a breach of warranty with regard to facts or circumstances warranted at completion which gives rise to a post-completion tax liability. For example, a seller may be prepared to warrant that the tax written down value of a target company's assets qualifying for capital allowances at completion will be not less than a certain agreed amount. A breach of this warranty is likely to increase a tax liability of the target company for a post-completion accounting period;
- tax warranties support tax due diligence by making key representations by the seller, or assumptions by the purchaser, terms of the contract on which the purchaser may then rely; and
- the purchaser may use tax warranties to force disclosure of information from the seller (see 8.7.5).

For whichever purpose they are applied, tax warranties should be as precise as possible. Very broad or vague warranties are likely to be resisted by the seller and may make proof of breach and consequent loss more difficult.

8.3.4. Tax assets (losses and other reliefs)

Sellers will often encourage purchasers to reflect a target's tax assets (tax losses in particular and, increasingly, corporation tax deductions on share option exercises or share awards in particular) in the purchase price, especially in auction sales.

The future availability of the target's tax assets is subject to a number of risks and is rarely certain (see 4.2.5 and 9.1). Purchasers should therefore generally resist pressure to attribute value to them, although it is sometimes appropriate to do so on a contingent basis, i.e. as and when the benefit of the losses is realised in future accounting periods.

Even where tax assets are not reflected in the purchase price, they may be available to shelter pre-completion tax liabilities of the target company or group. To this extent, pre-completion tax losses are essentially a cushion for historical tax exposures, reducing the extent of the purchaser's risk (and possibly also the scope of the purchaser's pre-acquisition tax due diligence – see 4.2.5). Sellers will wish to limit their exposure under any tax indemnity where a tax liability which could give rise to a potential indemnity claim can be sheltered by pre-completion tax losses. In response, purchasers will argue that this should only be the case where no value has been attributed to the pre-completion tax losses in arriving at the purchase price. See 4.2.5 and 9.1. In this regard, the seller will be anxious to ensure that, for the purposes of calculating any claim under the tax indemnity, pre-completion tax liabilities should be sheltered by pre-completion tax losses or reliefs in priority to any carry back of post-completion losses or reliefs.

In the rare situations where the purchaser has attributed value to tax losses in the purchase price, consideration should be given as to whether the seller should be required:

- to warrant the existence of the losses, or a minimum amount of losses, which will be available immediately before completion. The seller will understandably be unwilling to warrant the availability of any losses beyond completion because this will depend on circumstances beyond their control, such as the post-completion actions of the purchaser; and/or
- to indemnify the purchaser for any tax which becomes due in the event that the losses, or a minimum agreed amount of losses, is not available at completion. Again, the seller will be unwilling to provide an indemnity which protects the purchaser where the losses are not available as the result of some post-completion act or omission on the part of the purchaser.

In either case, the seller will insist that contractual protection should only be provided in respect of specific defined tax losses and that claims should not be permitted where relief for those losses is denied as a result of some post-completion event beyond the seller's control, e.g. a change by the purchaser in the nature or conduct of the loss-making trade.

Tax assets may be implicitly reflected in the price paid by the purchaser where that price is determined by reference to the net assets or net debt of the target company or group at an agreed date. See 9.14. Net assets or net debt will generally include provisions for current (and occasionally deferred) tax which in turn may have taken into account a certain level of tax assets. In these circumstances, the tax warranties and/or tax indemnity should be drafted so as to enable the purchaser to recover from the seller any tax which becomes due now or in the future as a result of the loss of such tax assets.

8.3.5. Reviewing the contract in auctions and contract races

In auctions and contract races there is a risk of over-amending the seller's proposed draft contract. A draft contract which is too heavily marked up by a potential purchaser can render that purchaser's bid uncompetitive. Auctions are sometimes won not by the highest bidder but by the bidder whose offer is subject to the fewest conditions.

This should obviously be borne in mind by the tax due diligence provider reviewing a contract in an auction situation; but it should not necessarily deter the tax due diligence provider from commenting on the matters described in 8.3 above as fully as would have been the case without the competitive tension of the auction. It should be left to the bidder to decide the extent of mark-up commercially desirable for the particular auction, with legal advice where appropriate.

8.4. Assignability of the benefit of tax warranties and indemnities

It is sometimes necessary to consider whether the benefit of tax warranties and indemnities is capable of being assigned to a party other than the one to whom they were originally given. This may be because the original beneficiary of the tax warranties and indemnities may wish to on-sell all or part of the acquired business or to transfer it to another company within the purchaser's group.

The assignability of tax warranties and indemnities is a legal matter with which the tax due diligence provider will have little or no involvement. It does, however, have implications for tax due diligence as follows.

A particular target company or group may have been acquired by the seller in a previous acquisition. When discussing with a potential purchaser how much tax due diligence is either desirable or permissible, a seller may claim:

- that up to a certain date the target company or group is already covered by tax warranties and indemnities provided to the seller by the party from whom the target was originally acquired; and
- that the benefit of these tax warranties and indemnities may be assigned to the purchaser in the current transaction.

Accordingly, a seller may argue that tax due diligence review of periods up to and including that date is unnecessary.

While this may be true, it cannot be relied on by the purchaser as a valid limitation of the scope of the tax due diligence review without careful consideration of the legal position. Even where it is true, before proceeding with the acquisition the purchaser is still likely to require some idea of the nature and scale of the potential tax risks inherent in the target company or group as well as an understanding of the financial position of the person giving the original tax warranties and indemnities.

In any event, the original tax warranties and indemnities provided to the seller may fall short of those required by the purchaser in the current transaction. They may be too limited in extent or too qualified by exclusions and limitations to be acceptable to the current purchaser. There is no reason why the current purchaser should necessarily accept terms and conditions accepted by the seller in a wholly different transaction in what might have been entirely different commercial circumstances.

Perhaps most importantly, payments under a tax indemnity to a party other than the original purchaser will not be protected from taxation by *Extra Statutory Concession D33 (ESC D33).* Such payments are therefore potentially taxable in the hands of the recipient. See 8.2.2.

A gross-up clause often applies to payments under a tax indemnity. Where a payment under the indemnity is taxable in the hands of its recipient, the gross-up clause requires the payer to increase the sum payable to an amount which after such taxation would leave the recipient in the same position as if no tax had been payable.

Where *ESC D33* does not apply, and where accordingly an indemnity payment is potentially taxable, under a gross-up clause the payer would be required to gross up the indemnity payment. For this reason, sellers providing tax indemnities governed by a gross-up clause will wish to limit the gross-up to no more than would have been payable had the indemnity payment been made to the original purchaser.

Where the gross-up clause is limited by the seller in this way, a payment under a tax indemnity will not therefore be protected from taxation, either by *ESC D33* or by a gross-up clause, where it is made to a person who was not the original purchaser but a person to whom the benefit of the tax indemnity was assigned.

8.5. Extending and supporting tax due diligence with warranties

Much useful tax due diligence is performed by means of interviews, meetings, discussions and telephone conversations etc. rather than by review of documents. Wherever possible, the important findings to emerge from these interviews, meetings, discussions and telephone conversations should be verified subsequently by review of supporting documentary evidence. But this is not always possible. The seller is unlikely to be in a position to provide documentary support for every statement made throughout the due diligence process. In particular, this is likely to be the case with regard to negative assertions that the facts which would otherwise give rise to a certain particular tax risk do not exist.

Where such representations or assertions are critical to the purchaser's investment decision, they should be given contractual effect by conversion into warranties. In this way, the purchaser is given a degree of comfort that the representation may be relied upon; and such course of action may also force disclosure of further relevant supporting information (see 8.7.5).

Tax warranties are also a useful means by which the purchaser can obtain some level of assurance with regard to post-completion tax exposures. The protection afforded by the tax indemnities is invariably limited to the period up to and including completion of the transaction. Tax warranties, on the other hand, are capable of continuing into the post-completion period and giving rise to a claim by the purchaser for a post-completion breach.

Areas in which tax warranties can provide a degree of comfort to a purchaser with regard to future events include:

- warranties in relation to the capital gains base cost of certain assets (see 8.11.12);
- warranties to support the provision for deferred tax in a defined balance sheet (see 8.11.2); and
- warranties to support the current level of instalment payments (see 8.11.3).

8.6. Limitations on claims under tax indemnities and warranties

The seller of the shares of a target company will clearly and reasonably wish to impose limitations on potential claims by the purchaser under the tax indemnities and warranties. Without such contractual limitations, the seller:

- would be potentially exposed to open-ended liability without time limit (subject only to general law time limits imposed by the *Limitation Act 1980*); and
- could face the administrative burden of dealing with large numbers of relatively trivial claims.

The purchaser, on the other hand, will be keen to ensure that the limitations on claims imposed by the seller will not be such as to prevent or limit claims under the tax indemnities and warranties for the very tax risks and exposures identified by due diligence as being of material concern.

The nature and extent of contractual limitations on indemnity and warranty claims will be a matter for commercial negotiation between the parties. In support of the purchaser's negotiation of contractual limitations which are fair and reasonable, the purchaser's tax due diligence adviser may be called upon to comment on the effect of particular limitations, usually suggested by the seller, in relation to tax exposures identified by due diligence.

Where the ability to make a claim for a specific tax exposure identified by due diligence is sufficiently important to a purchaser's negotiating position, it may be appropriate to exclude such a claim altogether from certain of the contractual limitations. This may be the case where the ability to make a claim is fundamental to the purchaser's view of the allocation of tax risk between purchaser and seller, for example where the tax exposure in question arises from some pre-sale reorganisation wholly for the seller's benefit.

8.6.1. Exclusions or carve-out clause of the tax indemnity

See 8.3.2.

8.6.2. Matters disclosed by the seller to the purchaser via the formal process of disclosure

Tax exposures which arise in connection with matters disclosed by the seller to the purchaser via the formal process of disclosure are excluded from claims under the tax warranties. See 8.7. However, disclosure should have no corresponding effect on claims under the tax indemnity. See 8.7.6.

8.6.3. Time limits for making tax claims

In the UK, the *Limitation Act 1980* imposes the following general time limits on contractual claims:

- six years from the date of the corresponding cause of action for claims under a simple contract (*Section 5*); and
- twelve years from the date of the corresponding cause of action for claims under a contract by deed, e.g. a deed of tax covenant (*Section 8*).

Paragraph 46(1) Schedule 18 Finance Act 1998 provides that 'Subject to any provisions of the Taxes Acts allowing a longer period in any particular class of case no assessment may be made more than six years after the end of the accounting period to which it relates.'

Accordingly, the generally accepted time limit for tax claims is commonly expressed as:

- six years plus the appeals period from the end of the accounting period in which completion takes place; or
- seven years from completion; or
- the period ending on the last day on which a valid tax assessment can be raised in respect of any accounting period up to and including the accounting period in which completion takes place.

The first two of these make the assumption that there are no circumstances which could constitute fraud or negligence and which could therefore extend the period in which HMRC could raise tax assessments from six to 21 years after the end of the accounting period to which they relate (*Paragraph 46(2) Schedule 18 Finance Act 1998*). In the absence of specific tax due diligence concerns to the contrary, this assumption is generally acceptable from a commercial perspective, in particular because a tax indemnity might otherwise represent a potential liability to a seller for a commercially unacceptable period of time from the date of the sale.

Nor will the first two of the above three time limits necessarily allow the purchaser to recover secondary tax liabilities which can effectively be assessed on a target company outside these time limits.

The last of the above three time limits has the advantage of potentially accommodating tax claims even if they arise as a consequence of an assessment outside the normal six year statutory time limit. For the reason given above, however, it is likely to be challenged by the seller.

The period within which valid tax assessments can be raised by the tax authorities varies considerably from jurisdiction to jurisdiction. Accordingly, where the target business has operations in a number of different jurisdictions, care should be taken by the purchaser to ensure that the time limit for valid claims under the tax indemnities or warranties is sufficiently long to permit such claims in whichever jurisdiction they might arise.

8.6.4. Financial limits on tax claims

Generally, there are three types of financial limitations or thresholds which are capable of applying to limit the ability to make claims under the tax indemnities and warranties.

- The de minimis amount per claim

  This is the financial amount below which claims are to be ignored altogether for the purposes of the tax indemnities and warranties. Its purpose is to prevent trivial claims.

- The claim threshold or 'basket'

  Even if an individual claim is for more than the de minimis amount described above, it is often still not possible to make a claim under the tax indemnities and warranties until the aggregate amount of all such individual claims passes a further claim threshold, sometimes referred to informally as 'the basket'. This is the total financial amount which all claims, validated in accordance with the terms of the contract, must exceed before a claim can actually be made. Its purpose is to prevent the administrative burden of a large number of separate small claims. The claim threshold should specify whether the purchaser is able to recover all valid claims once the threshold has been reached or only the excess of valid claims over the threshold.

- The cap

> This is the maximum amount of all claims (tax or otherwise) permitted by the contract. It is usually set at the amount of consideration paid by the purchaser (or a percentage of consideration) or at a fixed sum. Its purpose is to cap the seller's total liability at a fixed agreed amount so that the contract for sale shares risk between seller and purchaser on some commercially acceptable basis and does not leave the seller with a potentially open-ended and bottomless exposure.

These financial limits are largely a matter of commercial negotiation between the parties, but their significance to tax due diligence will be clear. Pre-acquisition tax due diligence will have identified and quantified the key tax risks which the purchaser will wish to address. One of the principal ways of addressing these risks is through the contract for the purchase of the target shares or business. Consequently, if the contract itself prevents claims for these risks on the basis of its financial limitations on claims, then the purchaser is left exposed to the very risks about which he or she is concerned and to identify which the tax due diligence was carried out in the first place. Unless these tax risks can be addressed in some other way, the value and purpose of the tax due diligence is accordingly undermined.

Financial limits which are set too high so as to exclude the principal areas of potential tax claims identified by due diligence also negate the cost and effort of negotiating tax indemnities and warranties. In short, there is little value to a purchaser in having successfully negotiated comprehensive and watertight tax indemnities and warranties if the financial limitations render them incapable of providing protection against the very risks which they are intended to cover.

Finally, if a purchaser gives early consideration to the level of the financial limits on claims which he or she would be prepared commercially to accept in the contract, this will help to define materiality for the purposes of due diligence and so correspondingly the scope of the tax due diligence review.

In appropriate circumstances, to avoid the above problems which can result from the imposition of financial limits on claims, it may be possible to exclude specific warranties, or more usually indemnities, from the application of the financial limits. This is often the case where tax due diligence has identified a material potential exposure which the seller does not dispute and which is fundamental to the purchaser's position with regard to risk and value.

8.6.5. Limitation of warranties by awareness or knowledge

Warranties are sometimes given by the seller subject to the awareness or knowledge of defined individuals.

Purchasers should always consider carefully whether such limitation is reasonable. Except with regard to traditional management buy-outs, it should generally be resisted. If accepted at all, the person whose awareness or knowledge is to limit the tax warranties must be someone who has a broad and deep understanding of the target's tax position.

With traditional management buy-outs, however, those giving the tax warranties will generally be the selling shareholders; those receiving the benefit of the tax warranties will be the target's management. In this situation, the selling shareholders can reasonably argue that the tax warranties should be limited to the sellers' reasonable, or even actual, awareness or knowledge on the basis that management benefiting from the tax warranties will usually know more about the target's tax position than the selling shareholders themselves.

Traditional management buy-outs are becoming less common. More typical now is the auctioning of a target business in which the management of that business (with its financial backers) is only one of several competing bidders. In this situation, the tax warranties and indemnities offered by the selling shareholders tend to be the same as those offered to any other bidder in the auction.

8.7. Tax disclosures

Matters disclosed by the seller through the formal disclosure process have the effect of limiting the ability of the purchaser to make claims for breach of the warranties. Very occasionally, tax disclosures are expressed so as also to limit the ability of the purchaser to make claims under the tax indemnities. However, any attempt by the seller to make disclosures against the tax indemnities in this way should be vigorously resisted (see 8.7.6).

8.7.1. The disclosure process

The normal procedure with regard to disclosure is as follows. At some time on or before signing of the contract, the seller will formally deliver to the purchaser details of all the information on the basis of which the purchaser will effectively be deemed to have entered into the contract for the purchase of the target shares.

The purchaser is thereby deemed to be aware of all disclosed information before entering into the contract. Accordingly, the purchaser is prevented from claiming subsequently that a loss has been suffered as a result of a breach of one or more of the warranties if that breach occurs as a result of a matter which has already been disclosed to the purchaser.

8.7.2. Reviewing disclosures

It is therefore critical that all disclosures made by the seller, including those relating to tax, are carefully reviewed by the purchaser and/or its advisers. Otherwise, a disclosure made by the seller could negate the benefit of a carefully negotiated warranty without the purchaser being aware of its effect.

Tax disclosures should be reviewed by whoever has carried out the tax due diligence review of the target. The purchaser's tax due diligence adviser should be in the best position to understand the implications of the tax disclosures. In an ideal world, such tax disclosures should not reveal anything of which the tax due diligence adviser is not already aware; they should merely confirm the tax due diligence findings and the consequent advice on how they might be addressed.

If tax disclosures do come as a surprise to the purchaser's tax due diligence adviser, their significance should be immediately assessed and reported to the purchaser with recommendations as to the appropriate course of action. In the majority of cases, such disclosures have only limited impact on the conclusions of the tax due diligence or the tax warranties and need not delay signing. But this is not always the case.

8.7.3. Voluminous or late disclosure

Perhaps the least pleasurable aspect of the tax due diligence adviser's role in this area is the matter of voluminous or late disclosure. In order to put pressure on the purchaser during the final negotiations leading up to signing, a seller will sometimes attempt to disclose large amounts of information very close to signing. The aim is often to limit the amount of time available to the purchaser for review of these disclosures. In extreme cases, extensive disclosure is attempted immediately prior to signing.

For the reasons described above, all disclosures made by the seller should be carefully reviewed by the purchaser and/or its advisers. In the case of tax disclosures, this usually means by the purchaser's tax due diligence adviser. As a general principle, disclosures which are unreasonable (either because they are too extensive or too late to be reviewed before signing) should therefore be resisted. Either such disclosures may be formally refused by the purchaser, rendering them ineffective, or signing of the contract may be delayed until such time as the disclosures can reasonably be considered. Neither course of action is ideal and neither is likely to be popular, especially when taken as principals and advisers are gathering, often late at night, to sign the contract. But either is preferable to signing a contract without full knowledge of the factual basis on which it is made.

8.7.4. Limiting disclosure

Sellers will wish to define the extent of their tax disclosures to the purchaser as widely as possible so as to limit the effect of the tax warranties to the maximum extent.

Accordingly, sellers will often try to define their tax disclosures to include:

- all the contents of a data room (whether virtual or otherwise – see 3.3) at any time provided for review by the purchaser and its advisers. While making formal disclosure to a purchaser via a data room is normal practice, the purchaser will wish to ensure that all its contents have been seen and considered by itself and/or its advisers. Additionally or alternatively, the purchaser may wish to limit such disclosure only:

    to certain defined data room contents; or

    to material placed into the data room up to a certain date;

- all information provided to the purchaser in response to any enquiry by the purchaser and/or its advisers. Again, the purchaser will wish to define such disclosure more narrowly to specific items of information;
- the contents of all reports prepared by the purchaser and/or its advisers in connection with the transaction, including any tax due diligence report. This should be resisted by the purchaser on the basis that such material is essentially proprietary to the purchaser. If accepted, such disclosure would undermine the purpose of tax warranties: the more the purchaser and/or its advisers investigate the tax position of the target company or group, the less valuable the tax warranties will become.

8.7.5. Forcing disclosure

In contrast to voluminous or late disclosure, which generally advantages the seller, the process of disclosure can be used earlier in the due diligence process to the purchaser's advantage.

As part of any tax due diligence exercise, the purchaser and/or its advisers will necessarily require information from the seller about the tax position of the target company or group. The seller may be unable or unwilling to provide some or all of this information. If provision of the requested information is material to the purchaser's investment decision, the purchaser may indicate to the seller that, if it is not provided, the factual conclusion to which the requested information was expected by the purchaser to give rise will need to be warranted. Once converted into a tax warranty as a term of the contract, the purchaser may rely on this factual conclusion as if it were true, always subject of course to the subsequent disclosure process described above.

This then shifts the burden to the seller who must either resist the giving of the warranty or provide the requested information. Resisting a purchaser's reasonable request for a warranty often weakens a seller's negotiating position and usually forces an explanation if not a full disclosure.

8.7.6. Attempts to disclose against tax indemnities

As explained at 8.2.1, a warranty is a contractual representation by the seller that certain particular circumstances do or do not exist or that certain particular facts are or are not true.

The disclosure process is the means by which the seller can limit the adverse impact of warranties by providing information to the purchaser. Accordingly, disclosure is clearly and firmly part of the process of negotiating warranties.

An indemnity, on the other hand, is an undertaking by the seller to meet a particular defined pre-completion liability of the target if and when it falls due. See 8.2.2. A tax indemnity is therefore a mechanism by which the risk of pre-completion tax exposures is divided between seller and purchaser on the basis of which the purchase price is struck. Knowledge of a particular pre-completion tax exposure should not therefore be relevant to a claim under a tax indemnity and accordingly disclosure should not as a matter of principle limit or prevent an indemnity claim.

Occasionally, however, a seller will attempt to make tax disclosures expressed in such a way as to do just that, i.e. as disclosures against **both** tax warranties **and** tax indemnities, thereby limiting or preventing a claim under the tax indemnities. This should be challenged vigorously.

8.8. Other contractual means of addressing tax risks identified by due diligence

It is not always commercially possible for a purchaser to obtain contractual protection in the form of warranties and indemnities for the tax risks inherent in a target company or group. Nor is such contractual protection necessarily always commercially acceptable to a purchaser.

In particular, in certain types of transaction the seller will be unable or unwilling to give tax warranties and indemnities, e.g. where the purchaser is buying shares of a listed company in the market; or where the seller is a private equity investor exiting from one of its portfolio investments. In the former case, the selling shareholders, often large in number with small individual shareholdings, would not be prepared to give such contractual protection which would, in any event, be too fragmented to be commercially valuable to a purchaser; and the mechanism for acquiring shares of a listed company cannot easily accommodate such contractual protection. In the latter case, the private equity seller will not be prepared to accept a long tail of potential future liability under tax warranties or indemnities given its need to realise certain funds for return to its investors.

Furthermore, even where tax warranties and indemnities are available to a purchaser, they will only be commercially acceptable if the purchaser is confident of the seller's ability to stand behind such warranties and indemnities and meet any claims made under them, i.e. where the purchaser is confident of the seller's creditworthiness and the ability to access sufficient funds or assets of the seller to meet any future claims. This will be of particular concern with regard to potential tax exposures in relation to which a future claim could be very substantial or where the seller's assets are held outside the purchaser's jurisdiction and/or in a holding structure of which the purchaser has limited visibility, e.g. offshore trusts.

In such situations, the purchaser will need to identify alternative means of protection against future tax risks inherent in the target. In addition to a straightforward adjustment to the purchase price in appropriate circumstances, these may include the following.

8.8.1. Retentions, withholdings and escrow

Where the tax exposure in question is high risk and can be quantified with sufficient certainty, the purchaser may wish to consider a reduction in the purchase price to reflect it. Inevitably, this is likely to be contentious with the seller so the nature and scale of the risk and the bargaining position of the purchaser should be such that this course of action is commercially appropriate. See 2.1.3.

As an alternative to a price reduction, the contract could provide that an amount of the purchase price equivalent to the tax exposure in question may be withheld by the purchaser in certain defined circumstances and for a specified period of time. After the expiry of this period, either the whole or an appropriate part of the amount so withheld is either paid to the seller or retained by the purchaser depending on the outcome of the tax risk in question.

So, for example, a company may have taken a particular tax filing position with regard to a material contentious tax matter. Assuming that the particular matter has been fully disclosed and only affects one particular tax return, the tax authorities in the relevant jurisdiction will have a finite amount of time in which to challenge it. In such a case, a purchaser of the company may seek to negotiate with the seller a retention of the purchase price equivalent to the amount of tax at risk until the time period for tax authority challenge has expired.

A method of withholding part of the purchase price which is often more acceptable to a seller is the use of escrow. Instead of withholding part of the purchase price, the purchaser will instead pay the equivalent amount into an escrow account, an account administered by a trusted third party over which neither the purchaser nor the seller has control. The funds are then retained in escrow until such time as the contract provides for them to be distributed depending on the outcome of the tax risk in question.

8.8.2. Warranty and indemnity insurance

Retentions, withholdings or escrow may not be commercially appropriate, either because the amount to be retained or withheld is too large a proportion of the purchase price to be acceptable to the seller or because the degree of risk of the particular exposure may not justify it. In these circumstances either seller or purchaser may wish to consider insurance cover for a particular tax risk. For many years, a limited number of specialist insurers have provided such cover which pays out to the policyholder in the event of crystallisation of the tax risk in question.

The tax risks which most readily lend themselves to insurance cover are those which are quantifiable and which arise from:

- tax treatments for which there is a commercial basis and a defensible filing position supported by advice (including counsel's opinion and tax due diligence where possible); but
- where there is uncertainty about the way in which relevant tax legislation will be applied in practice, assuming full disclosure to the tax authorities of all the pertinent facts.

As might be expected, premiums vary widely and can represent a material proportion of the sum insured. The underwriters will generally require full disclosure of all relevant facts and circumstances for the purposes of their own extensive due diligence into the insured risk. Typically, this will involve their instructing advisers of their own to review and assess the facts and supporting documents, including:

- the draft contract;
- any relevant tax or other due diligence reports commissioned by seller or purchaser;
- any tax counsel's opinion on the risk obtained by seller or purchaser (the underwriters may require tax counsel's opinion to be sought if this has not already been obtained).

8.9. What tax risks are suitable for contractual protection?

The tax exposures which are dealt with by means of contractual protection through the tax indemnities and/or tax warranties tend to be those:

- which are contingent, i.e. not certain liabilities of which the purchaser is already aware; and
- which are not sufficiently fundamental to cause a transaction to fail or to justify an immediate adjustment to price; and
- with a medium or low risk; or
- which, although high risk, cannot be quantified with sufficient certainty for a price adjustment.

8.10. Purchase price adjustments: completion accounts versus 'locked box' balance sheet

For a detailed consideration of the role of completion accounts and 'locked box' balance sheets in determining the final purchase price, together with a comparison between the two methods, see 9.14.

8.11. Standard tax warranties which are generally included in a typical UK contract for the sale/purchase of the shares of a target company or group

Listed below is a selection of those matters which are commonly the subject of tax warranties given by the seller to the purchaser in a typical market practice UK contract for the sale/purchase of the shares of a target company. This list is not intended to be comprehensive and in any particular case should be supplemented by specific warranties:

- to protect the purchaser against tax exposures identified by due diligence; and
- to provide contractual support for key representations by the seller, or assumptions by the purchaser, with regard to tax.

In particular, where the target has, or may have, tax exposures outside the UK, the matters listed should be extended either:

- by reference to the appropriate specific non-UK legislation; or
- by adding to UK legislative references words such as 'or its nearest equivalent legislation in any jurisdiction outside the UK'.

Furthermore, the list is intended only as a guide to the general areas in relation to a target's tax position which are typically the subject of warranty protection. It is not drafted in terms which are necessarily legally effective in any particular case and legal advice should always be sought in relation to the drafting of any particular contract.

There may be some duplication or overlap in the areas for warranty protection in the list. This is to provide an indication of alternative ways in which warranty protection may be sought to achieve the desired contractual result.

The list of areas for warranty protection assumes that the target of a particular acquisition comprises two or more legal entities. However, the list is equally applicable, *mutatis mutandis*, if the target comprises a single legal entity.

8.11.1. General

1. The defined target company(ies) has/have never been a member(s), nor treated as a member(s), of a group of companies, or of a consortium, or as owned by a consortium, or as a member of a partnership or any other unincorporated association, for any tax purpose.
2. None of the defined target companies has ever been the agent or representative of another person for any tax purpose.
3. None of the defined target companies has ever incurred, and none of the defined target companies has ever been liable to incur, any expenditure which is not, or will not be, wholly deductible in computing its taxable profits; in particular, all payments due under obligations which will continue to bind any of the defined target companies after completion will be fully deductible for tax purposes.
4. There is no proceeding by any tax authority pending or in progress in relation to any of the defined target companies which could adversely affect the seller's ability to enter into the agreement for the sale/purchase of the defined target companies or any related transaction.
5. There is no proceeding by any tax authority pending or in progress in relation to any of the defined target companies which could have the effect of creating any charge etc. on the shares or assets of any of the defined target companies.
6. The seller does not require the approval of any tax authority to enter into the agreement for the sale/purchase of the defined target companies or any related transaction; and neither the agreement nor any related transaction could be challenged by any tax authority on the basis of any outstanding tax liability.

8.11.2. Tax in the accounts

7. A defined set of financial statements makes full provision or reserve for all pre-completion tax (including deferred tax) for which the defined target companies could be liable or accountable.
8. A defined set of financial statements makes full provision or reserve for deferred tax calculated in accordance with generally accepted accounting principles in the jurisdiction(s) in which the defined target companies are resident for tax purposes.

8.11.3. Compliance

9. All tax returns, computations, claims etc., which have become due, and any other information required to be provided to any tax authority, have been

prepared on a proper and accurate basis and in accordance with all applicable legal requirements, remain accurate and complete in all material respects and have been duly submitted within any applicable statutory time limits.

10. The defined target companies have made and submitted all tax claims, consents, disclaimers, elections, notices, surrenders etc. assumed to have been made for the purposes of the tax balances in a defined set of financial statements.
11. None of the tax claims, consents, disclaimers, elections, notices, surrenders etc. assumed to have been made for the purposes of the tax balances in a defined set of financial statements have a time limit which expires within [three] months of the date of completion of the agreement for the sale/purchase of the defined target companies.
12. None of the tax returns, computations, claims etc., which have become due, and none of the other information required to be provided to any tax authority, is the subject of any [non-routine] audit, dispute, enquiry, investigation or review by any tax authority.
13. None of the tax returns, computations, claims etc., which have become due, and none of the other information required to be provided to any tax authority, is likely to become the subject of any [non-routine] audit, dispute, enquiry, investigation or review by any tax authority.
14. None of the defined target companies has ever been the subject of any [non-routine] audit, dispute, enquiry, investigation or review by any tax authority.
15. None of the defined target companies is aware of any [non-routine] audit, enquiry, investigation or review by any tax authority planned for the next [12] months.
16. None of the defined target companies has any reason to expect to be involved in any dispute in relation to tax.
17. There are no disputes or proceedings with any tax authority in relation to any asset acquired, held or owned by any of the defined target companies on or before completion which could have the effect of creating a charge on that asset or of rendering any transfer of it void.
18. The defined target companies have complied with all obligations and requirements imposed on them by tax legislation.
19. All tax which has become due from any of the defined target companies has been duly paid by the applicable time limit for its payment.
20. All amounts due to be paid to any tax authority, including all tax chargeable on benefits provided to employees, directors and officers (including former employees, directors and officers) of any of the defined

target companies, have been, or will be, paid within any required time limit necessary to avoid any interest or penalty.

21. Instalment payments on account of the current year's corporation tax liability are adequate and have been properly calculated.
22. None of the defined target companies is, or will become, liable to pay any fine, penalty, surcharge or interest to any tax authority.
23. There are no facts, circumstances or transactions in relation to any of the defined target companies which could give rise to a pre-completion tax liability in addition to tax already paid or provided for in a defined set of financial statements [other than a tax liability arising in the ordinary course of business].
24. The defined target companies have preserved and retained, and has within its control/possession sufficient records to meet all statutory requirements and to determine all tax liabilities for which they may be liable, including sufficient records to calculate the profit, loss, debit, credit, gain, balancing charge or balancing allowance which would arise on any disposal or realisation of any assets owned at the date of a defined set of financial statements and/or at the date of completion of the agreement for the sale/purchase of the defined target companies.
25. All records which any of the defined target companies are required to retain for tax purposes, or which would be required to substantiate any claim made or filing position taken, have been duly retained, including PAYE and NIC records, VAT records and documentation in relation to transfer pricing.
26. None of the defined target companies is aware of any failure to meet any material tax compliance obligation.
27. All obligations required under any applicable law to register for any tax have been met within any applicable time limit.
28. None of the defined target companies has ever requested an extension of any time limit in relation to any tax compliance obligation.
29. None of the defined target companies has ever waived any statute of limitations in relation to tax.
30. None of the defined target companies has ever requested or agreed to the extension of any time limit for the payment of any tax.
31. None of the defined target companies has ever been subject to a special tax regime or has ever benefited from a tax holiday etc.

8.11.4. Concessionary or informal tax treatments

32. None of the defined target companies has ever relied on any formal or informal unpublished concession, dispensation or practice (whether of general application or specific to a defined target company) which has

affected the amount of tax chargeable on any of the defined target companies or which has modified, or provided exemption from, any tax compliance obligation of any of the defined target companies.

33. The amount of tax in relation to which the defined target companies are chargeable for all periods still open to adjustment by any tax authority is not affected by any concessionary or informal agreement or arrangement (other than a concessionary or informal agreement or arrangement available to companies generally).

8.11.5. Deductions and withholdings of tax

34. The defined target companies have duly deducted/withheld and accounted for all tax which they have been obliged to deduct/withhold from any payment made or credited, or treated as having been made or credited.
35. Where required, certificates of tax deduction/withholding have been, or will be, provided within any required time limit necessary to avoid any interest or penalty.
36. All deductions, withholdings and payments required to be made under any tax legislation have been so made.
37. All payments made by any of the defined target companies which are required to have been made under deduction or withholding of tax have been so made and each of the defined target companies has, where required, accounted for the tax so deducted to the appropriate tax authority.
38. None of the defined target companies has received any notice from any tax authority requiring it to deduct or withhold tax from any payment made since the date of a defined set of financial statements in relation to which such tax has not been accounted for in full to the appropriate tax authority.

8.11.6. Tax planning

39. None of the defined target companies has ever been a party to any transaction or arrangement entered into wholly or mainly for the purposes of avoiding or deferring any tax liability.
40. None of the defined target companies has ever been a party to any transaction or arrangement which contains steps which have no commercial or business purpose.
41. None of the defined target companies has ever been a party to any transaction or arrangement which could be disregarded or recharacterised for tax purposes.
42. None of the defined target companies has ever been a party to any notifiable tax avoidance arrangements (*Part 7 Finance Act 2004* and the *Tax Avoidance Schemes (Prescribed Descriptions of Arrangements) Regulations 2006 (SI 2006/1543)*. See 9.12.

43. None of the defined target companies has ever been a party to any disclosable VAT avoidance scheme (*Section 58A* and *Schedule 11A Value Added Tax Act 1994*, the *Value Added Tax (Disclosure of Avoidance Schemes) Regulations 2004 (SI 2004/1929)*, and the *Value Added Tax (Disclosure of Avoidance Schemes) (Designations) Order 2004 (SI 2004/1933))*.
44. None of the target companies has ever applied for any clearance or ruling from any tax authority.

8.11.7. Residence and foreign tax matters

45. The defined target companies have always been, and will until completion remain, resident for all tax purposes only in [the UK/any other jurisdiction appropriate in the circumstances/the jurisdiction in which they were incorporated] and are eligible for any double tax treaty benefits available to residents of that jurisdiction.
46. None of the defined target companies is, or will become, liable to tax in any jurisdiction other than the jurisdiction in which it was incorporated. In particular, none of the defined target companies has ever had a branch, agency or permanent establishment in any jurisdiction other than the jurisdiction in which it was incorporated.
47. None of the defined target companies has ever been a controlled foreign company of any other company for the purposes of the UK CFC legislation (or its nearest equivalent legislation in any jurisdiction outside the UK) such that its profits could be apportioned to that other company.
48. None of the defined target companies has ever had any interest in a controlled foreign company (*Chapter IV Part XVII Income and Corporation Taxes Act 1988* or its nearest equivalent legislation in any jurisdiction outside the UK).
49. None of the defined target companies has ever had any interest in an offshore fund (*Chapter V Part XVII Income and Corporation Taxes Act 1988*).
50. None of the defined target companies is, or will become, liable for tax in the UK (or any other jurisdiction) as the permanent establishment, agent or representative of any person not resident for tax purposes in the UK (or in that other jurisdiction).
51. None of the defined target companies has ever been party to any migration (*Section 765(1) Income and Corporation Taxes Act 1988* or its nearest equivalent legislation in any jurisdiction outside the UK).
52. None of the defined target companies has ever been party to any movement of capital (*Section 765A Income and Corporation Taxes Act 1988* or its nearest equivalent legislation in any jurisdiction outside the UK).

8.11.8. Secondary liabilities

53. None of the defined target companies is, or will become, liable to pay,

reimburse or indemnify any pre-completion tax (or any amount representing tax) as a result of the failure of any other person to discharge that tax. See 8.3.2.

54. None of the defined target companies is, or will become, liable to tax chargeable or attributable primarily on any other person. See 8.3.2.

8.11.9. Distributions

55. None of the defined target companies has ever made, or agreed to make, any payment which is, or is treated for tax purposes as, a distribution, except dividends properly authorised and disclosed in its audited financial statements.
56. None of the defined target companies has ever issued, or agreed to issue, any share capital as paid up otherwise than by receipt of new consideration.
57. None of the defined target companies has made or declared, or will make or declare, a dividend or other distribution (deemed or otherwise) between the date of a defined set of financial statements and the date of completion of the agreement for the sale/purchase of the defined target companies.

8.11.10. Close companies

58. None of the defined target companies has ever been a close company or a close investment company in relation to any accounting period (*Sections 13A and 414 Income and Corporation Taxes Act 1988*).
59. None of the defined target companies has ever made any distribution within *Section 418 Income and Corporation Taxes Act 1988.*
60. None of the defined target companies has ever made any loan or advance giving rise to a charge under *Section 419 Income and Corporation Taxes Act 1988.*
61. None of the defined target companies has ever released or written-off any loan or advance giving rise to a charge under *Section 419 Income and Corporation Taxes Act 1988.*

8.11.11. Loan relationships

62. No tax liability or non-trading deficit would arise if the loan relationships to which the defined target companies are party were to be repaid to the extent of the amounts in relation to each such loan relationship included in the books of each of the defined target companies as at the date of the agreement for the sale/purchase of the defined target companies.
63. None of the defined target companies has ever been the debtor in connection with any loan relationship which has an unallowable purpose (*Paragraph 13 Schedule 9 Finance Act 1996*); or to which *Paragraphs 2, 11, or 11A Schedule 9 Finance Act 1996* could apply.

64. None of the defined target companies has ever released or waived any debt.

8.11.12. Capital gains

65. If each of the assets (apart from trading stock) of each of the defined target companies were to be disposed of at completion for consideration equal to the value at which it is included in a defined balance sheet (or, if acquired since the date of that balance sheet, were to be disposed of at completion at cost), then no chargeable gain under *Taxation of Chargeable Gains Act 1992* would arise.
66. If each of the assets (apart from trading stock) of each of the defined target companies were to be disposed of at completion, its base cost would not be treated, or deemed for any tax purpose, as reduced by any claim under *Sections 152, 153, 165 or 175 Taxation of Chargeable Gains Act 1992.*
67. If each of the assets (apart from trading stock) of each of the defined target companies were to be disposed of at completion, its base cost would not be determined by virtue of *Sections 17 or 126 to 140 Taxation of Chargeable Gains Act 1992.*
68. None of the defined target companies has ever entered into any transaction which is, or could be treated for any tax purpose as, a transaction otherwise than by way of a bargain made at arm's length (*Section 17 Taxation of Chargeable Gains Act 1992*); in particular none of the defined target companies has ever entered into any transaction with a connected person (*Sections 18* and *286 Taxation of Chargeable Gains Act 1992*).
69. None of the defined target companies owns any depreciating asset in relation to which a heldover gain could be triggered (*Sections 154(2)* and/or *175(3) Taxation of Chargeable Gains Act 1992*).

8.11.13. Tax groupings etc.

70. None of the defined target companies has ever been associated with another company (*Section 13(4) Income and Corporation Taxes Act 1988*) other than with another of the defined target companies.
71. None of the defined target companies has ever surrendered or claimed any amounts by way of group relief in the six years prior to the date of the agreement for the sale/purchase of the defined target companies.
72. None of the defined target companies is, or will become, liable to make any payment for group relief (*Section 402(6) Income and Corporation Taxes Act 1988*) except to another of the defined target companies.
73. None of the defined target companies is, or will become, liable to make any payment for a transferred tax refund (*Section 102(7) Finance Act 1989*) except to another of the defined target companies.
74. None of the defined target companies is, or will become, liable to make any

balancing payment (*Paragraph 7A Schedule 28AA Income and Corporation Taxes Act 1988*) except to another of the defined target companies.

75. Except to another of the defined target companies, none of the defined target companies is, or will become, liable to make any refund of any payment of the type referred to in 72 to 74 above received by any of the defined target companies before completion.

8.11.14. De-grouping charges

76. None of the defined target companies owns any asset which was acquired from another company then in the same group for the purposes of *Section 170 Taxation of Chargeable Gains Act 1992* [other than from another of the defined target companies which will leave the seller's group at the same time in the circumstances envisaged by *Section 179(2) Taxation of Chargeable Gains Act 1992*].
77. Within the last six years none of the defined target companies has acquired (other than as trading stock) any tangible or intangible asset from any company which was at that time a member of the same group as defined in *Section 170 Taxation of Chargeable Gains Act 1992* or *Paragraphs 46 to 54 Schedule 29 Finance Act 2002*.
78. No member of any group of which any of the defined target companies is, or has been, the principal company, as defined in *Section 170 Taxation of Chargeable Gains Act 1992* or *Paragraphs 46 to 54 Schedule 29 Finance Act 2002*, has acquired (other than as trading stock) any tangible or intangible asset from any company which was at that time a member of the same group as defined in *Section 170 Taxation of Chargeable Gains Act 1992 or Paragraphs 46 to 54 Schedule 29 Finance Act 2002*.
79. The entering into/completion/execution of the agreement for the sale/purchase of the defined target companies (whether alone or in conjunction with any other events or circumstances) will not trigger any profit, gain or tax charge in any of the defined target companies for the purposes of *Section 179 Taxation of Chargeable Gains Act 1992* or for any other tax purpose.
80. Within the last six years, none of the defined target companies has ceased to be a member of a group of companies for the purposes of *Section 179 Taxation of Chargeable Gains Act 1992*.
81. None of the defined target companies has ever made, or will make, any election under *Section 171A, 179A* or *179B Taxation of Chargeable Gains Act 1992*.

8.11.15. Transfer pricing and transactions not at arm's length etc.

82. All transactions entered into by any of the defined target companies with any related party (including transactions with an unrelated party which

are guaranteed by a related party) have taken place on arm's length terms and in compliance with the transfer pricing requirements of any relevant jurisdiction.

83. None of the defined target companies has ever been a party to any transaction to which the provisions of *Schedule 28AA Income and Corporation Taxes Act 1988* could apply.
84. None of the defined target companies has ever been a party to any transaction not on arm's length terms.
85. None of the defined target companies has ever entered into any transaction or arrangement in relation to which the actual consideration given or received could be replaced for any tax purpose by a different consideration.

8.11.16. Appropriations to or from stock

86. None of the defined target companies has ever made any appropriations to or from trading stock (*Section 161 Taxation of Chargeable Gains Act 1992*).

8.11.17. Depreciatory transactions

87. None of the defined target companies beneficially owns any shares or securities in relation to which it has been party to any depreciatory transaction (*Sections 176 and 177 Taxation of Chargeable Gains Act 1992).*

8.11.18. Value shifting

88. None of the defined target companies has ever entered into any transaction which could constitute value shifting (*Sections 29 to 34 Taxation of Chargeable Gains Act 1992*).

8.11.19. Tax depreciation (capital allowances and intangible assets)

89. Each of the defined target companies has met, and continues to meet, all necessary conditions for the availability of all capital allowances which each has claimed.
90. If each of the assets (apart from trading stock) of each of the defined target companies were to be disposed of at completion for consideration equal to the value at which it is included in a defined balance sheet (or, if acquired since the date of that balance sheet, were to be disposed of at completion at cost), then no balancing charge would arise (*Capital Allowances Act 2001*).
91. All fixtures in any property (as defined in *Section 173 Capital Allowances Act 2001*) belong to the defined target companies and no person other than the defined target companies is entitled to capital allowances in relation to expenditure incurred on them.
92. None of the defined target companies has acquired or created on or after 1 April 2002 any intangible fixed assets. [Alternatively, full details of all such intangible fixed assets (including the total amount of expenditure on each

and the amount of such expenditure for which tax relief has already been claimed) are provided by way of the disclosure letter].

8.11.20. Reorganisations, reconstructions, changes of ownership, changes to trades or businesses etc.

93. None of the defined target companies has ever been party to any transaction involving a reorganisation or reconstruction of its share capital (including any bonus issue, buy-back, redemption, reduction, repayment, or repurchase of shares), of any trade or trades which it has ever carried on or of any group of which it has ever been a member.
94. There have never been any changes in the ownership of any of the defined target companies or to any of the trade(s) or business(es) carried on by any of the defined target companies.

8.11.21. Period between the date of a defined set of financial statements and completion

95. None of the defined target companies has entered into any transaction outside the ordinary course of business between the date of a defined set of financial statements and the date of completion of the agreement for the sale/purchase of the defined target companies.
96. None of the following has occurred in relation to any of the defined target companies since the date of a defined set of financial statements:

    any acquisition, disposal or revaluation of any intangible fixed asset;

    any deemed acquisition, disposal or supply of assets, goods, services or business facilities;

    any of the defined target companies ceasing, or being deemed to cease, to be a member of any group or to be associated with any other company for any tax purpose;

    any disposal or supply of assets, goods, services or business facilities for a consideration which is treated for any tax purpose as greater than the actual consideration;

    any acquisition or supply of assets, goods, services or business facilities for a consideration which is treated for any tax purpose as less than the actual consideration;

    any distribution (*Sections 209 to 211 and 418 Income and Corporation Taxes Act 1988*);

    any event which results in any of the defined target companies being liable for tax for which it is not primarily liable;

    any event in relation to which a tax liability arises as a result of a failure by any of the defined target companies to deduct, withhold or account for tax;

any event giving rise to a liability under any of the anti-avoidance provisions of *Income and Corporation Taxes Act 1988* (*Part XVII*);

any event giving rise to a balancing charge.

8.11.22. Employment taxes

97. The defined target companies have always accurately, correctly and properly operated the PAYE system and the NIC system (or their nearest equivalents in any jurisdiction outside the UK) by:

    maintaining records and submitting returns as required by law;

    deducting income tax and NIC as required by law from all payments made, or treated as made, to its employees, directors and officers (including former employees, directors and officers); and

    accounting to HMRC for all income tax and NIC so deducted and for all income tax and NIC chargeable on income and benefits provided to its employees, directors and officers (including former employees, directors and officers).

98. The defined target companies have maintained and retained such books and records in relation to PAYE and NIC in such manner and for such time as required by law.

99. All payments made, or agreed to be made, in remunerating employees, directors and officers (including former employees, directors and officers), including by way of salary, bonus, emolument and any gratuitous payment, shall be subject to all deduction/withholding required by law; and none of the defined target companies is, or will be, required to gross-up any such payments to ensure that the net amount received by any employee, director or officer (including any former employee, director or officer) will be equal to the full amount which would have been received had no such deduction/withholding been required.

100. None of the defined target companies has ever been granted any dispensation by any tax authority in relation to the taxation of its employees, directors or officers (including former employees, directors or officers) or in relation to the reporting of benefits provided to them.

101. All expenditure incurred or agreed to be incurred in remunerating any employee, director or officer (including any former employee, director or officer) of any of the defined target companies, including any salary, bonus, emolument or gratuitous payment, is or will be fully deductible for tax purposes.

8.11.23. Bonus, share and option schemes

102. None of the defined target companies has ever participated in any bonus, share or share option scheme etc. for the benefit of its employees, directors

and officers (including former employees, directors and officers).

103.None of the employees, directors or officers (including former employees, directors or officers) of any of the defined target companies has ever exercised or surrendered any share options.

104.None of the employees, directors or officers (including former employees, directors or officers) of any of the defined target companies holds any share options the future exercise or surrender of which could result in a liability to apply and account for PAYE and/or NIC.

105.Since 6 April 2003, there have been no reportable events within the meaning of *Section 421K Income Tax (Earnings and Pensions) Act 2003.*

106.Since the date of a defined set of financial statements:

there has been no charge on any of the defined target companies to income tax or NIC by reference to income deemed to arise under *Part 7 Income Tax (Earnings and Pensions) Act 2003* (or its nearest equivalent legislation in any jurisdiction outside the UK);

nor have there been any circumstances liable to give rise to such a charge; and

nor will such a charge arise by reason of any outstanding employment-related security or securities option (*Part 7 Income Tax (Earnings and Pensions) Act 2003*).

107.None of the defined target companies has ever:

operated any approved SAYE option scheme *(Chapter 7 Part 7 Income Tax (Earnings and Pensions) Act 2003);*

operated any approved CSOP scheme (*Chapters 8 Part 7 Income Tax (Earnings and Pensions) Act 2003*);

operated any approved share incentive plan (*Chapter 6 Part 7 Income Tax (Earnings and Pensions) Act 2003*);

granted any qualifying enterprise management incentive options (*Chapter 9 Part 7 Income Tax (Earnings and Pensions) Act 2003*); or

operated a qualifying employee share ownership trust (*Schedule 5 Finance Act 1989*).

8.11.24. Value Added Tax

108.Each of the defined target companies is registered for VAT in the UK (*Schedule 1 Value Added Tax Act 1994*)

109.None of the defined target companies has ever been treated as a member of a VAT group.

110.No application by any of the defined target companies to be treated as a member of a VAT group has ever been refused.

111. None of the defined target companies is registered, or required to be registered, for VAT or its nearest local equivalent tax in any jurisdiction outside the UK.
112. Each of the defined target companies is fully taxable for VAT purposes.
113. Each of the defined target companies has complied in all respects with the requirements of all applicable VAT legislation.
114. Each of the defined target companies has retained all records required to be retained by VAT legislation and all such records are accurate, complete and up-to-date.
115. None of the defined target companies has ever been subject to any liability, notice, penalty, or warning under *Part IV (Administration, Collection and Enforcement) Value Added Tax Act 1994.*
116. None of the defined target companies has ever been required by HMRC to give any security for the purposes of VAT.
117. None of the defined target companies is, or will become, liable for VAT under *Sections 47* or *48 Value Added Tax Act 1994.*
118. In relation to each VAT period since the date of a defined set of financial statements, none of the defined target companies has made any exempt supplies which would prevent it from obtaining credit for all input VAT paid by it.
119. In relation to each VAT period since the date of a defined set of financial statements, no credit for input VAT of any of the defined target companies could be prevented or disallowed in whole or in part by virtue of *Section 26A Value Added Tax Act 1994.*
120. No option to tax land (*Part 1 Schedule 10 Value Added Tax Act 1994)* has been made by, or otherwise binds, any of the defined target companies or any associate (as defined in *Paragraph 3 Schedule 10 Value Added Tax Act 1994*); and no such option will be made on or prior to completion.
121. There are no arrangements or circumstances in existence whereby any option to tax land (*Part 1 Schedule 10 Value Added Tax Act 1994)* could be disapplied by reason of the application of *Paragraphs 12* to *17 Schedule 10 Value Added Tax Act 1994.*
122. None of the defined target companies has any assets falling within the VAT Capital Goods Scheme (*Regulations 112* to *116 Value Added Tax Regulations 1995 (SI 1995/2518)*).
123. None of the defined target companies has ever been a party to a transfer of a business as a going concern (*Article 5 Value Added Tax (Special Provisions) Order 1995 (SI 1995/1268)*).
124. None of the defined target companies has ever entered into any transaction which could be treated as a self-supply for VAT purposes.

8.11.25. Customs duty

125. Each of the defined target companies has paid in full all VAT and customs and excise duties payable to HMRC in relation to any imported goods or assets.

8.11.26. Stamp taxes and transfer taxes

126. All stampable documents have been stamped and all Stamp Duty liabilities have been paid.
127. All SDLT returns have been submitted within the appropriate time limits and all SDLT liabilities have been paid.
128. All pre-1 December 2003 land transfers have been stamped and all related Stamp Duty liabilities have been paid.
129. Where required, all stamp tax, transfer tax or any similar tax or duty has been paid in relation to all transactions to which any of the defined target companies has ever been a party.
130. All documents which relate to the right, title or interest of any of the defined target companies to or in its properties, undertakings or assets and which attract stamp taxes have been stamped within the requisite time limit for stamping; and there are no such documents outside the UK which, if remitted to the UK, would give rise to stamp taxes.
131. No liability to stamp tax, transfer tax or any similar tax or duty will arise in consequence of the entry into or completion of the agreement for the sale/purchase of the defined target companies.

8.11.27. Inheritance tax

132. None of the defined target companies has ever made any transfer of value (*Section 3 Inheritance Tax Act 1984*).
133. None of the defined target companies is, or will become, liable for inheritance tax as the donor or donee of any gift or as the transferor or transferee of any transfer of value.
134. None of the defined target companies is, or will become, liable for inheritance tax as the result of any disposition, chargeable transfer or transfer of value by any other person.
135. There is no liability to, or charge for, unpaid inheritance tax attached to or over any of the assets or shares of any of the defined target companies (*Sections 237* and *238 Inheritance Tax Act 1984*).
136. There are no circumstances in existence in which any of the powers to raise inheritance tax could be exercised in relation to any shares, securities or other assets of any of the defined target companies (*Section 212 Inheritance Tax Act 1984*).

8.11.28. Other

137. None of the defined target companies is or will become liable to reimburse any party in relation to tax.
138. All outstanding matters relevant to tax have been disclosed.

9. Dealing with Specific Risk Areas

For the reasons explained in its introduction, this book is not, and cannot be, an exhaustive guide to all the specific circumstances which can give rise to tax exposures under the tax code of any jurisdiction in which due diligence might be performed.

However, certain tax issues or exposures tend to arise in due diligence more often than others. This chapter describes issues or exposures commonly encountered in practice and explains how a tax due diligence review might address them.

9.1. Tax losses and other assets

Sellers will often encourage purchasers to reflect a target's tax assets (losses in particular) in the purchase price, especially in auction sales.

9.1.1. Tax losses

The future availability of the target's tax losses is rarely certain and purchasers should generally resist pressure to attribute value to them, although it is sometimes appropriate to do so on a contingent basis, i.e. as and when the benefit of the losses is realised in future accounting periods.

Although pre-acquisition tax due diligence can and should focus on the likelihood of the purchaser realising value from these tax losses, the purchaser's ability to carry forward and utilise pre-completion tax losses will always be subject to a number of risks, including:

- pre-completion tax liabilities of the target company or group which may absorb pre-completion tax losses. To this extent, pre-completion tax losses are essentially a cushion for historical tax exposures, reducing the extent of the purchaser's risk (and possibly also the scope of pre-acquisition tax due diligence – see 4.2.5 and 8.3.4);
- anti-avoidance provisions in many jurisdictions which deny or restrict the ability of a company to carry forward tax losses following a change of ownership (e.g. *Section 768 Income and Corporation Taxes Act 1988* in the UK);
- legislation in many jurisdictions in accordance with which tax losses (and sometimes also other tax assets) will expire after a certain fixed period of time (e.g. Netherlands, Spain, Italy); or
- restrictions in some jurisdictions on the amount of profits in any one year which can be sheltered with brought forward tax losses (e.g. Germany). Whilst such restrictions are not strictly risks to the losses themselves, they

will inevitably affect how quickly the losses can be utilised and therefore their potential value to a purchaser.

Tax due diligence with regard to losses therefore usually comprises:

- determination of the amount and type of the losses and the manner in which they arose, analysed by company and by year;
- confirmation of the extent to which the losses have already been agreed by any tax authority; or the extent to which claims to use part of the same or similar losses have already been agreed by any tax authority;
- identification of any circumstances already in existence which might trigger a denial of, or restriction on, the ability to carry forward the losses, e.g. in the UK, a major change in the nature or conduct of the trade in respect of which trading losses are carried forward within three years of the change of ownership which the proposed transaction is likely to represent (*Section 768 Income and Corporation Taxes Act 1988*); and
- advice on any other restrictions imposed by the tax law of the relevant jurisdiction on the ability to carry forward or utilise the tax losses, either following a change of ownership or control or otherwise.

See 8.3.4 for commentary on the extent to which tax losses and other assets should be protected by tax warranties and indemnities.

9.1.2. Tax written down value of expenditure qualifying for capital allowances (i.e. tax depreciation) in future periods

In the UK, the tax asset represented by a company's pool of capital expenditure available for tax relief in future periods by way of capital allowances (i.e. tax depreciation) is not affected by a change of ownership of the company.

Tax due diligence in relation to such assets will not generally extend to a detailed review of the qualifying basis for all the expenditure which a target company has claimed as eligible for capital allowances. This would potentially require detailed analysis of a target company's records (including original invoices) going back many years, assuming that these even still exist.

However, where capital allowances are a material feature of the tax profile of a particular target company or group, or where their future availability is material to a particular investment decision, tax due diligence procedures will often include:

- analysis and summary of the target's qualifying capital expenditure by each category of asset qualifying for capital allowances (obtained from the latest available corporation tax return and computation and supplemented by any available data in relation to the target's subsequent capital expenditure);

- review of the target's processes and systems for identifying qualifying capital expenditure (e.g. the application of certain percentages to total capital expenditure to determine the qualifying amount) and for making appropriate capital allowances claims;
- review of any external advice provided to the target in connection with its claims for capital allowances;
- investigation of the extent to which the target's qualifying capital expenditure itself, or the principles according to which it has been identified as qualifying, have been queried or agreed by HMRC;
- review of the qualifying basis and disclosure to HMRC of specific items of capital expenditure in relation to which the target derives a material proportion of its capital allowances;
- review of the qualifying basis and disclosure to HMRC of specific items of capital expenditure in relation to which there is particular doubt or risk, e.g. claims for capital allowances in relation to items of plant and machinery which on the face of it appear to be more in the nature of business premises;
- identification and review of any capital allowances planning carried out by the target which affects the target's tax position for any period still potentially open to enquiry by HMRC;
- investigation of the target's future capital expenditure commitments and their impact on future capital allowances; and
- determination of whether there is any scope for a target company carrying forward trading losses to reduce its historical claims for capital allowances (and therefore its tax losses carried forward) without adverse consequences. Where this is possible, the target company will carry forward at completion of the acquisition/disposal of its shares:

    fewer trading losses (which are potentially subject to the *Section 768 Income and Corporation Taxes Act 1988* risk described above); and

    more capital expenditure available for relief in future periods by way of capital allowances (which is not affected by a change of ownership of the target company).

Additional bespoke due diligence procedures focused on capital allowances may be desirable in relation to transactions in certain business sectors (e.g. plant and machinery leasing) or asset acquisitons involving real estate or where capital allowances are identified as an area of particular risk or opportunity. Such procedures would typically aim to:

- confirm the target's entitlement to capital allowances;

- confirm that the target has used appropriate asset valuation techniques for capital allowances purposes;
- identify potential restrictions on the target's capital allowances claims; and
- identify any unclaimed allowances to which the target may be entitled.

9.2. De-grouping charges

9.2.1. The basis of the UK de-grouping charge

In the UK, wherever a company or sub-group is to be acquired from a larger selling group, the risk of de-grouping charges will invariably exist.

Section 171 Taxation of Chargeable Gains Act 1992 provides that where one company within a capital gains group transfers a chargeable asset to another, the transfer takes place on a tax neutral basis such that no gain or loss will arise for the transferor company and the transferee company will assume the transferor's tax basis in the asset (plus any indexation up to the date of the transfer).

However, if within six years of the original intra-group transfer, the transferee company leaves the capital gains group still holding the asset transferred, any gain which was effectively deferred at the time of the intra-group transfer will be triggered in the hands of the transferee company by virtue of *Section 179 Taxation of Chargeable Gains Act 1992*, unless the intra-group transferor and transferee qualify for the associated companies exemption in *Section 179(2)*. See below.

Where *Section 179* applies, the transferee company is deemed to have sold and re-acquired the asset in question at its market value on the date of the original intra-group transfer. See *Section 179(1) and (3)*. Any resulting gain is taxed in the hands of the transferee company and is deemed by *Section 179(4)* to have arisen at the later of:

- the beginning of the accounting period in which the transferee company leaves the capital gains group; or
- the time of the intra-group transfer.

In fact, *Section 179* can apply even if the original transfer did not occur under *Section 171*. For example, if a no gain/no loss transfer happened under *Section 140A Taxation of Chargeable Gains Act 1992* at a time when the transferor and transferee companies were not part of a capital gains group, but they subsequently became members of the same group prior to the transferee company being sold, then *Section 179* can still apply.

Under *Section 179(2)*, where the parties to the original tax-neutral intra-group transfer are associated companies, i.e. where they are in a sub-group relationship, no de-grouping charge arises. Although HMRC were known to hold a contrary view, it was widely believed for many years that this exemption applied where the transferor and transferee companies left the capital gains group together as associated companies and that their relationship at the time of the original intra-group transfer was not relevant. However, the Court of Appeal decision in *Johnston Publishing (North) Ltd v Revenue and Customs Commissioners [2008] STC 3116* has endorsed HMRC's view that the exemption only applies where the transferor and transferee companies:

- leave the capital gains group together as associated companies; and
- were also associated companies at the time of the original intra-group transfer.

Accordingly, a de-grouping charge cannot be avoided simply by transferring the shares of the transferor company into the transferee's sub-group after the date of the original intra-group transfer but before the sale of the transferee sub-group to the third party purchaser.

9.2.2. De-grouping charges in the context of tax due diligence

So if a purchaser is to acquire one or more target companies from a selling group, any transfers of chargeable assets to the target company or companies at no gain/no loss from companies to be retained in the selling group could give rise to de-grouping charges when the target company or companies leave the selling group. See Example 13.

Because they accrue in the seller's period of ownership of the target, de-grouping charges are usually accepted as being for the seller's account. Accordingly, a market practice tax indemnity should generally ensure that the purchaser is able to recover from the seller any tax liability to which they give rise. See 8.3.2. However, this is not always the case. Alternatively, it may be possible for the purchaser to agree with the seller that a joint election should be signed between the target company and another company in the seller's group under *Section 179A Taxation of Chargeable Gains Act 1992* to reallocate any gain to the seller group.

In any event, even where the seller does provide indemnification against de-grouping charges, a purchaser will still wish to be aware of the likelihood and potential scale of any de-grouping charges for which an indemnity claim may be necessary. At the very least, the purchaser will wish to know whether limitations elsewhere in the contract could undermine such a claim.

So the potential incidence of de-grouping charges should be a focus of the purchaser's pre-acquisition tax due diligence. This will necessitate a thorough understanding of the seller's group in order to identify the range of potential transferor companies which might have made transfers to a target company qualifying for tax neutral treatment within the preceding six years. Sources of potential information from which such transfers might be identified or inferred include:

- audited financial statements;
- management reports and accounts;
- board minutes which often record such transactions. These are often reviewed as part of the legal due diligence, so co-operation between tax and legal due diligence advisers can sometimes avoid duplication of effort; and
- interviews with management themselves.

However, while identifying the potential incidence of a de-grouping charge can be achieved by one or more of the above, quantifying the charge is notoriously difficult, and often impossible to achieve without a valuation exercise which would generally not fall within the normal scope of a market standard tax due diligence review. This is because a de-grouping charge is calculated by reference to the market value of the asset in question at the date of the transfer to the target. There would generally have been no reason for the selling group to have given any consideration to this value at that time because the transfer would have been tax neutral. So a purchaser is faced with the task of estimating retrospectively a market value at a point in time up to six years before the present. Unless some extraneous evidence exists from which a reasonable estimate may be deduced, some form of valuation exercise may be the purchaser's only option if reliance on a tax indemnity for a claim of uncertain size does not provide sufficient comfort.

Example 13

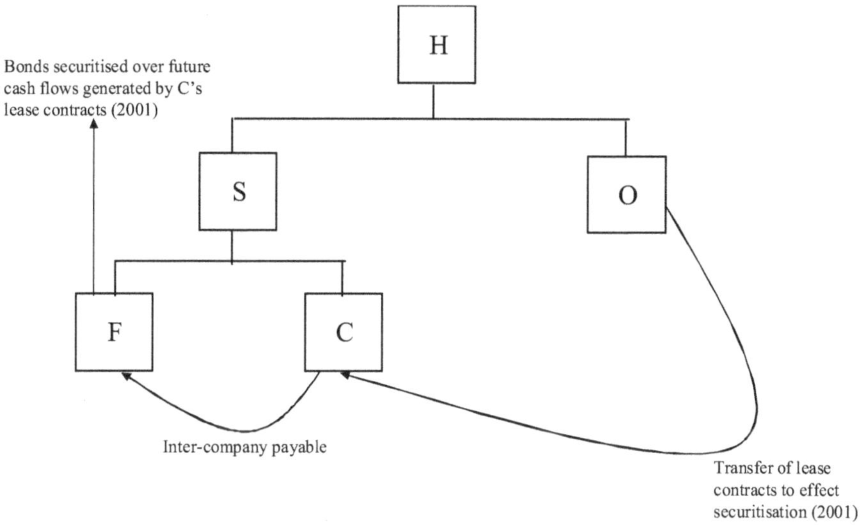

The H group was a landlord of public houses.

In 2001, the S sub-group was formed to facilitate a securitisation of the cash flows generated by the H group's pub leases. To effect this securitisation: the lease contracts were transferred from O to C; and F issued bonds on the Luxembourg Stock Exchange lending the proceeds to C.

In 2004, the H group experienced financial difficulties and the business was put up for sale.

Because of their financial circumstances, the potential purchaser was reluctant to acquire the shares of H or O but wished instead to acquire S.

However, due diligence identified that the transfer of the lease contracts from O to C in 2001 had involved the transfer of the considerable goodwill associated at the time with those contracts.

This transfer of goodwill had taken place on a no gain/no loss basis under *Section 171 TCGA 1992*. Accordingly, a disposal of the shares of S within six years would have triggered a substantial tax charge in C under *Section 179 TCGA 1992* by virtue of C (the recipient of the original *Section 171* transfer) leaving the H group with assets transferred to it from O in 2001.

Solution

The purchaser acquired the bonds issued into the market by F (which essentially represented all the economic value of the target business) together with an option to acquire the shares of S which was capable of being exercised at a point in the future after the six-year time limit for *Section 179 TCGA 1992* had expired.

There is an equivalent de-grouping charge under *Paragraph 58 Schedule 29 Finance Act 2002* where the asset which is the subject of the tax neutral transfer is an intangible fixed asset created or acquired on or after 1 April 2002 in the circumstances described in *Paragraph 118 Schedule 29 Finance Act 2002*.

There are also de-grouping charges for the purposes of Stamp Duty Land Tax.

9.3. Substantial Shareholdings Exemption ('SSE')

9.3.1. The exemption

With effect from 1 April 2002, *Section 192A and Schedule 7AC Taxation of Chargeable Gains Act 1992* provide an exemption from tax for disposals by UK companies of substantial shareholdings. Specifically, *Paragraph 1 Schedule 7AC* provides that:

'A gain accruing to a company ('the investing company') on a disposal of shares or an interest in shares in another company ('the company invested in') is not a chargeable gain if the requirements of this Schedule are met.'

These requirements are set out in Parts 2 and 3 of *Schedule 7AC*:

- Part 2 sets out the requirements which must be satisfied in relation to the substantial shareholding which is the subject of the disposal; and
- Part 3 sets out the requirements which must be satisfied in relation to both the investing company (i.e. the company making the disposal) and the company invested in (i.e. the company whose shares are the subject of the disposal).

Where these conditions are met, not only will a gain arising on the disposal of a substantial holding of shares be exempt from corporation tax on chargeable gains, but a loss arising on such a disposal will not be allowable where a gain on the same disposal would have been exempt. See *Section 16(2) Taxation of Chargeable Gains Act 1992*.

9.3.2. The key conditions which must be satisfied for the SSE to apply

- The investing company must have held at least 10% of the share capital in the company being disposed of for a continuous period of 12 months in the period beginning not more than two years prior to the date of the disposal. However, the investing company is not required to have disposed of a shareholding of 10% or more in order to qualify for the SSE; nor is it required to hold a shareholding of 10% or more at the date of the disposal in relation to which the SSE is claimed.
- The 10% holding requirement refers to:

  at least 10% of the ordinary share capital of the company invested in;

beneficial entitlement to at least 10% of the profits available for distribution to equity holders of the company invested in; and

beneficial entitlement to at least 10% of the assets available for distribution on a winding-up of the company invested in.

- All shareholdings within the investing company's worldwide group are aggregated in assessing the 10% holding requirement.
- For the purposes of the SSE, a group is defined as for *Section 170 Taxation of Chargeable Gains Act 1992* with the 75% shareholding requirement in that section replaced by a 51% shareholding requirement, i.e. a group for these purposes essentially comprises a principal company and its 51% subsidiaries.
- The investing company must be a sole trading company or a member of a trading group:

  throughout the period which begins at the start of the latest 12 month substantial shareholding qualifying period (see above) and ends with the sale of the substantial shareholding; and also

  immediately after the disposal. Where the investing company is not a sole trading company or a member of a trading group because of the sale of the target shareholding, HMRC accept, based on the subsidiary exemption in *Paragraph 3(3)(b) Schedule 7AC,* that the SSE can still apply provided that the investing company is liquidated as soon possible after the disposal.
- The group for these purposes potentially includes the entire worldwide group of which the investing company is a member and is not limited to the UK companies within the group.
- The company invested in must have been a trading company or the holding company of a trading group or sub-group:

  throughout the period which begins at the start of the latest 12 month substantial shareholding qualifying period (see above) and ends with the sale of the substantial shareholding; and also

  immediately after the disposal.

For the purposes of the SSE, a trade is defined by *Paragraph 27* of *Schedule 7AC* as 'anything that:

> (a) is a trade, profession or vocation, within the meaning of the *Income Tax Acts*, and
>
> (b) is conducted on a commercial basis with a view to the realisation of profits.'

There is no statutory definition of what is considered to be a trade, so the definition of 'trading' must be considered in light of UK case law.

Case law makes a distinction between a trade and an investment business. An investment business (i.e. the receipt of passive income from an investment) is often considered not to be trading. Whether an asset is held for trading or investment purposes will generally depend on the nature of the underlying asset and on the way in which the asset is exploited in the business. For example, a business of holding investments which produce a yield (e.g. holdings of shares or land) is likely to fail the trading test.

In order to satisfy the SSE's trading requirements, a company or group must not carry on **to a substantial extent** activities other than trading activities. Specifically:

- according to *Paragraph 20* of *Schedule 7AC*, a trading company is 'a company carrying on trading activities whose activities do not include to a substantial extent activities other than trading activities.'
- according to *Paragraph 21* of *Schedule 7AC*, a trading group is 'a group:

  (a) one or more of whose members carry on trading activities, and

  (b) the activities of whose members, taken together, do not include to a substantial extent activities other than trading activities.'
- according to *Paragraph 22* of *Schedule 7AC*, a trading sub-group is 'a sub-group:

  (a) one or more of whose members carry on trading activities, and

  (b) the activities of whose members, taken together, do not include to a substantial extent activities other than trading activities.'

HMRC have stated that 'substantial' in this context means more than 20% having regard to the following measures:

- turnover from non-trading activities;
- the non-trading asset base of the company; and
- time and resources spent and expenses incurred by officers and employees of the company/group in undertaking non-trading activities.

HMRC have also indicated that these 20% tests should not be applied mechanically and that each will be considered on its own merits. Nevertheless, analysis of the above three criteria should provide a useful indication of whether or not a company or group is trading.

Transactions between members of a sub-group are disregarded for the purposes of determining whether or not the sub-group is trading.

Any investment activities, including temporary activities such as the investment of surplus cash which has arisen as the result of a disposal or from the rental of surplus property, could if they are substantial prevent the 'trading company' or 'trading group' requirements from being satisfied. However, this is not an automatic presumption because HMRC have confirmed that there may be circumstances in which the temporary holding of surplus cash will not be construed as a non-trading activity.

HMRC have also confirmed that it is not necessarily the case that all non-trading income or assets derive from an 'activity.' For example, income arising on an intra-group loan might not derive from an activity; but it might derive from an activity if the intra-group loan is made as part of a Treasury function. In other words, a 'non-activity' is unlikely to utilise significant time and resources of officers and employees; and so is unlikely to contribute significantly to a group failing the time and resources test.

For the purposes of the SSE, a group comprises a principal company together with its 51% subsidiaries (*Paragraph 26* of *Schedule 7AC*). A sub-group is similarly defined. Companies without share capital (e.g. certain corporate partnerships) can break a group for these purposes because they cannot qualify as a 51% subsidiary for UK tax purposes. In the case of some corporate entities (e.g. guarantee companies), it is clear that they can never issue share capital and so they will always break a SSE group. For other entities (e.g. a US LLC), the characteristics of the entity can vary depending on how it is constituted and in such cases the decision as to whether such an entity has issued share capital has to be considered on a case-by-case basis. *HMRC Brief 54/07* is helpful in this regard.

9.3.3. The SSE in the context of tax due diligence

A pre-acquisition tax due diligence review may identify that a target company or group had made a share disposal in the past for which the SSE was claimed such that no chargeable gain arose on the disposal. If the conditions for the SSE to apply were not satisfied with regard to this disposal, then a material chargeable gain could have arisen which would now represent a material unprovided pre-acquisition tax exposure. As part of the pre-acquisition tax due diligence, it will therefore be necessary to form a view on the validity of the SSE claim, specifically on the extent to which there is a risk that the SSE conditions may not have been met.

It may also be the case that a purchaser of a target group may have plans for a post-acquisition transfer of some part of the acquired group to another part of its own acquiring group. Where this transfer would otherwise be taxable (for example where it would not be protected by *Section 171 Taxation of Chargeable*

Gains Act 1992 because the transferee is not within the UK capital gains group), the purchaser will wish to form a view in advance of whether the SSE is likely to apply. This may require consideration of whether the transferred company was the holding company of a trading group or sub-group throughout the 12 month qualifying period which may include a period when it was part of the seller's group.

Determining whether or not the SSE applies to a historical disposal by a target company or to a prospective disposal after completion is generally not straightforward. Whether or not a company/group is trading is often particularly difficult to determine. Answering these questions usually necessitates a separate exercise which would not normally be included as a matter of course in a market practice UK tax due diligence review and which requires careful consideration of the factors described above, some of which will depend on the circumstances prevailing within the seller's group of which the purchaser will have little or no visibility.

Nevertheless, a preliminary assessment of the likelihood of the applicability of the SSE to a particular disposal can often be made as part of a tax due diligence review as the following case study demonstrates. See Example 14.

It should be noted that all is not necessarily lost if it is not possible to determine with certainty whether a transferred company was previously part of a qualifying trading group or sub-group. In such circumstances, other reliefs may be available, e.g. under *Paragraph 18(4) Schedule 7AC*.

Example 14

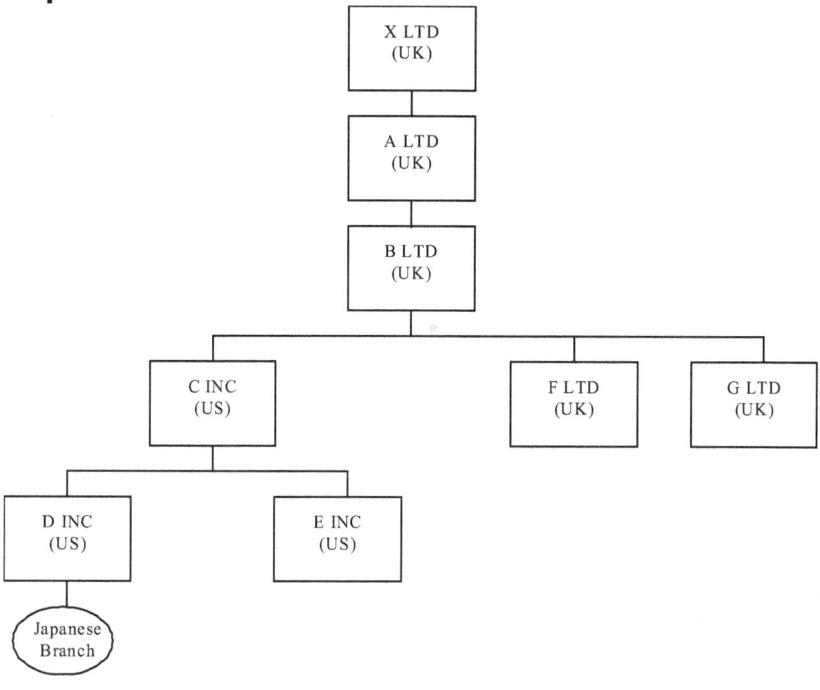

It is mid-2007 and the target group illustrated above ('the A group') is put up for sale.

The seller, X Ltd (a UK limited company) wishes to sell the shares of A Ltd, the UK holding company of the A group.

A purchaser is identified who is happy to acquire the shares of A Ltd (via a subsidiary in the purchaser's group, Y Ltd) but would prefer to acquire the A group's US sub-group directly into its own US sub-group.

This would involve a separate sale of C Inc (the US company which heads the A group's US sub-group) by B Ltd (the UK holding company of this US sub-group).

The seller may be willing to entertain such a split sale provided that B Ltd could sell C Inc with the benefit of the SSE such that no UK tax charge would arise on the disposal.

As part of its general pre-acquisition tax due diligence of the A group, the purchaser wishes specifically to form a preliminary view of whether the sale by B Ltd of C Inc would qualify for the SSE.

Legal due diligence has established that A Ltd/B Ltd has held a 100% shareholding in C Inc since April 2005. The substantial shareholding test therefore appears to be satisfied. The only other information available to the purchaser on which to base an assessment of the applicability or otherwise of the SSE is limited to:

- FY06 management accounts;
- FY06 group consolidation schedule;
- FY06 draft accounts for B Ltd, F Ltd and G Ltd;
- PE05 tax computations and returns for B Ltd, F Ltd and G Ltd.

Clearly, this is not sufficient information on which to base a full SSE review but it is sufficient to support the following preliminary analysis.

Application of the trading test to the company invested in, C Inc

The company invested in, C Inc, is not a sole trading company. Accordingly, for the SSE to apply, C Inc must be the holding company of a trading sub-group.

To establish whether this might be the case, the activities of the C sub-group must be considered, i.e. the activities of C Inc, D Inc, E Inc and D Inc's Japanese branch.

Any intra-group transactions wholly within this C sub-group may be disregarded, but transactions between members of the C sub-group and members of the wider X group will need to be considered.

Turnover analysis
According to the FY06 group consolidation schedule, D Inc recognises turnover of $8.5 million. No turnover is booked for C Inc or E Inc.

The FY06 management accounts indicate that all turnover arises from the provision of a service which prima facie appears to be a trade and which C sub-group management confirms (and is prepared to warrant) has been treated as a trade for all tax purposes in the past. This service is provided to members of the wider X group as well as to third parties.

The above analysis would suggest that D Inc's turnover does not substantially include turnover relating to non-trading activities.

Asset base analysis
According to the FY06 group consolidation schedule, D Inc has:

- tangible operating assets of $4.8 million;
- debtors of $2.7 million; and

- cash of $0.9 million.

According to the FY06 group consolidation schedule, E Inc has:

- tangible operating assets of $1.5 million;
- debtors of $0.4 million; and
- cash of $0.8 million.

A reasonable assumption can be made in the particular circumstances of D Inc and E Inc that their debtors relate to trading activities rather than to financing activities and largely arise in connection with trading transactions with the wider X group. C Inc's recognition of a $15.5 million investment in D Inc is disregarded for these purposes. D Inc and E Inc have current creditors of $4.1 million and $1.3 million respectively.

Given the general trading nature of the C sub-group's activities, there appears to be no significant non-trading activity to which its assets could be attributed. It is therefore reasonable to assume that its assets are employed for the purposes of trading activities. The only assets with a risk of non-trading status are the cash balances on the balance sheets of D Inc and E Inc at the end of FY06 on the basis that in certain circumstances cash can be considered to be a non-trading asset.

The total cash in the C sub-group, i.e. $1.7 million, comprises approximately 15% (approximately) of the sub-group's total assets of $11.1 million. On this basis, and assuming that surplus cash does not increase between the end of FY06 and the date of disposal of C Inc, then it is reasonable to draw the conclusion that the surplus cash on the consolidation balance sheet is unlikely to impact adversely the application of the trading test to C Inc.

Employee analysis

It is clearly not possible to determine from the limited information available how staff time is spent. However, given that the C sub-group does not appear to undertake activities other than trading activities (see assumption made with regard to the asset base analysis above), it is reasonable to assume that all employee time and expenses are applied to trading activities.

Preliminary conclusion

Given that the C sub-group prima facie only undertakes trading activities, it is reasonable to make the working assumption that it should pass the trading test. Although the level of surplus cash on the balance sheet may be a concern in this regard, this should only be problematic if the cash is not working capital or is not otherwise used for trading requirements. In any event, because the C sub-group appears not to undertake non-trading activities to any material extent, it is likely that HMRC would take the view that the sub-group should pass the trading test.

Application of the trading test to the investing company, B Ltd

The investing company, B Ltd, is not a sole trading company. Accordingly, for the SSE to apply, B Ltd must be a member of a trading group. To determine whether or not this is likely to be the case, the activities of all companies within the X group will need to be considered. Intra-group transactions are disregarded for these purposes.

The limited information available indicates that the activities of the X group are principally undertaken by B Ltd itself, F Ltd and G Ltd. According to the FY06 consolidation schedule, the turnover of these three entities represents approximately 90% of group turnover. Accordingly, it is reasonable to base preliminary analysis of trading status on these entities on the assumption that, apart from the C sub-group, the activities of the other entities in the X group are either immaterial or comprise only intra-group transactions.

A preliminary review of the activities of B Ltd, F Ltd and G Ltd suggests that their activities comprise, at least in part, the exploitation of rights to intellectual property giving rise to royalty income. There could be some doubt about whether these represent trading activities for the purposes of the SSE on the basis that the royalty income derived could be said to be passive income. However, all three companies actively manage the intellectual property rights, provide services to third party customers and undertake marketing and advertising activities. Furthermore:

- the X group's advisers confirm that B Ltd, F Ltd and G Ltd have filed tax returns on the basis that they undertake a trade and this has never been questioned by HMRC; and
- X group management has represented, and is prepared to warrant, that B Ltd, F Ltd and G Ltd are trading for tax purposes.

On this basis, it is reasonable to make the working assumption that the X group should pass the trading test.

Turnover analysis

From the information available, in particular from the PE05 tax computations and returns, it appears that B Ltd, F Ltd and G Ltd have no sources of income other than the activities described above. Accordingly, all of the turnover of each can reasonably be attributed to these activities.

Asset base analysis

The above analysis has so far suggested:

- that the activities of the X group are principally undertaken by B Ltd, F Ltd and G Ltd; and
- the activities of B Ltd, F Ltd and G Ltd relate solely to the activities described above.

It is therefore reasonable to conclude that the X group's assets (with the possible exception of any surplus cash) must relate to trading activities. The X group has cash of £12.7 million according to the FY06 consolidation schedule. This surplus cash represents approximately 11% of total assets which should not give cause for concern, especially if the cash is used for working capital or is related to the group's trading activities.

Employee analysis

It is reasonable to assume that employee time is spent on the activities described above, i.e. on predominantly trading activities.

Preliminary conclusion

On the basis of the above analysis, it is reasonable to make the working assumption that the X group should pass the trading test.

Overall conclusion

It is reasonable to make the working assumption that both the X group and the C sub-group are likely to be considered as trading for the purposes of the UK's Substantial Shareholdings Exemption. The risk that the X group's activities might be characterised as the exploitation of rights to intellectual property yielding passive (i.e. non-trading) income is low.

9.4. Roll-over and hold-over of chargeable gains into replacement business assets

Sections 152 to 159 Taxation of Chargeable Gains Act 1992 provide relief from tax on chargeable gains on the disposal of an asset falling within one of the classes of assets listed in *Section 155,* the most important of which in practice are:

- any building or part of a building and any permanent or semi-permanent structure in the nature of a building, occupied (as well as used) only for the purposes of a trade (other than a trade of dealing in or developing land or of providing services for the occupier of land in which the person carrying on the trade has an estate or interest - *Section 156(2)*);
- any land occupied (as well as used) only for the purposes of a trade (other than a trade of dealing in or developing land or of providing services for the occupier of land in which the person carrying on the trade has an estate or interest - *Section 156(2)*);
- fixed plant or machinery which does not form part of a building or of a permanent or semi-permanent structure in the nature of a building.

Broadly, the relief applies where the consideration for the disposal of a *Section 155* asset ('the old asset') is re-invested in the acquisition of another *Section 155* asset ('the new asset'). Both the old asset and the new asset must be used only for the purposes of the trade of the person making the disposal and reinvestment. The new asset must be acquired (or an unconditional contract for its acquisition must be entered into) within the period beginning 12 months before and ending three years after the disposal of the old asset (or at such earlier or later time as HMRC may allow).

Where the relief applies:

- if the new asset is a non-depreciating asset (i.e. an asset with a predictable life of more than 60 years), any gain on the disposal of the old asset is rolled-over under *Section 152*, i.e. it is deducted from the tax base cost of the new asset and effectively only becomes chargeable by increasing any chargeable gain or reducing any allowable loss when that new asset is eventually disposed of (at which time further roll-over or some other relief may be available); or
- if the new asset is a depreciating asset (i.e. an asset with a predictable life of 60 years or less - *Section 154(7)* in conjunction with *Section 44 Taxation of Chargeable Gains Act 1992*) any gain on the disposal of the old asset is held-over under *Section 154*, i.e. it is deferred until the earliest of the following:

  the date on which the new asset is itself disposed of;

  the date on which the new asset ceases to be used for the purposes of a trade; and

  the expiry of a period of ten years from the date of the acquisition of the new asset.

A gain held over against a depreciating asset can subsequently be rolled-over against a new non-depreciating asset which is acquired before the crystallisation of the held-over gain on the earliest of the above three occasions (*Section 154(4), (5) and (6)*).

Partial roll-over or hold-over relief is possible and is provided for by *Section 153*.

Section 175 Taxation of Chargeable Gains Act 1992 extends the scope of the above roll-over and hold-over relief by providing that, for the purposes of *Sections 152 to 158 Taxation of Chargeable Gains Act 1992*:

- all the trades carried on by a group of companies may be treated as if they were a notional single trade (to the extent that they are trades the profits of which are within the charge to UK corporation tax); and
- all the members of a group of companies may be treated as a notional single person (provided that they are resident in the UK or that any new or old asset is a chargeable asset in relation to them).

In particular:

- where a non-trading group company owns an asset used for the purposes of a trade carried on by another group company, that non-trading company may be treated as if it were carrying on the notional single trade of the group (*Section 175(2B)*);

- where a group company makes a claim to hold-over a gain against a new depreciating asset, all members of that group may be treated as the same person (*Section 175(3)*) and all trades carried on by group members may be treated as the same trade (*Section 175(1)*). Accordingly, the gain deferred by hold-over relief will only crystallise on the earliest of the following:

    the date on which the new depreciating asset is disposed of outside the group (and not the date of any earlier intra-group disposal of the asset);

    the date on which the new asset ceases to be used for the purposes of a trade by any and every group member (and not the date on which the new asset ceases to be used for the purposes of the trade carried on by the owner of the depreciating asset);

    the expiry of a period of ten years from the date of the acquisition of the new asset.

A claim for roll-over/hold-over relief must be made within six years (*Paragraph 55 Schedule 18 Finance Act 1998*) of the later of:

- the end of the accounting period in which the disposal of the old asset takes place; or
- the end of the accounting period in which the new asset is acquired.

Where a new asset has not yet been acquired, a provisional claim for roll-over/hold-over relief may be made in accordance with the provisions of *Section 153A*. This requires a declaration in the corporation tax return for the accounting period in which the disposal of the old asset occurs to the effect that a qualifying acquisition of a new asset will be made. Such provisional claims expire four years after the end of the accounting period in which the disposal of the old asset takes place.

9.4.1. Roll-over and hold-over of chargeable gains into replacement business assets in the context of tax due diligence

Historical roll-over or hold-over relief claims can materially affect the future tax position of a target company or group. In particular:

- they may adversely affect a purchaser's post-acquisition plans for the disposal of any major assets of the target against which past chargeable gains have been rolled-over or held-over; and

- any past chargeable gains deferred by means of hold-over relief will automatically crystallise within a period of ten years or less without appropriate action in the intervening period.

Accordingly, tax due diligence can be used:

- to identify and quantify any material roll-over or hold-over relief claims made by the target company or group;
- to investigate the validity of such claims, i.e.:

    whether the claim has been agreed by HMRC;

    whether the disposal of the old asset and the acquisition of the new asset appear to satisfy the requirements of the relief; and

    whether the claim was properly made within the required time limit and provided HMRC with the required information etc. (This can be more complicated where the claim has been made within a group using the extension of the relief provided by *Section 175*);
- to determine the date on which any held-over gain will crystallise in future, assuming that the new asset against which it is held-over does not cease to be used in a trade or is not sold; and
- to investigate the basis of any provisional claims for roll-over or hold-over relief; or of any representations by target management that a chargeable gain which has already arisen will be sheltered by roll-over or hold-over into qualifying new assets which have yet to be acquired.

The long period of time for which they need to be maintained, together with staff turnover in tax and finance departments, mean that target company base cost, roll-over and hold-over records are often poor. Where this is the case, there will always be a risk that tax due diligence will not be able to identify historical roll-over and hold-over relief claims and appropriate tax warranties and indemnities will be critical.

9.5. Transfer pricing

9.5.1. Generally

Transfer pricing is currently acknowledged by most multinational companies as their most important international tax issue. However, in the comparatively recent past, it was common practice for a tax due diligence review to cover transfer pricing only in passing; and it was not uncommon for transfer pricing to be excluded from the scope of tax due diligence altogether. Since then, a number of factors have increased the importance of transfer pricing within the context of tax due diligence. These include:

- increasing focus on transfer pricing by tax authorities generally as a result of the continuing globalisation of business;

- the growing compliance burden, increasingly backed by documentation regimes and tax-geared penalties, placed on companies to demonstrate compliance with the arm's length principle;
- increased audit activity by tax authorities in the area of transfer pricing;
- the greater number of jurisdictions adopting formal and penalty-backed transfer pricing regimes, in particular some of the more recently admitted European Union member states;
- the incorporation of a UK company's transfer pricing arrangements within its Corporation Tax Self Assessment ('CTSA') filing obligations;
- the extension with effect from 1 April 2004 of the UK's transfer pricing rules to transactions between two related UK companies. In the year or so after this change any consequent risk was often dismissed on the basis that it was unlikely to have given rise to a material exposure in so short a time period. Sufficient time has now passed since 1 April 2004 to make this assumption unsafe; and
- the increasing focus of the UK tax authorities on highly-geared private equity acquisitions and attempts to apply transfer pricing principles to their leverage, culminating in *Paragraph 4A Schedule 28AA Income and Corporation Taxes Act 1988*.

Most tax authorities now have domestic rules requiring transactions between entities under common control to be priced for tax purposes as though they had taken place between independent entities acting at arm's length. These rules may be couched in different terms and have different thresholds before they apply, but all have at their core the need to price at arm's length in calculating taxable profits or losses. This requirement is commonly reinforced through the obligation to prepare and maintain documentation supporting compliance with the arm's length principle; and there is often a prescriptive format for this documentation (e.g. the documentation requirements under §6662 of the US tax code). In some territories, the tax authorities go one step further and require a separate transfer pricing return (e.g. Australia). Penalties may be imposed for failure to comply with transfer pricing documentation requirements or where a transfer pricing adjustment is conceded on audit.

In the UK, the requirement to transfer price at arm's length for the purposes of corporation tax and income tax returns is contained in *Schedule 28AA Income and Corporation Taxes Act 1988*. Documentation in support of entries in a return must be retained in accordance with *Section 12B(1)(a) Taxes Management Act 1970* for pre-CTSA periods and *Paragraphs 21 to 23 Schedule 18 Finance Act 1998* for CTSA periods. These provisions apply to transfer pricing and HMRC have issued their own guidance on transfer pricing documentation compliance and what they expect this to include. Where there has been neglect (i.e. a careless or deliberate inaccuracy) in considering the question of arm's length pricing, HMRC will usually seek tax-geared penalties.

Transfer pricing is also generally addressed in bi-lateral tax conventions. In the OECD *Model Tax Convention on Income and on Capital, Article 9* (dealing with the issue of associated enterprises) applies the arm's length principle to transactions between two enterprises under common control by providing that where:

> '...conditions are made or imposed between the two enterprises in their commercial or financial relations which differ from those which would be made between independent enterprises, then any profits which would, but for those conditions, have accrued to one of those enterprises, but, by reason of those conditions, have not so accrued, may be included in the profits of that enterprise and taxed accordingly.'

Where a tax treaty applies the arm's length principle, it will often also contain a Mutual Agreement Procedures Article which provides a mechanism for seeking redress for any double taxation which may arise from a transfer pricing adjustment made by the tax authorities of one or other of the treaty states.

Some territories have transfer pricing rules which apply also to intra-country transfer pricing. The UK has been one such territory following the changes to *Schedule 28AA Income and Corporation Taxes Act 1988* with effect from 1 April 2004. However, HMRC approach UK to UK transfer pricing with a lighter touch in practice than cross-border transfer pricing, in particular because of the compensating adjustment which is often available under *Paragraph 6 Schedule 28AA*. However, this compensating adjustment may not be available where intra-UK related party transactions give rise to a particular tax advantage to one or other of the parties to them, e.g. accelerated utilisation of tax losses. Generally, intra-country transfer pricing is seen as less likely to give rise to tax exposures and this section therefore concentrates on transfer pricing in the cross-border context.

9.5.2. Transfer pricing in the context of tax due diligence

Transfer pricing should clearly be a focus of tax due diligence in relation to any target which enters into transactions with related parties to any material extent; the related party transactions of very few target groups are demonstrably on arm's length terms with full and unambiguous documentation to support their arm's length nature. Equally clear is that the cost and time required mean it is simply not feasible to include a full transfer pricing review, including functional analysis and benchmarking study, within the scope of normal market practice tax due diligence.

This is not to say, however, that, in relation to any target with related-party transactions, tax due diligence need simply do no more than conclude, as was customary until ten or so years ago, that a risk of tax authority adjustment to transfer prices must inevitably exist and that accordingly appropriate contractual protection should be secured from the seller.

Where related-party transactions are extensive and transfer pricing is perceived to be a critical risk, it may be appropriate to extend the scope of tax due diligence to include a more formal study of a target's transfer pricing circumstances. However, as a minimum, tax due diligence should generally:

- identify the main types of transactions entered into by the target with related parties. Generally, these comprise:

    intra-group loans and related interest payments;

    loan guarantees provided by related parties to third party lenders and related fees;

    intra-group trading (e.g. intra-group sales of finished goods, raw materials, components);

    charges for the provision of group services (e.g. management services, technical services, sales & marketing services); and

    intra-group royalties for the use of group intangible assets or intellectual property (e.g. trademarks, licences, know-how);

- provide some indication of the scale of these related-party transactions over the course of the last one to three years and any trends in their movement;
- report and comment on any challenge by any tax authority to the target's transfer pricing arrangements;
- describe any action taken by management to ensure or confirm that the target's related-party transactions take place on arm's length terms, including comparison with any similar transactions entered into by the target with third parties;
- describe the nature and extent of any documentary evidence to support the arm's length nature of the target's related-party transactions;
- comment on any potential risks arising from the above facts and circumstances; and
- provide specific recommendations for addressing these risks, contractually or otherwise.

But it is often possible to achieve more than this within the confines of tax due diligence given the broader range of techniques and sources of information now available to assess transfer pricing risks. It may, for example, be possible to form a view as to the profit and loss profile of group companies and to comment on areas of potential exposure where profits or losses appear to be inconsistent with any transfer pricing policy in place or with a characterisation (e.g. as a low risk distributor) of the parties to known transactions.

Sources of information

The following sources of information may be helpful in assessing a target group's transfer pricing position as part of a tax due diligence review:

- the documentary evidence retained by each member of the target group in order to satisfy the local country transfer pricing documentation requirements in each territory in which the target group operates;
- any transfer pricing master file held at the target group's head office documenting the group's transfer pricing principles and policies on a group-wide basis, together with any local customisation for particular territories;
- any statement of the target group's pricing policy;
- any reconciliations of pricing policy to the actual results;
- segmented financial statements for each business or service line;
- financial statements for each entity within the target group;
- the target group's consolidated 'glossy' financial statements including the chairman's and other statements;
- the target group's website, investment and analysts' reports, press releases or articles available to the public describing the business, historical changes and future prospects; and
- any other documents which may be of use in understanding the global business and how the separate businesses within it operate.

The years to be considered

Based on whatever information is available, the objective will be to form a view (as limited by the scope of the tax due diligence review) as to whether there has been general compliance with the arm's length principle for all open years, or years which could be opened on a subsequent enquiry by the relevant tax authorities.

In this regard, it is worth noting that UK tax legislation does not require a separate transfer pricing return. The absence of such a requirement effectively means that in the UK all in-date accounting periods remain open and subject to discovery notices and assessment in relation to transfer pricing on the basis that it is rarely clear from a corporation tax return and the underlying financial statements how compliance with the arm's length principle has been achieved or tested.

Whether or not such a discovery is possible will depend on the particular circumstances. In the Special Commissioners case *Newidgets Manufacturing Ltd v Jones (Inspector of Taxes) [1999] STC (SCD) 193*, HMRC made discovery assessments in relation to the payment of an intra-group royalty for the use of technology and other intellectual property for years where appeals had already been settled by agreement under *Section 54 Taxes Management Act 1970*. However, on appeal against the further assessments raised by HMRC under the discovery provisions of *Section 29 Taxes Management Act 1970*, the Special Commissioners found that HMRC were not entitled to make a discovery given the extent of the information already disclosed to them from which full details of this royalty could be determined. Specifically, almost everything about the royalty had already been provided to HMRC in the course of correspondence in relation to withholding taxes. In particular, HMRC already had copies of the licence agreement; knew the royalty rates applied and when these were changed; and knew the total amount of the royalties paid. Given the extent of information available to HMRC at the time when the original appeals were considered, HMRC were unable to make discovery assessments having come to a different view of the matter subsequently.

Whilst there is no separate return requirement for transfer pricing in the UK, some other jurisdictions, Australia in particular, have comprehensive transfer pricing return requirements. Whatever these requirements, in quantifying potential transfer pricing exposures, it is necessary to consider for any territory what years could be affected by the outcome of a transfer pricing enquiry.

Overall due diligence approach

The conventional wisdom for transfer pricing is that those entities responsible for routine services, such as selling, should generally receive a routine return, with the residual return, whether profit or loss, accruing to the principal. For these purposes, the principal will usually be the holder of the valuable intellectual property within the supply chain.

If the functions, assets held and risks assumed and managed by entities within the target group are evident from the information available for due diligence, it may be possible to form a high level view as to whether profits actually accrue within the target group where and to the extent they might be expected to accrue. If the available documentation is sufficiently clear and robust, it may also be possible to form a high level view as to whether the results returned by the various target group entities are consistent with the results or pricing shown as compliant with the arm's length principle in that documentation.

In practice, transfer pricing documentation, where it exists, is normally far from comprehensive. It often omits certain transactions or territories and on occasion it is necessary to judge compliance with the arm's length principle not by what appears in the available documentation but by what has been omitted from it.

Furthermore, the characterisation of entities used by the target group as the basis for its compliance with the arm's length standard is sometimes open to challenge, e.g. where a principal trading company, to which residual profits accrue, could be said to have no real substance, relying instead on bought-in services from other group companies. In such situations, some or all of the profits accruing to the principal company could more properly be attributed to other parts of the supply chain. See Example 15.

Example 15

A manufacturing company within a target group undertakes all research and development on behalf of the group and employs all the group's senior management. This manufacturing company sells its product to group sales entities around the world (including a separate sales entity in the same territory of residence as its own) at unit cost plus 10%.

The target group has an independent report, supported by some comparable data and analysis, showing that such pricing was, at least at the time the report was prepared, compliant with the arm's length standard. The report is now five years old.

In recent years, the manufacturer has reported declining profits and for the last two years has made losses. However, the sales entities have fared rather better. Their operating margins have grown in recent years from 2%-3% to 15%-18% in the latest year. It has been confirmed that throughout this period the pricing policy of cost plus 10% has been applied consistently.

On the basis only of these limited facts, the target group's transfer pricing policy appears prima facie to have given rise to results which are difficult to reconcile with the arm's length standard. In particular:

- the manufacturer appears to be the principal in the supply chain and on this basis the residual profit (after any routine returns to other entities) would normally be expected to accrue to it. To estimate any transfer pricing exposure, it might perhaps be sensible in these circumstances to assume that the report was broadly right when written and to apply (say) a 3% margin to the sales entities throughout the period;

- it is possible, however, that the characterisation of the manufacturer as principal is wrong. This might be the case if its intellectual property is not the real driver of the business but instead this is actually brand awareness generated by the marketing and sales efforts of the local sales entities. In these circumstances the manufacturer might be expected only to earn a routine return and the sales entities would be entitled to the residual, or most of the residual, profit. In practice, however, many other factors are likely to complicate the analysis and the final outcome would be dependent on who owned the brands, how the sales entities had contributed to the value of the brands and whether this is consistent with the legal rights of the various parties, in particular the distribution rights granted to the distributors.

It is rarely possible to undertake a detailed review of a target group's transfer pricing from first principles as part of a tax due diligence review. However, a thorough understanding of the target's business can help to identify transfer pricing which prima facie may not be consistent with the arm's length principle.

Indicators of potential transfer pricing risk

Certain facts or circumstances are often indications that a target group's transfer pricing may not accord with the arm's length principle. These could usefully be borne in mind when performing tax due diligence and include:

- transactions with an entity in a low tax jurisdiction;
- profits accruing in an entity where they are sheltered, e.g. by tax losses brought forward;
- entities which do not obviously appear to be the principal but which persistently make losses;
- changes in business structures which appear to have had the effect of transferring risk from one related entity to another, e.g. the creation of contract or toll manufacturers or commissionaires and limited risk distributors;
- employment of senior staff other than by the principal;
- routine service providers with wide fluctuations in margins or a trend towards diminishing margins; and
- transactions involving intangibles such as licences and cost-sharing arrangements.

If any of the above circumstances are relevant, further enquiry should be made of the target to establish:

- whether they have yet become the subject of audit or enquiry by any tax authority; and
- what evidence exists to defend the arm's length status of the resulting transfer pricing, including in particular any documentation prepared, or advice obtained, by the target in advance to defend the transfer pricing in the event of any such audit or enquiry.

A tax authority audit or enquiry may already be pending or in progress. Where this is the case, tax due diligence should attempt to estimate the likely outcomes both:

- in the jurisdiction of the entity which is subject to audit or enquiry; and
- in the territory of any other related entities which have transacted with the entity subject to audit or enquiry on terms which may not be arm's length.

This will involve consideration of the tax treaty position.

Treaty Relief

Exposures to transfer pricing adjustments may be mitigated through the availability of corresponding adjustments on making a claim under the mutual agreement procedure of any applicable tax treaty or, within the European Union, under the EU Arbitration Convention. Where a tax due diligence review has identified related-party transactions at risk of a transfer pricing adjustment, it should go on to determine whether these transactions are covered by the provisions of a tax treaty. In turn, this will involve consideration of the wording of the relevant treaty and its interpretation by the tax authorities of the contracting states. Where the treaty follows the OECD Model, the published commentary on the Model Treaty should be consulted. Given the often imprecise language in treaty articles themselves, the commentary is useful in confirming, where OECD members are concerned, what the contracting states believe the words to mean.

The drawback with almost every tax treaty is that the competent authorities appointed to administer any mutual agreement procedure are not required to come to an actual agreement so as to eliminate double taxation. Most treaties require that the competent authorities should simply use their best endeavours. In many cases, agreement will be reached; but this will not always be the case. In some instances, no relief at all, or only partial relief, from double taxation will be achieved. The eventual outcome will depend to a large extent on the tax authorities involved and a view will therefore need to be taken of the extent to which any transfer pricing exposures are likely to be mitigated through use of the mutual agreement procedure article in the relevant treaty.

Where the related parties to a non-arm's length transaction are both located within the European Union, it should be possible to make a claim under the EU Arbitration Convention concurrently with, or instead of, a treaty claim. A claim under the convention will be similar in form and process to a treaty claim but may differ from country to country. However, after a period of two years the relevant competent authorities under the convention are obliged to refer the matter to binding arbitration. This typically has the effect of forcing the parties to reach agreement so as to avoid the binding arbitration stage.

In determining the net exposure in relation to any transfer pricing adjustment within the European Union, the availability of the EU Arbitration Convention should always be considered, although relief may not be available where serious penalties are in point.

While the availability of convention or treaty relief should always be taken into account in relation to transfer pricing exposures identified by tax due diligence, it should not be assumed that, where available, such relief will necessarily result in no net payment of tax. In particular, the approach of the relevant competent authorities to the admission and prosecution of claims should be considered; and, even where a convention or treaty claim is successful, it will not necessarily mitigate the effect of penalties.

9.5.3. Private equity investments

Questions of thin capitalisation commonly arise in relation to private equity investments, given their highly leveraged nature. Accordingly, thin capitalisation is invariably a focus of tax due diligence where the target is a private equity investee company or group.

The target's thin capitalisation position will depend on the rules of the jurisdiction in which it is resident for tax purposes. The UK and many other territories have thin capitalisation rules within their general transfer pricing provisions. The UK's thin capitalisation rules were subsumed within *Schedule 28AA Income and Corporation Taxes Act 1988* by *Finance Act 2004*. Accordingly, it is necessary in the UK to consider the arm's length position in relation both to the total amount of debt and to the interest rate applied. Some jurisdictions, however, have specific rules or agreed financial ratios to determine allowable interest for tax purposes.

Most territories apply their transfer pricing rules where there is control between associated entities, i.e. where one entity controls the other or where both are under common control. However, some territories have transfer pricing provisions which can apply where such a control test is not fully met. In the UK, for example, the transfer pricing rules can apply to joint ventures where two parties each control at least 40% of the relevant entity. In addition, when applying transfer pricing to the funding arrangements of any entity, typically in relation to thin capitalisation, the UK rules are further extended to situations where a number of parties have acted together in relation to those funding arrangements (*Paragraph 4A Schedule 28AA Income and Corporation Taxes Act 1988*). This is of particular relevance to private equity investee companies since this 'acting in concert' extension was introduced principally to counter thinly capitalised private equity structures where several partnerships were involved, none of which individually controlled the acquisition vehicle.

Tax due diligence with respect to thin capitalisation should, among other things, establish whether any advance agreement in relation to the tax deductibility of interest has been obtained from the relevant tax authorities. In the UK, advance thin capitalisation agreements are often obtained from HMRC to provide some degree of certainty with regard to the level of interest which will be deductible for tax purposes. Such UK agreements will generally be based on the criteria which third party banks would typically apply and will be couched in terms similar to third party bank covenants in connection with the achievement of certain financial ratios on a prospective basis.

In considering whether or not a UK company is thinly capitalised, HMRC will typically consider the following financial ratios in addition to the Debt : Equity ratio itself:

- Debt : EBITDA; and
- EBITDA : Interest Cover.

Other financial ratios, or variations of the above ratios, may be relevant in particular industries.

9.6. Permanent establishments ('PEs')

Most tax jurisdictions have statutory provisions for the taxation of non-resident companies having operations within their territory.

A taxable presence of a non-resident corporation in a particular territory is generally referred to in tax treaties as a permanent establishment ('PE'). This term may sometimes also be found in domestic tax legislation, as has been the position in the UK following *Finance Act 2003*.

Tax treaties will normally give taxing rights to a jurisdiction in relation to the profits arising from a business or trade carried on through a PE situated in that jurisdiction. In particular, the *OECD Model Tax Convention on Income and on Capital* contains:

- *Article 5, Permanent Establishment,* which sets out when and in what circumstances a PE will exist in a particular contracting state; and
- *Article 7, Business Profits,* which sets out how the profits accruing to a PE in

a particular contracting state (and therefore taxable in that state) are to be determined.

9.6.1. PEs in the context of tax due diligence

As with transfer pricing, there has been increased focus on PEs by many tax authorities over recent years. This may be attributable to the active consideration of PEs by the OECD which has brought PEs increasingly to the attention of tax authorities. It may also in part be due to globalisation and the increasing trend of restructuring businesses along global or regional lines. This typically entails the creation of a principal trading company, often in a low-tax jurisdiction, responsible for intangibles, ongoing R&D, strategy and other key value drivers, with routine functions (e.g. manufacturing and sales) undertaken by low-risk entities such as contract manufacturers and limited-risk distributors or agents. This has resulted in the erosion of the tax base of jurisdictions in North America, Europe and Asia Pacific as profits move offshore. One of the responses of tax authorities to the creation of low-risk entities in their respective jurisdictions has been to assert that permanent establishments of the principal enterprise may have been created so as to give those tax authorities taxing rights on profits over and above the profits attributable to the routine functions of the low-risk entity.

Given this focus on PEs by the OECD and by many tax authorities, the following risks should be considered as part of any tax due diligence review of a multi-national business:

- where a PE is already acknowledged to exist by a target company, and tax returns are submitted accordingly, the risk that the profits attributable to the PE have not been properly determined; and
- the risk that the operations of a target company have created a PE, and thus an exposure to tax, which has not yet been acknowledged by the target company. In relation to this latter risk, it will also be necessary to determine how profits attributable to the PE ought to be calculated so that any resulting tax exposure may be estimated.

Assessment of the above risks will generally involve consideration of:

- the domestic rules for taxing PEs, branches or agencies. In a particular case, it may be that there are no such domestic rules and that consequently no liabilities in fact arise; or that the domestic rules in relation to PEs, branches or agencies are very different from the OECD approach. If there is no tax treaty in point, the domestic rules will be the only provisions governing the existence of a PE and how its profits are to be calculated;
- the provisions of any applicable tax treaty; and

- where an OECD Model Treaty is in point, and depending on the territories involved, the guidance provided by the existing commentary on the Model Treaty current at the time and the revised commentary published in final form in July 2008 as well as Parts I to IV of the *OECD Report on the Attribution of Profits to Permanent Establishments,* also published in July 2008 and to which the revised commentary refers. Caution is required in this regard: some fiscal authorities treat the drafts published by the OECD over recent years as dictating how treaties are to be interpreted; while other tax authorities do not apply the revised commentary to treaties signed before it was published in final form. The position is set to grow in complexity with planned revisions to the actual wording of *Article 7* of the Model Treaty leading to the existence side by side of different commentaries depending on the Model in point.

9.6.2. The existence of a PE

The question of whether or not a PE exists will depend on the domestic law of the relevant jurisdiction as modified by any applicable tax treaty. Where an OECD Model Treaty is in point, this will provide that a PE exists where there is a fixed place of business through which the business of the enterprise is wholly or partly carried on. *Article 5(2)* of the Model Treaty gives examples of what is included within this definition, e.g. a branch, office or factory. At *Article 5(4),* the Model Treaty also lists examples of what is specifically excluded from the definition of a PE, generally activities of a preparatory or auxiliary character.

Article 5(5) of the Model Treaty confirms that a PE may also be created where a dependent agent acting on behalf of an enterprise has, and habitually exercises, authority to conclude contracts. This is the 'Agency PE' and is often more problematic than the 'Fixed Place PE' described above. For an agency PE to be created, all that is necessary is for the dependent agent to be able to bind the principal. Consequently, wherever a target includes one or more group sales agents, tax due diligence should consider the risk that an Agency PE may have been created.

9.6.3. Attributable profits

Article 7 of the Model Treaty confirms that only those profits attributable to the PE may be taxed in the contracting state in which the PE is situated. It goes on to confirm that these will be limited to the profits which the PE might be expected to make if it were a distinct and separate enterprise engaged in the same or similar activities under the same or similar conditions and dealing wholly independently with the enterprise of which it is a part.

In the case of intangibles, however, it is not possible to apply this approach by imputing a hypothetical licence of intangibles between the PE and the enterprise of which it is a part. Consequently, where a PE is created by the existence of a salesforce in a particular territory, and where this salesforce sells intellectual property such as software, the profits attributable to the PE could be:

- local revenues from the sale of the intellectual property

  less
- local costs

  less
- the costs associated with the maintenance of the intellectual property incurred during the year.

This could produce profits considerably in excess of a hypothetical arm's length licence royalty.

9.7. Tax residence

A target company's tax residence is clearly fundamental to its tax position; and the overall tax profile of a target group will crucially depend on the tax residence of its individual member companies.

The rules applied to determine tax residence in a particular territory vary from jurisdiction to jurisdiction and generally include tests based on the location of one or more of the following:

- place of incorporation or law of establishment;
- place of variously interpreted management and/or control;
- voting power control;
- legal or corporate seat;
- place of registration, registered address, registered office, head office, legal or business headquarters, administrative office; and/or
- place where the business or principal activity is carried on.

These differing tests of tax residence give rise to the possibility that a company may be resident for tax purposes in more than one jurisdiction at the same time. Where a tax treaty applies, the tie-breaker article will determine tax residence.

Target companies will file tax returns, pay tax, carry forward and utilise losses, claim treaty benefits etc. on the basis that they are resident for tax purposes in one or more particular jurisdictions, and only in those jurisdictions. Often, a target company's tax residence will be a matter of little doubt, e.g. where the relevant residence tests clearly coincide in a single territory. In some cases, however, circumstances may suggest that the tax residence of one or more target companies should be tested through due diligence. This will be the case, for example:

- where the tax residence of particular companies within a target group structure is crucial to the overall tax efficiency of the group as a whole;
- where a target company is treated as tax resident in one jurisdiction (often where it benefits from a favourable tax regime) but there are indications that a degree of management or control may be exercised in another jurisdiction which applies a test of residence based on management or control; or
- any other situation where the risk that a target company might not be solely resident for tax purposes where it files returns etc. would have a material adverse impact on a transaction.

9.7.1. The position in the UK

A UK-incorporated company is automatically resident in the UK for tax purposes by virtue of *Section 66 Finance Act 1988*.

However, a company incorporated outside the UK may still be resident in the UK for tax purposes if its central management and control is exercised in the UK. This 'central management and control' test has never been statutorily defined but has been established through case law.

The leading case of *De Beers Consolidated Mines v Howe (Surveyor of Taxes) [1906] AC 455* defined a company's residence as the place 'where its real business is carried on' and established that this is 'where [its] central control and management actually abides'[24]. Cases since *De Beers* have endorsed the central management and control test and have defined the principles by which the location of central management and control is to be determined. In summary:

- to establish whether or not a company incorporated outside the UK is in fact resident in the UK for tax purposes, it is necessary to determine whether central 'management and control of the company is exercised through its own constitutional organs (the board of directors or the general meeting)'; or whether 'the functions of those constitutional organs are "usurped" – in the sense that management and control is exercised independently of, or without regard to, those constitutional organs'[25];
- to establish whether or not the functions of a company's own constitutional organs have been usurped by an outsider (i.e. by 'a person

---

[24] *De Beers Consolidated Mines v Howe (Surveyor of Taxes) [1906] AC 455 per Lord Loreburn at page 458.*

[25] *Wood and another v Holden (Inspector of Taxes) [2006] STC 443.*

who is not, himself, a participant in the formal process…through which the relevant constitutional organ fulfils its function') it is necessary to determine whether that outsider is 'proposing, advising and influencing the decisions which the constitutional organs take in fulfilling their functions' or whether the outsider is in fact dictating such decisions[26];

- 'In all normal cases the central control and management is identified with the control which a company's board of directors has over its business and affairs, so that the principle almost always followed is that a company is resident in the jurisdiction where its board of directors meets'[27];
- however, 'it is possible for a company to be resident in one territory even if it does not hold directors' meetings there'[28].

Statement of Practice 1/90 sets out HMRC's approach to determining company residence in general and in particular articulates HMRC's view of the case law principles (up to 1990) for determining central management and control:

- 'central management and control is, in broad terms, directed at the highest level of control of the business of a company. It is to be distinguished from the place where the main operations of a business are to be found, though those two places may often coincide.'
- 'the place of central management and control is wholly a question of fact.…It follows that factors which together are decisive in one instance may individually carry little weight in another.'
- 'a series of decisions has attached importance to the place where the company's board of directors meet.…But the location of board meetings, although important in the normal case, is not necessarily conclusive.…In some cases, for example, central management and control is exercised by a single individual.…In those cases the residence of the company is where the controlling individual exercises his powers.…In general the place of directors' meetings is significant only insofar as those meetings constitute the medium through which central management and control is exercised.…the conclusion in any case is wholly one of fact depending on the relative weight to be given to various factors. Any attempt to lay down rigid guidelines would only be misleading.'
- 'Generally, however,…the Revenue adopt the following approach -

---

[26] *Wood and another v Holden (Inspector of Taxes) [2006] STC 443.*

[27] *Wood and another v Holden (Inspector of Taxes) [2006] STC 443 per Park J.*

[28] *Wood and another v Holden (Inspector of Taxes) [2006] STC 443 per Park J* referring to the authority of *Unit Construction Co Ltd v Bullock [1960] AC 351.*

they first try to ascertain whether the directors of the company in fact exercise central management and control;

if so, they seek to determine where the directors exercise this central management and control (which is not necessarily where they meet);

in cases where the directors apparently do not exercise central management and control of the company, the Revenue then look to establish where and by whom it is exercised.'

In the *Inland Revenue International Manual at 120060*, HMRC express the view that, exceptionally, a company may have divided or multiple residence. Apart from a suggestion to this effect in *Swedish Central Railway Co Ltd v Thompson (Inspector of Taxes) [1925] AC 495*, there has been no development in case law of the concept of divided or multiple residence.

9.7.2. UK tax residence in the context of tax due diligence

The target of a transaction may include one or more companies:

- which are material to the tax profile of a target group;
- which were incorporated outside the UK (and so are not UK tax resident by virtue of *Section 66 Finance Act 1988*); and
- which have been treated historically as resident for tax purposes in a jurisdiction outside the UK.

Early-phase tax due diligence, often at the scoping and planning stage, may identify a risk that such companies may in fact be managed and controlled in the UK.

From the case law and HMRC's interpretation of it, it is clear that the location of a company's central management and control is:

- a question of fact; and
- heavily influenced by the substance and location of board meetings.

Accordingly, the location of a target company's central management and control is commonly the subject of tax due diligence which should include consideration of the following matters.

- Do the company's board minutes and any other evidence available for due diligence purposes appear to be comprehensive?
- In particular, does the number and content of board meetings recorded appear to be consistent with the company's level of activity[29]?

---

[29] It should be borne in mind that the 'degree of activities is not considered to be part of the [central management and control] test' and the degree of activity of the board can be

- Do the board minutes appear to record important policy and strategy decisions? Such decisions might relate to:

  approval of accounts;

  dividend policy;

  financing matters, including the raising of debt or share capital;

  major investments and other material transactions, including acquisitions, disposals, restructuring and reorganisations;

  material contracts;

  approval of budgets;

  appointment and remuneration of senior members of staff, including directors.

- Does the board of directors of the company in question appear from board minutes and other available evidence to fulfil its proper functions effectively? In particular, do all board members appear to possess sufficient knowledge, skill and experience etc. for this purpose[30]?
- Where, according to board minutes and other available evidence, are board meetings held?
- What proportion of the company's board is represented by UK resident directors? Is their influence disproportionate? Do non-UK resident

---

commensurate with the activities of the company being governed (*News Datacom Ltd and another v Atkinson (Inspector of Taxes) [2006] STC (SCD) 732*). Park J. in *Wood and another v Holden (Inspector of Taxes) [2006] STC 443*: 'it is possible (and is common in modern international finance and commerce) for a company to be established which may have limited functions to perform, sometimes being functions which do not require the company to remain in existence for long....They can and do fulfil important functions within international groups, and they are principals, not mere nominees or agents, in whatever roles they are established to undertake. They usually have board meetings in the jurisdictions in which they are believed to be resident, but the meetings may not be frequent or lengthy. The reason why not is that in many cases the things which such companies do, though important, tend not to involve much positive outward activity. So the companies do not need frequent and lengthy board meetings...' Furthermore, depending on the circumstances, it is possible for board meetings of a purely administrative or housekeeping nature to be disregarded when determining central management and control (*News Datacom Ltd and another v Atkinson (Inspector of Taxes) [2006] STC (SCD) 732*).

30 The decision in *Wood and another v Holden (Inspector of Taxes) [2006] STC 443* provides support for the view that, where the board of a company incorporated outside the UK is fulfilling its duties and making effective decisions which are fully considered, the company resides where its board meetings take place.

directors represent a majority of the board and do they appear to have sufficient knowledge, skill and experience etc. to fulfil their functions effectively? Where is the chairman of the board resident for tax purposes? Does he or she have a casting vote at board meetings?

- Do all directors (in particular any UK resident directors) attend board meetings outside the UK in person[31]; or do they participate by telephone? If they participate by telephone, how often, from where and for what reason? Do the company's rules allow a director dialling in to a board meeting to count towards the quorum for the meeting and to participate fully in the decision-making process?
- Does it appear from the evidence available for due diligence that any important decision affecting the company may have been made outside board meetings? If so, what were the circumstances? Was this decision pre-agreed by the board (at least in principle or subject to certain conditions)? Was the decision subject to, or conditional upon, subsequent approval or ratification by the board?
- Where decisions are made by directors outside normal board meetings, what constitutes a quorum for the purposes of such decisions? Must this comprise a majority of non-UK resident directors? Can UK-resident directors by themselves form a quorum?
- Does it appear from the evidence available for due diligence that any single individual has excessive influence over the company? Is any individual able to control the board, to override its decisions or alone to make important business decisions? In particular, do the company's articles of association or any other document confer any extraordinary powers on any individual?
- Where the board of directors considers proposals and advice originating from outside the board, is there evidence of adequate and independent consideration of such proposals and advice by the board? Where documents are put to the board as part of this process, are these clearly drafts for the board's consideration?
- Has the board delegated any of its authority for any purpose? If so, is such delegation subject to appropriate checks, balances and continual review? In particular, is it limited in time or extent (e.g. to specific transactions or to transactions up to a specified financial limit)? Is the exercise of any

31 In some cases, it may be appropriate to review evidence to support travel to, and attendance at, specific board meetings by particular directors. Such evidence might include diary extracts, travel documents, expense claims etc.

delegated authority pre-agreed or subject to subsequent approval or ratification by the board?

- Where do shareholder meetings take place?
- Where is the company seal held; who may authorise its use and in what circumstances?
- Where are the company's books of account and statutory records held?
- Where is the function of company secretary (including the preparation of formal documents) performed?

9.8. Special pension contributions

Generally, pension contributions paid by an employer company under a registered pension scheme are deductible for tax purposes in the accounting period in which they are paid (*Section 196 Finance Act 2004*).

However, *Section 197 Finance Act 2004* contains rules governing the tax treatment of exceptionally large or special pension contributions which can require the tax relief for such contributions to be spread over a number of years.

Broadly, spreading applies where:

- an employer company makes pension contributions under a registered pension scheme in two consecutive periods of account (referred to in the legislation as 'the previous chargeable period' and the 'current chargeable period'); and
- the amount of the contributions paid in the current chargeable period exceeds 210% of the amount of the contributions paid in the previous chargeable period; and
- this excess is £500,000 or more.

Where this is the case, spreading applies to the tax relief for so much of the contributions paid in the current chargeable period as exceeds 110% of the contributions paid in the previous chargeable period.

If the current chargeable period and the previous chargeable period are not of equal length, for these purposes the amount of the contributions paid in the previous chargeable period is adjusted proportionately.

Section 197(5) Finance Act 2004 requires tax relief for such excess to be spread as follows:

Excess of current chargeable period contributions over 110% of previous chargeable period contributions	The excess is treated for tax purposes as having been paid as follows:
£500,000 or more but less than £1,000,000	½ in the current chargeable period ½ in the following chargeable period
£1,000,000 or more but less than £2,000,000	⅓ in the current chargeable period ⅓ in the following chargeable period ⅓ in the second following chargeable period
£2,000,000 or more	¼ in the current chargeable period ¼ in the following chargeable period ¼ in the second following chargeable period ¼ in the third following chargeable period

9.8.1. Special pension contributions in the context of tax due diligence

Tax due diligence is often required to establish the following:

- whether a special pension contribution made by a target company in the past has been, and/or is being, treated for tax purposes in accordance with the the above rules;
- where a special pension contribution is required to make good a pension scheme deficit at completion, the period over which tax relief for such contribution is likely to be obtained; and
- whether the contribution has been made by a company which can justifiably claim a tax deduction for the contribution, e.g. an employer company, or some other company which is liable under the scheme rules to make the payment.

Historical pension contributions

The otherwise taxable profits of a target company for a pre-closing accounting period may have been sheltered by a special pension contribution. Tax due diligence may establish that this pension contribution had not been spread in accordance with the legislation and that tax would have been due for the accounting period in question if this failure were to be corrected. Ultimately such a failure will only give rise to a timing exposure on the basis that tax relief for the full special contribution will be obtained eventually whatever spreading is required. However, interest and penalties may be due if the failure has caused tax to have been underpaid in any particular accounting period.

Pension contributions at completion

Purchaser and seller may agree, or the Regulator may determine, that a pension deficit at completion is to be made good by one or other of the parties putting the target company in funds to make a special pension contribution.

If the purchaser provides the funding, the seller will argue that the purchase price which would otherwise have been paid should only be reduced by the net amount of the contribution on the basis that the target company will obtain tax relief for the contribution. For the same reason, a seller providing the funding will argue that only the net amount of the contribution need be paid to the target company.

Tax due diligence may therefore be required by the purchaser to establish how quickly, based on forecasts and projections, tax relief for the contribution is likely to be obtained. The seller's argument outlined above should be rebutted if in fact the target company is unlikely to have sufficient taxable profits to absorb the special pension contribution fully for some considerable time into the future.

There may be advantages in the purchaser funding a contribution post-completion because any tax losses created by such a contribution, if accruing in a pre-completion accounting period, might be subject to additional restrictions on their use, e.g. under *Section 768 Income and Corporation Taxes Act 1988,* whereas such restrictions might not apply if the contribution is made post-completion.

9.9. Tax treatment of self-employed consultants

The case of *Demiboune Ltd v Revenue and Customs Commissioners [2005] STC (SCD) 667* potentially increased the exposure in relation to payments made outside PAYE to self-employed consultants from approximately 12.8% to approximately 53.8%[32]. However, its effect has to some extent been mitigated by recent amendments to the PAYE Regulations which take effect from 6 April 2008.

Following *Demibourne,* where HMRC re-categorised a worker from a self-employed consultant to an employee, it would claim the full amount of PAYE due from the employer without any allowance for tax already paid by the worker on the same income taxed through self-assessment.

---

[32] i.e. in the worst case, if PAYE is due at the higher rate, the composite rate of PAYE, employer's NIC and employee's NIC would be 53.8% at current rates.

It was still possible for the employer to offset tax already paid by the worker against the PAYE due. However, in order to do so, the individual worker had to sign a mandate which effectively allocated to the employer any refund due to the individual for tax paid under self-assessment. Accordingly, any offset was entirely contingent on the co-operation of the individual worker; and the amount of tax available for offset would depend on how much that individual had already paid via self-assessment. Problems could arise where the individual no longer worked for the employer. In particular, where the termination of the relationship between the worker and employer was not amicable, full co-operation could be in doubt.

If a mandate could be successfully agreed and if full tax and Class 2 and 4 NIC had been paid via self-assessment, then any exposure for the employer would be limited to the employer's NIC, currently 12.8% (no offset is available against the employer's NIC).

However, recent amendments to the PAYE Regulations once again permit tax paid by the individual worker via self-assessment to be set off against the PAYE due from the employer without the need for signed mandates.

The amended regulations apply from 6 April 2008 and can be applied to tax years prior to this date, provided that certain events have not already taken place before 6 April 2008, e.g. provided that HMRC has not already issued a Notice of Determination to recover PAYE before 6 April 2008. However, even where the amended regulations cannot be applied to a pre-6 April 2008 tax year, it should still be possible to offset tax already paid by the worker using the mandate described above.

Interest and penalties will apply to the PAYE and NIC due before any offset, whether by mandate or under the new regulations.

9.10. Employee share/security ownership

The introduction of *Part 7 Income Tax (Earnings and Pensions) Act 2003 (Employment income: income and exemptions relating to securities)* has meant that it is now more necessary then ever to understand what employee share schemes the target company has in place and to understand the history of any employee share/security ownership. Even though introduced in 2003, companies still often underestimate the scope and complexity of the provisions in *Part* 7 and do not always take sufficient professional advice in relation to them. Accordingly, it is generally recommended that any tax due diligence review of employee share/security ownership should be conducted by specialists in this particular area of tax law.

Circumstances where *Part 7 Income Tax (Earnings and Pensions) Act 2003* is relevant vary widely. The provisions of *Part 7* may apply in the relatively simple case where the target company is a quoted company with a number of unapproved and HMRC-approved share option schemes and long term incentive plans which the company secretary operates efficiently. Equally, they will need to be taken into account in a complex situation where security-based bonus planning arrangements have been implemented (which may be in process of negotiation with HMRC) or where numerous transactions have been undertaken each involving employee share (and perhaps security) ownership, for example cases of multiple private equity backed buy-outs or companies operating a buy and build strategy.

If any of the value, or growth in value, of any employee shares falls within *Part 7 Income Tax (Earnings and Pensions) Act 2003*, the potential exposure to the target company increases from 0% (where only capital gains tax for the shareholder is in point) to as much as 53.8%[33] at current rates (without including interest, penalties and any 'gross-up' charges). Some of this may be deductible for corporation tax purposes, but there are situations where the amount subject to PAYE and NIC is not deductible. Furthermore, whether for legal or practical reasons, it may not always be possible for the target company to recover any of the PAYE and employees' NIC from the employees.

Where it is found that PAYE should have been operated, if the employees do not make good the tax to the employer within 90 days of the tax point, a further charge to tax is crystallised under *Section 222 Income Tax (Earnings and Pensions) Act 2003* together with a further Class 1 NIC charge. If these charges are crystallised, the employer may have to settle the further income tax on behalf of employees on a grossed-up basis and Class 1 NIC will be due on the grossed-up tax.

There is additional complexity where the target company is unquoted. The potential charges arising under the different chapters which make up *Part 7 Income Tax (Earnings and Pensions) Act 2003* are all based on the difference in the value of the shares before and after a particular event. With an unquoted company, there may not be any third party transactions or valuation advice to assist in quantifying the potential exposure.

Research into a number of publicly available sources of information at the planning stage of a tax due diligence review will indicate the extent to which employee share/security ownership should be included within the scope of the review:

---

[33] i.e. in the worst case, if PAYE is due at the higher rate, the composite rate of PAYE, employer's NIC and employee's NIC would be 53.8% at current rates.

- the target company's financial statements should disclose whether the directors have any interests in the company and, in various notes to the financial statements, there should be an outline of any employee share schemes which the target company has implemented;
- the target company's website will often include details of the history of the company and the ownership of its shares;
- the Articles of Association, annual returns, etc. may also be helpful in this regard.

If such initial research suggests that employee share/security ownership may be material to the tax due diligence, the seller can be asked at an early stage for additional information and documents such as Form 42s, etc.

In evaluating the tax risks of a target company in relation to employee share/security ownership, the following questions will be of particular relevance:

- What professional advice has been taken in relation to the target company's employee share/security ownership arrangements? Has the target company followed the advice: when implementing the arrangements; throughout the life of the arrangements; and where new awards have been made? Not only will this assist in understanding any risks associated with the arrangements but it can provide comfort that management is aware of the potential PAYE and NIC exposures throughout their life.
- Are the shares/securities within the PAYE regime? In the case of an unquoted company, shares are only within the PAYE regime if they are readily convertible assets or are deemed to be readily convertible assets (as no corporate tax deduction is available). Other securities, such as debt instruments, will always be deemed to be readily convertible assets even if in fact they are not readily convertible[34].

---

[34] PAYE/NIC is applicable to taxable receipts which are readily convertible assets ('RCAs'). The definition of RCAs generally means that the securities can be converted into cash. This will normally be the case where there is a market for the securities, e.g. an employee benefit trust or arrangement to sell to a third party. In addition to this general rule, there are specific provisions in *Section 702 Income Tax (Earnings and Pensions) Act 2003* which deem securities to be RCAs where the cost of providing them is not deductible for UK corporation tax purposes under statutory rules set out in *Schedule 23 Finance Act 2003*. This deeming rule can result in several anomalous situations where PAYE/NIC applies to assets which are not readily marketable, but which are deemed to be RCAs. Common examples include employees receiving interests in investment partnerships and shares in companies controlled by private

- In the case of an unquoted target, what valuation work has the target company undertaken and/or what valuation advice has it obtained in relation to the amount of income likely to be taxable? PAYE has to be operated on the basis of the best estimate which can reasonably be made of the amount of income likely to be taxable. If the target company has made such an estimate, either by undertaking its own valuation, obtaining a professional valuation or agreeing the value with HMRC for PAYE purposes, the risk of any exposure to the target company will be reduced. Any difference in value is then recovered from the individual employees via their self-assessment tax returns.
- Will a corporation tax deduction be available for any PAYE and NIC liabilities identified to reduce the net exposure? There are various reasons why a corporation tax deduction may not be available. For example, the arrangements may involve a security other than ordinary shares, or, particularly in the case of a private equity-backed company, the target company may be under the control of another company. It should be noted in this regard that the corporation tax deduction will arise in the employing company which may not be the parent company whose shares are part of the arrangements.
- What amounts can be recovered from the employees, legally and practically? Generally, for non-cash consideration to be recoverable from an employee, that employee has to have agreed to such recovery. This may be in the rules for the arrangements or in a separate document such as an investment agreement. Recovering employer's NIC is generally only possible in specific circumstances where joint elections can be entered into to transfer the liability to the employee (e.g. in the case of share option gains). To the extent that indemnities are in place or are to be sought, a purchaser should ensure that their wording includes interest, penalties and any 'gross-up' charges under *Section 222 Income Tax (Earnings and Pensions) Act 2003* (if the employee has not made good the PAYE liability within 90 days).

9.11. VAT treatment of a target's historical transaction costs

The direct tax treatment of any material transactions (acquisitions, disposals, reorganisations etc.) of a target company or group in historical periods still potentially open to audit or adjustment by the tax authorities should clearly be a focus of tax due diligence.

---

equity funds. Both of these are normally deemed to be RCAs and therefore subject to the operation of PAYE/NIC, regardless of their commercial marketability.

The indirect tax treatment of such transactions, and in particular the recovery of VAT on the related transaction costs, often represents a higher risk and accordingly should not be overlooked. Such transaction costs can include financial adviser's fees, arrangement fees, lawyers' fees, the costs of due diligence, other adviser's fees etc. If not treated correctly at the time, the VAT effect of these costs when aggregated over a number of transactions can amount to a potentially material historical tax exposure.

The increased level of risk associated with a target's VAT treatment of past transaction costs arises from the fact that the management of many targets often has a lower level of awarenesss, and tends to take less professional advice, in this area than with regard to direct tax risks.

See 12.2 for details of the UK VAT treatment of the costs of buy-side and sell-side due diligence in relation to both share transactions and asset deals.

9.12. Tax planning arrangements disclosable under *Part 7 Finance Act 2004* and the *Tax Avoidance Schemes (Prescribed Descriptions of Arrangements) Regulations 2006 (SI 2006/1543)*

Finance Act 2004 introduced into UK tax legislation a regime requiring the details of certain types of tax planning to be disclosed to HMRC separately from, and in advance of, a company's corporation tax return.

This regime was substantially revised in 2006 (with effect from 1 August 2006) and in relation to income tax, corporation tax and capital gains tax, is now contained within *Part 7 Finance Act 2004* and the *Tax Avoidance Schemes (Prescribed Descriptions of Arrangements) Regulations 2006 (SI 2006/1543).*

The requirement to disclose under the regime applies to certain categories or descriptions of tax planning arrangements specifically prescribed by the *2006 Regulations* which give rise to a tax advantage where that tax advantage is a main benefit of the arrangements.

Depending on the circumstances, disclosure is required:

- either by a promoter of tax planning arrangements (essentially, anyone who designs, markets or manages the implementation of the arrangements); or
- by in-house tax teams who implement such arrangements.

Promoters are required to make disclosure to HMRC:

- in relation to 'off-the-peg' tax planning within five days of making tax planning arrangements available for implementation; and
- in relation to 'bespoke' tax planning within five days of becoming aware

of any transaction which forms part of such tax planning arrangements.

In-house tax teams are required to make disclosure to HMRC within 30 days of the commencement of implementation of tax planning arrangements.

The specific categories or descriptions of tax planning arrangements prescribed by the *2006 Regulations* are informally referred to as the seven 'hallmarks' of notifiable tax planning arrangements.

9.12.1. The seven hallmarks of notifiable tax planning arrangements

1. Confidentiality where a promoter is involved

The first hallmark covers circumstances where it might reasonably be expected that a hypothetical promoter of tax planning arrangements might wish to keep those arrangements confidential either:

- from other promoters; or
- from HMRC itself;

between the date of the commencement of implementation of the arrangements to the date on which the promoter's client would be required to file a tax return reporting them.

Specifically, disclosure to HMRC is required where an element of the tax planning arrangements gives rise to a tax advantage in circumstances:

- where it might reasonably be expected that the promoter of the tax planning arrangements would wish to keep confidential from other promoters details of how the particular element of the arrangements gives rise to a tax advantage; or
- where, but for this disclosure requirement:

    the promoter of the tax planning would wish to keep details of how the particular element of the tax planning arrangements gives rise to a tax advantage confidential from HMRC; and

    a reason for wanting such confidentiality from HMRC is to facilitate repeated or continued use of the same or a similar element in future.

In the case of confidentiality from HMRC, the hallmark is not an objective or hypothetical test but a subjective one applicable to the specific wish for confidentialty of a particular individual promoter. HMRC have indicated that explicit warnings from promoters to their clients about the risk of a limited 'shelf life' of tax planning arrangements, or specific confidentiality obligations imposed by promoters on their clients in relation to tax planning arrangements, will be considered as indicative of a desire to keep those arrangements confidential from HMRC.

2. *Confidentiality where no promoter is involved, i.e. 'in-house' tax planning*

Disclosure to HMRC is required where an element of the tax planning arrangements gives rise to a tax advantage and where:

- there is no promoter of the arrangements;
- the intended user of the arrangements is not a small or medium-sized enterprise as defined in *Regulation 4*;
- the user wishes to keep details of how the particular element of the tax planning arrangements gives rise to a tax advantage confidential from HMRC between the date of commencement of implementation of the arrangements and the date on which the user would have been required to notify HMRC of them if a promoter had been involved; and
- a reason for wanting such confidentiality is to facilitate repeated or continued use of the same or a similar element in future.

3. *Premium fee*

Disclosure to HMRC is required where a promoter, or a person connected with a promoter, of arrangements giving rise to a tax advantage would, but for this disclosure requirement, be able to charge a premium fee in relation to them.

A premium fee is defined for these purposes as a fee:

- which is chargeable in connection with any element of the arrangements from which the expected tax advantage arises; and
- which is to a significant extent attributable to that tax advantage; or
- which is to any extent contingent upon the obtaining of that tax advantage.

However, this hallmark does not apply where:

- there is no promoter; and
- the tax advantage is intended to be obtained by a small or medium-sized enterprise.

4. *Off-market terms*

This is essentially a version of the premium fee hallmark applicable to banks which sell financial products priced on the basis of their tax advantages.

Disclosure to HMRC is required where:

- the tax advantage expected to be derived from the tax planning arrangements more than incidentally arises from the inclusion of one or more financial products;
- a promoter, or a person connected with a promoter, becomes a party to one or more of those financial products; and

- the price of those financial products differs significantly from the price which might reasonably be expected to apply in the open market.

Financial product is defined in *Regulation 9(2)*.

5. Standardised tax products

Under this hallmark, disclosure to HMRC is required in relation to generic tax planning schemes made available to more than one user with standardised, or substantially standardised, documentation provided by the promoter requiring little or no modification before implementation. Specifically, disclosure is required where:

- the promoter of the scheme makes available to a client standardised, or substantially standardised, documentation the purpose of which is to facilitate the implementation of the tax planning arrangements by the client;
- the client is required to enter into a specific transaction (or series of transactions) which are standardised, or substantially standardised, in form; and
- it would be reasonable for an informed observer to conclude that the main purpose of the tax planning arrangements was to enable the client to obtain a tax advantage.

This disclosure requirement applies only where there is an immaterial amount of tailoring of the arrangements to fit a particular client's facts and circumstances. Nor is disclosure required if a tax planning scheme has already been made available to clients prior to 1 August 2006.

Regulation 11 provides a list of inoffensive standardised tax products which are excluded from the disclosure requirement.

6. Loss schemes

The disclosure requirement under this hallmark is aimed at individuals who participate in loss-making schemes, specifically where:

- the promoter of the scheme expects more than one individual client to implement the same, or substantially the same, tax planning arrangements; and
- the arrangements are such that an informed observer could reasonably conclude that the main benefit expected to be derived from them takes the form of tax losses relievable against an individual's income tax or capital gains tax liability.

According to HMRC, this hallmark is targeted at schemes which create excessive tax relief for losses and not at arrangements which provide tax relief for losses on what might be considered as a normal basis.

7. Leasing arrangements

The disclosure requirement under this hallmark applies where a tax advantage is expected to be derived from tax planning arrangements involving a plant & machinery lease with a duration of more than two years:

- where the value of any single leased asset is at least £10 million; or
- where the aggregate value of all the leased assets is at least £25 million.

Before disclosure is necessary, however, one or more of a number of other factors indicative of tax avoidance needs to be present. These are set out in *Regulation 15* and broadly comprise:

- arrangements where one party to the plant & machinery lease is able to claim UK capital allowances and the other party is not within the charge to UK corporation tax;
- arrangements designed to remove from the lessor, by the provision of money or a money debt, the majority of the risk of default by the lessee; or
- arrangements involving:

    a sale and finance leaseback within the meaning of *Section 221 Capital Allowances Act 2001*; or

    a lease and finance leaseback within the meaning of *Section 228F(5) Capital Allowances Act 2001.*

9.12.2. Disclosable tax planning arrangements in the context of tax due diligence

The aim of the UK tax planning disclosure regulations is to provide HMRC with early warning of tax avoidance schemes together with greater detail on how they achieve their particular tax advantage. Thus armed, HMRC are in a much better position to monitor overall trends in the tax planning environment and to take early and targeted action to counteract schemes which they consider to be offensive.

Whether or not a tax avoidance scheme has, or should have, been disclosed to HMRC is therefore an important focus of tax due diligence. Specifically, such disclosure will have implications for the extent to which it is appropriate to recognise tax benefits emanating from the scheme in the target's financial statements and/or the purchaser's valuation model.

In relation to tax-motivated planning, tax due diligence should therefore consider the following questions:

- Has the target disclosed to HMRC all tax planning which is required to be disclosed under the UK tax planning disclosure regulations; and, if not, what are the implications?

- What assumptions should be made by a purchaser about the longevity of the tax benefits deriving from tax planning which has been disclosed to HMRC under the UK tax planning disclosure regulations?
- Is any remedial action required by a purchaser in relation to tax planning which has been disclosed to HMRC under the UK tax planning disclosure regulations?

9.13. The general tax control environment of the target company or group

Quite apart from the identification of specific tax risks, tax due diligence enables a purchaser to assess the overall quality of the target's tax control environment. Specifically, tax due diligence will consider:

- whether the target's tax function is adequately resourced and whether, as a whole, it has sufficient technical expertise;
- whether the target's tax function is sufficiently integrated in the target's business and management;
- whether the target's tax function is made aware of, and consulted on, material non-routine transactions at a sufficiently early stage;
- the robustness of the target's procedures and systems for capturing reliable information for the purposes of meeting its tax compliance and accounting obligations and to support effective tax planning;
- the quality of the target's tax disclosures generally;
- the target's ability to reconcile information in tax returns to financial statements and underlying books and records;
- who prepares and reviews the target's tax returns (i.e. are both preparation and review performed in-house or is an independent adviser involved in either process?);
- the target's appetite for risk in relation to tax planning;
- the extent to which the target takes advice in relation to tax matters, in particular with regard to VAT/sales tax and employment taxes;
- whether any part of the target's tax compliance is outsourced (e.g. payroll administration);
- the nature and quality of the target's relationship with the tax authorities. In the UK, this would include the outcome of any HMRC Risk Review of

the target, including the Risk Rating and Risk Review Summary Template[35];
- etc.

This aspect of tax due diligence provides a purchaser with an early opportunity:

- to evaluate the target's overall risk profile with regard to tax, with consequent implications for other tax due diligence, price and contract negotiations etc. A weak tax control environment would tend to suggest that the tax due diligence should be broader and deeper than might otherwise have been the case and that price and contractual protection should reflect an increased level of risk; and
- to plan the post-acquisition integration and management of the target's tax affairs.

When reporting due diligence findings in relation to a target's general tax control environment, it is vital to be objective, to ground all conclusions in fact and to confine commentary to observations on processes and procedures (rather than the competence etc. of any particular individual members of the target's tax department).

9.14. Completion accounts versus 'locked box' balance sheets to determine purchase price

9.14.1. Purchase price adjustments based on completion accounts

Until the advent of 'locked box' pricing mechanisms (see 9.14.2) which have come to predominate in recent years, the pricing of a share sale was typically determined by means of the following mechanism provided for in the contract for the sale and purchase of the target's shares.

- The potential purchaser determines the enterprise value of the target, usually based on a multiple of EBITDA, i.e. on a cash-free, debt-free basis and assuming a normal (or sometimes an estimated or forecast) level of working capital. (A seller who expects working capital to be lower than normal at completion, will sometimes choose not to include a working capital adjustment explicitly in the purchase price adjustment mechanism).
- This enterprise value is then adjusted for an estimate (made before signing) of the level of net debt (including debt-like items, e.g. tax) at completion, based on a pre-signing reference date, to give the equity purchase price agreed at signing but not actually paid until completion, i.e.

---

[35] See *H.M Revenue & Customs 'Tax compliance risk management: Guidance for LBS customers and staff – Review of Links with Large Business', December 2007.*

Equity Purchase Price Agreed at Signing but Paid at Completion

=

Enterprise Value

+

Estimated cash at completion

-

Estimated debt at completion

Specifically, the equity purchase price agreed at signing but not actually paid until completion is calculated as follows.

Enterprise Value		X
less: Estimated net debt at completion		(X)
plus: Estimated working cap at completion	X	
less: Normal working capital	(X)	
	---	
plus/(minus): Working capital adjustment		X

Equity purchase price paid at completion		X
		==

- Post-completion, the equity purchase price paid at completion is adjusted by means of completion accounts to arrive at the final equity purchase price. Specifically, the completion accounts are used to true-up net debt and working capital from the estimated balances assumed in the purchase price paid at completion to the actual completion balances.

Equity Purchase Price Paid at Completion		X
Actual net debt at completion	X	
less: Net debt assumed in the purchase price paid at completion	(X)	
	---	
plus/(minus): Net debt adjustment		X
Actual working capital at completion	X	
less: Working capital assumed in the purchase price paid at completion	(X)	
	---	
plus/(minus): Working capital adjustment		X

Final equity purchase price		X
		==

Purchasers will generally prefer completion accounts mechanisms for determining the final equity purchase price because, as their name implies, completion accounts will be drawn up at the date when economic ownership effectively passes and so provide an element of certainty for the purchaser. Furthermore, the process by which completion accounts are drawn up and agreed enables purchasers to influence their content and thereby potentially to reduce the purchase price.

Completion accounts need not be audited. However, they are usually prepared in accordance with detailed provisions set out in the contract for the sale and purchase of the target's shares, subjected to scrutiny by both seller and purchaser and agreed through a process of negotiation.

Completion accounts in the context of tax due diligence

Where the purchase price paid at completion is to be adjusted subsequently for net debt and working capital adjustments derived from completion accounts as outlined above, the purchaser's tax due diligence should focus on the following.

- Whether the tax creditors/provisions (or debtors) in the completion accounts fairly reflect the target's tax liabilities (or assets) as at that date, including, where appropriate, provision for pre-completion tax exposures identified by due diligence. Generally, the contract for the sale/purchase of the target's shares will require the tax creditors/provisions (or debtors) in the completion accounts to be prepared on the basis that the period between the date of the last financial statements and completion will be treated as if it were an accounting period for tax purposes.
- Whether the net debt and working capital adjustments should include tax balances. While this is a matter for negotiation between the parties, as a general rule it is commercially accepted that:

  current corporation tax liabilities (or current corporation tax assets, e.g repayments due) are included within net debt as debt-like items;

  deferred corporation tax liabilities (or deferred corporation tax assets, e.g tax losses and general provisions) are excluded from net debt on the basis that they are non-cash items; and

  PAYE and VAT liabilities are a component of working capital.

9.14.2. 'Locked box' price determination

As an alternative to allowing for a price adjustment based on completion accounts, sellers in a strong bargaining position will sometimes require potential purchasers to agree the equity purchase price of a target by reference to a 'locked box' balance sheet drawn up as at a certain date before signing of the contract, often the last audited balance sheet.

Where this is the case, the price is agreed on the basis of that balance sheet and cannot be adjusted subsequently for any balance sheet movements between the balance sheet date and completion. Accordingly, purchasers must make their own estimates of such movements in their calculation of the equity purchase price to be paid at completion.

However, the seller will commonly warrant that the 'locked box' balance sheet is complete and correct. Where this is the case, the agreed equity purchase price paid at completion is effectively adjusted for successful claims under such a warranty, although this is a more onerous process than a traditional completion accounts adjustment.

Where a 'locked box' is used to determine price:

- the purchase price itself is still paid at completion (i.e. not at the 'locked box' date); but
- the risk (or, conversely, the reward) of movements in tax balances between the 'locked box' date and completion will effectively pass to the purchaser (unless, of course, these have already been taken into account in the purchaser's calculation of the equity purchase price to be paid at completion).

Accordingly:

- the seller will usually agree not to extract value from the target (commonly referred to as 'leakage' or 'non-permitted leakage') from the 'locked box' date to completion except for specifically defined and permitted extractions of value ('permitted leakage'); and
- the purchaser will correspondingly:
  - reduce the price for permitted leakage; and
  - require indemnification for any leakage in excess of permitted leakage; and
- the seller will require some form of recompense to reflect the fact that, although determined at the 'locked box' date, the purchase price is not received until completion and (subject to permitted leakage – see above) value will have accrued in a profitable target between these two dates.

This latter additional component of the purchase price (commonly referred to as the 'value accrual') is essentially an estimate, based on forecasts of the position at completion, of the change in net debt and working capital which would have been adjusted for had completion accounts been used to determine price.

The value accrual is commonly defined in the contract for the sale of the target's shares as:

- an effective rate of interest applied to the price determined on the basis of the 'locked box' balance sheet; or
- some daily, weekly or monthly rate of forecast profit; or
- if the date of completion is certain, a lump sum; or
- some combination of the above, e.g. a lump sum for the period between the 'locked box' date and signing (for which the change in net debt may be known with some certainty) and a rate of interest or daily rate of forecast profit for the period between signing and completion.

From a tax perspective, it is likely to be important for the seller that this additional component of the purchase price should be treated as additional capital sale proceeds (i.e. as additional purchase price) and not some type of income receipt. Additional purchase price is likely to qualify for various capital gains reliefs or participation exemptions available in a number of jurisdictions; whereas an income receipt may be taxable immediately, possibly at a higher rate, and/or subject to withholding tax. Sellers will therefore be keen to ensure that, in the contract for the sale of the target's shares, the definition of any additional component of the purchase price is carefully drafted to support the desired tax treatment.

In summary, with a 'locked box' price determination mechanism, the final equity purchase price (which is paid at completion and which is not adjusted subsequently) is calculated as follows.

Enterprise Value		X
plus/(minus): Net debt at the 'locked box' date		(X)
plus: Actual working cap at the 'locked box' date	X	
less: Normal working capital	(X)	
	---	
plus/(minus): Working capital adjustment		X
plus/(minus): Value accrual		X

Final equity purchase price paid at completion		X
		==

Provided that the purchaser's contractual protection in relation to pre-completion tax liabilities (in particular the tax indemnity) is comprehensive and reliable, the difference between a completion accounts mechanism and a 'locked box' mechanism for determining price should in principle only be a question of timing:

- with completion accounts, the purchaser will be compensated for tax liabilities existing at completion faster and more directly because the purchase price will automatically be adjusted to reflect them; whereas
- with a 'locked box' mechanism, the purchaser will have to make an indemnity or warranty claim for any pre-completion tax liabilities which are not reflected in the final equity purchase price based on the 'locked box' balance sheet and paid at completion.

In practice, however, even assuming comprehensive contractual protection, the difference between a completion accounts mechanism and a 'locked box' mechanism may be more than timing once the inconvenience and expense of making warranty and/or indemnity claims, and all the restrictions to which such claims may be subject (see Chapter 8 in general and 8.6 in particular), are taken into account.

Sellers will generally prefer 'locked box' balance sheets for determining the final equity purchase price and their use has become increasingly common in the sellers' market which has prevailed in recent years. A 'locked box' balance sheet avoids the administrative burden and cost of providing for a completion accounts mechanism in the contract for the sale and purchase of the target's shares and subsequently drawing up, negotiating and agreeing completion accounts. More significantly, it provides greater price certainty for the seller by avoiding the risk that the purchaser will use negotiation of completion accounts to chip away at the purchase price. In other words, the risk of over-pricing passes to the purchaser. This is of particular importance to financial sellers and in auctions, e.g. private equity exits. Correspondingly, the purchaser may benefit from under-pricing, although this is less likely to occur in practice given the seller's geater knowledge of the target.

There is no general requirement that a 'locked box' balance sheet should be audited, although, if not audited, it will generally have been reviewed by the provider of any sell-side due diligence carried out on behalf of the seller. Commonly, however, the 'locked box' balance sheet will be the latest available audited balance sheet on the basis that purchasers will generally require the additional comfort which an audited balance sheet provides in relation to the accuracy and completeness of the 'locked box' balance sheet position, given how important these are to determining the price.

'Locked box' balance sheets in the context of tax due diligence

Where a 'locked box' mechanism applies, the purchaser will require from the seller sufficient information from which to determine:

- whether the tax creditors/provisions (or debtors) in the 'locked box' balance sheet fairly reflect the target's tax liabilities (or assets) as at that date, including, where appropriate, provision for pre-completion tax exposures identified by due diligence;
- whether net debt and working capital should include tax balances. While this is a matter for negotiation between the parties, as a general rule it is commercially accepted that:

  current corporation tax liabilities (or current corporation tax assets, e.g repayments due) are included within net debt as debt-like items;

  deferred corporation tax liabilities (or deferred corporation tax assets, e.g tax losses and general provisions) are excluded from net debt on the basis that they are non-cash items; and

  PAYE and VAT liabilities are a component of working capital;
- the tax implications of any leakage by the seller, whether permitted or otherwise, in the period between the 'locked box' date and completion; and whether, in the case of non-permitted leakage, this will be covered by the terms of the indemnity provided by the seller. In this regard, certain tax-specific matters may themselves constitute non-permitted leakage (e.g. a change of tax residence) and the indemnity provided by the seller for these should include drafting to cover them, e.g. 'The seller shall procure that, from the 'locked box' date up to and including completion, each target company will conduct its business in the ordinary course and on arm's length terms and that, without the prior written consent of the purchaser, none of the target companies will do, or agree to do, anything outside the ordinary course of its business or on terms other than arm's length terms, including, but not limited to, any of the following:

  changing its residence for tax purposes; or

  making any tax election, or settling or compromising any tax liability, or submitting any tax return which is inconsistent with past practice, or incurring any liability for tax other than in the ordinary and usual course of business;'
- whether, in the period between the 'locked box' date and completion, the target might be required to pay a pre-'locked box' date tax liability which is not recorded in the 'locked box' balance sheet. Such a payment is likely to constitute non-permitted leakage. Conversely, there may be:

tax refunds etc. which are received in the period between the 'locked box' date and completion but which are not recorded in the 'locked box' balance sheet; and

other refunds etc. which are received in the period between the 'locked box' date and completion but which are not recorded in the 'locked box' balance sheet. These may need to be included in the purchase price on an after-tax basis, subject to the purchaser's decision whether or not to give the seller full value for them ; and

- what movements there are likely to be in the target company's or group's tax liabilities between the date of the 'locked box' and the date of completion. Any increases would be for the purchaser's account unless taken into account in the purchaser's calculation of the equity purchase price to be paid at completion.

The choice of date for the 'locked box' balance sheet will have implications for tax due diligence:

- where the 'locked box' balance sheet is the last audited balance sheet, the tax balances are likely to be more reliable on the basis that they will have been audited. Accordingly, it may be possible to include tax audit working papers in the scope of the purchaser's pre-acquisition tax due diligence. Furthermore, the seller may be willing to warrant the tax balances to a greater extent than would be the case for non-audited tax balances. However, the last audited balance sheet may not disclose tax balances in sufficient detail for the purchaser's purposes; and the tax balances may fall below the level of audit materiality. In any event, the last audited balance sheet may be too long ago before the expected date of completion for seller and/or purchaser to be able to derive comfort from it;
- a more recent 'locked box' balance sheet date (e.g. a balance sheet prepared for the purposes of the last management accounts) would avoid this latter problem. However, unless the balance sheet is audited (e.g. a special purpose audited balance sheet), the tax balances recorded in it are likely to be less reliable or detailed. Accordingly, the seller may be unwilling to warrant them to the same extent as audited tax balances. In such cases, the purchaser may insist on a more extensive due diligence review of the tax balances. As noted above, if not audited, a 'locked box' balance sheet will generally have been reviewed by the provider of any sell-side due diligence carried out on behalf of the seller; but the level of comfort which this provides to the purchaser is limited.

9.15. Money laundering and proceeds of crime

The *Proceeds of Crime Act 2002* extended money laundering to all crimes, including tax evasion.

Furthermore, the *Proceeds of Crime Act 2002* provides that money laundering includes conduct outside the UK which, whilst it may not be criminal in the jurisdiction in which it takes place, would be criminal if it occurred inside the UK.

The *Money Laundering Regulations 2003* (since replaced by the *Money Laundering Regulations 2007 (SI 2007/2157)*) expanded the range of professional advisers within the money laundering reporting regime to include accountants and tax advisers. Specifically, the *2007 Regulations* include within their scope:

- 'external accountants', i.e. 'a firm or sole practitioner who by way of business provides accountancy services to other persons' (*Regulation 3(1)(c) and (7)*); and
- 'tax advisers', i.e. 'a firm or sole practitioner who by way of business provides advice about the tax affairs of other persons' (*Regulation 3(1)(c) and (8)*).

Accordingly, since 1 March 2004 accountants and tax advisers have had a duty to make a report to the Serious Organised Crime Agency ('SOCA') whenever they know or suspect, or have reasonable grounds for knowing or suspecting, that anyone anywhere in the world is in possession of the proceeds of a crime.

One important area of their work where accountants and tax advisers are perhaps more likely in practice to come across circumstances giving rise to such knowledge or suspicion is tax due diligence. This is not to suggest that instances of money laundering are commonly encountered during the course of tax due diligence. In fact, the reverse is true and such instances are mercifully rare. But tax due diligence necessarily comprises an investigation to identify potential tax liabilities which have not been paid as at the date of a particular transaction.

There are, of course, many reasons why such unpaid tax liabilities may exist without dishonesty or criminal intent. The person potentially liable for a particular liability identified by tax due diligence may simply not have been aware of its possible incidence. (This is often the case where the liability is not immediately obvious to a non-specialist because it is highly technical in nature). Or the particular liability may genuinely have been overlooked. In either case, a willingness on the part of the liable party to disclose and pay the liability as soon as reasonably possible after its discovery would confirm the absence of any dishonesty or criminal intent.

Equally indicative of an absence of dishonesty or criminal intent may be a belief on the part of the potentially liable party that there is a reasonable case to rebut the particular tax liability identified by tax due diligence. Broadly, provided that a person has a defensible filing position in relation to the matters from which the liability could be said to arise, then there is no reasonable basis for suspicion that that person is in possession of the proceeds of a crime.

Very occasionally, however, tax due diligence will uncover an overlooked liability, or a filing position for which there is no reasonable basis, combined with a reluctance on the part of the liable party to correct the oversight, or to amend the relevant return, by means of disclosure to the relevant tax authorities. In such rare cases, careful consideration (based on consultation and advice, where appropriate) should be given to the need to make a money laundering report to SOCA via the Money Laundering Reporting Officer of the firm undertaking the tax due diligence. It should be borne in mind that the due diligence provider generally has no duty to make further investigations to confirm the existence or absence of dishonesty or criminal intent.

9.16. Stamp taxes

A tax due diligence review does not generally include stamp taxes as a matter of course but its scope is sometimes extended specifically to include them. Even when they are outside the scope of a tax due diligence review, stamp tax exposures are often identified during the course of other tax due diligence. Where this occurs, such exposures should be raised for appropriate attention, always being careful to make clear that the formal scope of the tax due diligence is not thereby extended.

9.16.1. Background

Stamp taxes are transfer taxes charged on the transfer of certain assets and generally payable by the purchaser. There are three stamp taxes in the current UK tax regime, Stamp Duty, Stamp Duty Reserve Tax ('SDRT') and Stamp Duty Land Tax ('SDLT'). Stamp Duty and SDRT broadly arise on transfers of shares and securities. With effect from 1 December 2003, SDLT is charged on transfers of UK land and buildings. In light of the recent timescale of the introduction of SDLT to replace Stamp Duty on transfers of UK land and buildings, it is still possible that there are land assets governed by the old Stamp Duty regime. In addition to the abolition of Stamp Duty on transfers of UK land and buildings with effect from 1 December 2003, at the same time intangible assets such as goodwill were also removed from the charge to Stamp Duty.

9.16.2. Stamp Duty

Stamp Duty is a tax on documents of transfer of certain 'stock and marketable securities' (*Schedule 13 Finance Act 1999*) and certain partnership interests where the partnership owns securities. A charge will always arise on documents of transfer relating to UK situs assets, usually a stock transfer form. A charge will only arise on documents of transfer relating to non-UK situs assets (e.g. a non-UK incorporated company) where the document of transfer is executed in the UK or relates to a 'matter or thing to be done' in the UK. The concept of 'matter or thing to be done' is very wide and is extremely difficult to identify in practice. For example, the simple transfer of funds through a UK bank account may bring a transfer of a non-UK situs asset within the scope of UK Stamp Duty. Similarly, the execution of a share purchase agreement in the UK which under local law also acts to transfer the shares would bring a transfer within the scope of UK Stamp Duty and a charge could arise accordingly. This identification of the document of transfer is a matter of fact and a legal matter which must be confirmed by lawyers of the relevant jurisdiction.

Where a transfer is within scope, Stamp Duty is charged at 0.5% (rounded up to the nearest £5) of any consideration given. For Stamp Duty purposes, consideration given includes consideration in the form of cash, shares or the release or assumption of liabilities. The document of transfer in relation to UK situs assets must be stamped by the Stamp Office in order to settle any Stamp Duty liability and to allow the Company Secretary to update the appropriate asset register. This stamping also allows any charge to SDRT to be cancelled (see 9.16.4 below). Interest and penalties arise where the document of transfer is not presented for stamping to the Stamp Office, and any Stamp Duty liability is not paid, within 30 days from the date of execution.

Stamp Duty is not reportable or assessable. It is therefore possible to leave a document of transfer in relation to the transfer of non-UK in-scope assets unstamped and leave any Stamp Duty unpaid. However, a document of transfer on which a charge to Stamp Duty has arisen which remains unstamped cannot be used for any formal purpose such as in a UK court of law or in support of a tax claim. This does not usually cause concern on the basis that, should the transfer ever need to be proven, it should be possible to rely on an agreement to transfer and the relevant asset register. An unstamped document can be stamped at a later date, if and when this becomes necessary. However, interest will arise from the date of execution and penalties on the late stamping from the date on which the document was first brought into the UK.

Various reliefs provide complete exemption from the charge to Stamp Duty for certain transfers.

- Group relief may apply where the transfer of any Stamp Duty assets is for consideration between group companies within an effective 75% beneficial ownership body corporate group structure. Anti-avoidance rules deny relief where, at the time of transfer, there are arrangements in existence by virtue of which, at that or some later time, any person has, or could obtain, control of the transferee but not the transferor. Furthermore, for the relief to apply, there must be no arrangements in place at the time of the intra-group transfer under which:

- the consideration, or any part of the consideration, for the conveyance or transfer was to be provided or received, directly or indirectly, by a person outside the group; or
- the assets being transferred were previously conveyed or transferred, directly or indirectly, by a person outside the group; or
- the transferee and transferor were to cease to be associated with each other by reason of the transferor or a third body corporate ceasing to be the transferee's parent.
- Reconstruction relief may be relied upon in group reorganisations, essentially where a holding company is inserted such that there is a transfer of shares in one company (the target company) to another company (the acquiring company). This is often done for bone fide transactions where the insertion of a clean company facilitates subsequent group reorganisations. However, the numerous conditions for this relief to apply are onerous and strictly enforced by the Stamp Office, including in particular:

    that the acquiring company must acquire the whole of the issued share capital of the target company; and

    that the consideration for the acquisition must consist only of the issue of shares in the acquiring company to the shareholders of the target company.

There are no clawback provisions in force relating to the Stamp Duty relief regime apart from the remote possibility of clawback of group or acquisition relief under *Sections 111 and 113 Finance Act 2002*. These provisions could only apply in the rare situation where the original transfer of land to which group or acquisition relief applied was agreed before the introduction of SDLT (i.e. before 1 December 2003) but where formal completion was delayed to a date less than three years before any transaction which might now potentially trigger a clawback of such relief.

9.16.3. Stamp Duty Reserve Tax ('SDRT')

SDRT was introduced in 1986 in order to catch paperless share transactions and is a tax on agreements to transfer 'chargeable securities' (*Section 99 Stamp Taxes Act 1986*). This has the effect of capturing share transactions which would otherwise not have been chargeable to Stamp Duty because of the nonexistence of a stampable transfer document. It is important to note that, whilst Stamp Duty is charged on **documents** of transfer, SDRT is charged on **agreements** to transfer. A chargeable security for the purposes of SDRT is any security issued by (or paired with) a UK incorporated company, or, when issued by a non-UK company, any security where a register is maintained in the UK.

SDRT is charged at 0.5% of the consideration given in 'money or money's worth' and, as with Stamp Duty, any liability rests with the purchaser. Unlike Stamp Duty, however, SDRT is assessable and reportable, a difference which is of particular relevance in relation to any transfer of shares which constitute chargeable securities. Any SDRT must be paid to the Stamp Office no later than seven days from the end of the month in which the agreement for transfer was entered into in order to prevent interest and penalties arising.

SDRT is generally the least understood of the UK stamp taxes. However, its wider definition of consideration, its non-territorial scope and, most importantly, the fact that SDRT is reportable and assessable mean that SDRT is generally considered as a greater area of risk than Stamp Duty.

9.16.4. Interaction of Stamp Duty and Stamp Duty Reserve Tax

On the basis of the above, certain transfers, such as the purchase of shares in a UK incorporated company, would appear to give rise to a double charge to stamp taxes, with a Stamp Duty liability arising on the document of transfer and an SDRT liability on any agreement to transfer. However, stamp tax legislation provides that where a document of transfer is executed pursuant to an agreement on which a charge to SDRT arose and is stamped (for whatever reason) within six years of the date on which the agreement was entered into, any charge to SDRT is cancelled (*Section 92 Finance Act 1986*). It should be noted that this is the only way in which to cancel the compulsory SDRT.

Provided, therefore, that a share transfer is dealt with correctly for Stamp Duty purposes, the SDRT charge should be cancelled with the stamping of the document of transfer. The majority of non-UK share purchases should not have any SDRT implications because the share register is unlikely to be maintained in the UK. Where this is the case, it is possible to leave the document of transfer unstamped because there is no SDRT liability to cancel, and because Stamp Duty is a non-reportable tax. In practice, it is unusual to stamp a document of transfer relating to non-UK shares.

A charge to SDRT may arise on the agreement to transfer chargeable securities, without a charge to Stamp Duty arising. In these instances, it is necessary proactively to request the stamping of a document of transfer, not to facilitate the payment of Stamp Duty, but to cancel the SDRT.

9.16.5. Stamp Duty Land Tax ('SDLT')

SDLT is a tax on transactions involving UK land and buildings, more specifically transfers of 'chargeable interests'. A chargeable interest is an estate, interest, right or power or the benefit of an obligation, restriction or condition affecting the value of any such estate, interest, right or power (*Section 48 Finance Act 2003*). Broadly, this comprises any freehold or leasehold interest (or equivalent interests in Scotland or Northern Ireland) over UK land and buildings. Certain other interests are specifically not chargeable interests, namely a licence to use or occupy, a security interest (i.e. an interest or right, other than at rent, held for securing payment of money or fulfilment of an obligation), a tenancy at will, advowson, franchise or manor.

Transfers of freeholds and the majority of assignments of leasehold interests are charged to SDLT at a staggered rate of up to 4% of the chargeable consideration given in 'money or money's worth'. In the majority of cases, the rate varies according to the consideration given for the property. Where the consideration falls within a rate band, the whole amount of the consideration is charged at that rate.

Consideration (£)	**SDLT (%)**
0 - 150,000 (£125,000 for residential properties)	0
150,001 - 250,000	1
250,001 - 500,000	3
Over and above 500,001	4

The calculation of SDLT on the grant of a lease differs in that SDLT is paid on the premium and rental elements individually and both liabilities are then added together to arrive at a total SDLT liability.

SDLT is charged at 4% of any premium given. A 'premium' is not defined in legislation and is referred to only by the words 'consideration other than rent.' A reverse premium is a premium paid by a landlord to a tenant in relation to the grant of a lease, or a premium paid by the assignor to the assignee in relation to the assignment of a lease, or a premium paid by the tenant to the landlord in relation to the surrender of a lease and is specifically not consideration for SDLT purposes.

SDLT is charged at 1% of the net present value ('NPV') of any rent to the extent that it exceeds £150,000 for commercial properties (or £125,000 for residential properties). There are complex rules with regard to determining the exact amount of the 'rent' for the purposes of calculating the SDLT which may not be the figure prescribed in the rental agreement. The correct rent figure is then discounted to provide the NPV using a discount factor of, broadly, 3.5%.

The grant of a lease may be exempt from SDLT under a sale-and-leaseback transaction (*Section 57A Finance Act 2003*) where a vendor sells a freehold (or another major interest) to a purchaser and the purchaser grants a lease out of that interest over land back to the vendor. If certain other conditions are met, for example if the vendor and purchaser are not connected group companies, the granting of the leaseback element of the structure is exempt from SDLT.

There are times when the assignment of a lease will be treated as the grant of a lease for the purposes of calculating SDLT on the assignment. *Paragraph 11 Schedule 17A Finance Act 2003* applies to SDLT leases (i.e. those granted post-1 December 2003) where the grant of the lease was exempt from SDLT as a result of the availability of a relief. *Paragraph 11* deems the first assignment of a lease for which no relief is available to be the grant of that lease. Accordingly, any SDLT will not be calculated on the consideration given in money or money's worth, but on the premium and rent as described above.

Special market value rules apply when the seller and purchaser are connected and the purchaser is a company. Where these rules apply, SDLT is charged on the higher of the actual consideration and the market value of the land interest, and, if a lease at rent, that rent (*Section 53 Finance Act 2003*). For example, where a property is transferred for £1 between group companies, the market value rules apply, calculating any SDLT on the market value of the interest, not the £1 as would have been the case had the two group companies not been connected. Special market value rules also apply in relation to the granting of a lease between two group companies for the commonly used nominal or peppercorn rent.

Companies making changes to their group structures involving asset reorganisations including transfers of land and buildings may wish to make use of one of the available SDLT reliefs. The three most commonly relied on reliefs are:

- group relief *(Schedule 7 Part 1 Finance Act 2003)*;
- reconstruction relief *(Schedule 7 Part II Finance Act 2003)*; and
- acquisition relief *(Schedule 7 Part II Finance Act 2003)*.

A brief description of each is given below.

- Group relief provides a complete exemption from the charge to SDLT on transfers of UK land and buildings between group companies within an effective 75% beneficial ownership structure, provided that the transfer does not fall foul of the anti-avoidance provisions. The SDLT group relief anti-avoidance provisions are much more onerous than those for Stamp Duty group relief.

- Reconstruction relief provides a complete exemption from SDLT where the acquiring company acquires the whole or part of the undertaking (broadly the 'business') of another company pursuant to a scheme for the reconstruction of the target company and where certain other conditions are met.
- Acquisition relief provides a reduction from the 4% SDLT charge to a 0.5% charge on the consideration given. Broadly, it will apply where the acquiring company acquires the whole or part of the undertaking of the target company and where certain other conditions are met.

Like the other stamp taxes, SDLT is a liability of the purchaser. For SDLT purposes, a purchaser is defined as the person in a transaction giving the consideration for the acquisition of the chargeable interest. In addition to having the obligation to pay any SDLT liability, a purchaser must also submit a land transaction return (SDLT 1) for every notifiable transaction (providing details of the transaction, the interest transferred, the consideration given and additional seller/purchaser details) no later than 30 days from the effective date (see below). There are certain instances, however, where a land transaction return is not required.

Supplementary return pages may also be required to be submitted with the SDLT 1:

- an SDLT 2 should accompany the SDLT 1 where there are two or more sellers and/or two purchasers;
- an SDLT 3 should accompany the SDLT 1 where there is insufficient space on the SDLT 1; and, most commonly seen in practice,
- an SDLT 4 should be used for complex commercial transactions and transactions involving leases. A typical 'complex' transaction would be where the purchaser is a company. The SDLT 4 must show the company registration number, tax reference number and registered address (if non-UK).

Each return has a unique reference number. The original return must be submitted; photocopies must not be used. To accommodate the Stamp Office's computerised system, the return should be completed in black ink, signed by the purchaser and sent to the Stamp Office unfolded in an A4 envelope. It is also possible to file SDLT returns online which may be preferable in cases where there is a requirement for the land transfer to be registered with the respective land registry within a short space of time.

The due date for the Stamp Office to receive an SDLT return and payment of any SDLT is no later than 30 days from the 'effective date' of the transaction, i.e. the **earlier** of 'substantial performance' (*Section 44(5) Finance Act 2003*) or completion. Substantial performance is broadly regarded as possession being taken of the interest transferred. This might occur, for example, when the landlord becomes entitled to rent, or when the first payment of rent is made, both of which in practice may be before legal completion. Determination of the effective date is critical because interest and penalties arise on any unpaid SDLT and late submission of the appropriate returns respectively after this date.

Once the SDLT return has been processed and the appropriate amount of SDLT has been received, the Stamp Office will issue a land transaction return certificate (SDLT 5) in relation to the land transfer. The SDLT 5 certificate replaces the previous impressed stamp used under the old Stamp Duty regime. The SDLT 5 should be forwarded to the appropriate Land Registry in England and Wales or Northern Ireland or to the Registrars of Scotland in order to register the land transfer and update the Land Registry.

9.16.6. Stamp taxes in the context of tax due diligence

Where stamp taxes are included within the scope of a tax due diligence review of a UK target company, there are two areas of risk to be considered:

- the creation of a charge to stamp taxes as a result of the purchase of the target company's shares; and
- the assumption of any inherent charges to stamp taxes already in existence in the target company.

Creation of a charge to stamp taxes

The purchase of shares in the target company can create a charge to all three UK stamp taxes, each of which is considered in turn below. Some of these charges arise solely as a result of the transfer of the target's shares, regardless of any pre-existing facts or circumstances. Accordingly, they do not strictly fall within the province of tax due diligence but are more closely associated with the structure of the transaction. Others, however, will only arise because of the combination of the transfer of the target company's shares with one or more historical events which tax due diligence may be required to identify.

In the absence of any relief, Stamp Duty will be payable on the purchase of UK shares and may be payable on the purchase of non-UK shares. SDRT may also apply, although, for the reasons explained above, this is unlikely provided that the transfer is dealt with appropriately.

The most important stamp tax to consider is therefore SDLT on the basis that the act of purchasing a company holding UK land and/or buildings may itself trigger a charge as a result of clawback provisions in connection with a previous transfer in relation to which a relief was claimed by the target company.

The SDLT relief most commonly clawed back in practice is group relief. Clawback of group relief occurs where:

- the transferee of the UK land and buildings (i.e. the target company for the purposes of present tax due diligence) or a 'relevant associated company' (*Paragraph 3(1) Schedule 7 Finance Act 2003*);
- ceases to be a member of the same group as the transferor (i.e. as a result of the acquisition of the target company's shares);
- within three years from the 'effective date' (being the earlier of completion and substantial performance - broadly possession - see 9.16.5) of the land transfer in relation to which group relief was claimed (or at any time pursuant to arrangements made before the end of this period);
- whilst still holding the land interest.

Finance Act 2008 introduced new anti-avoidance measures to prevent claims for group relief on the set up of popular OpCo- PropCo structures with the PropCo subsequently being sold to a third party whilst still holding the land interest.

Where a relief is withdrawn, an SDLT liability arises as if such relief had never been available. The liability rests with the transferee of the interest and is charged on the interest's market value. If the transfer was the grant of a lease at rent, then SDLT will be charged on that rent at the time of the grant.

Tax due diligence in relation to the potential acquisition of a target company's shares should therefore establish:

- whether the target company purchased a land interest where the effective date was within the last three years; and
- whether, at the time when the land interest was purchased, the target company relied on an SDLT relief.

Where the above circumstances are identified, clawback of this SDLT relief is likely to occur if the acquisition of the target company's shares will break the group relationship with the transferor of the land interest.

Inherent liabilities

There may also be inherent liabilities to all three stamp taxes within the target company.

As noted above, Stamp Duty is not reportable or assessable. From a tax due diligence perspective, it is not therefore as much of a concern as the other stamp taxes. However, there may have been past intra-group transfers of UK shares where the document of transfer was never stamped and where the Stamp Duty remains unpaid. Should this be the case, interest will be accruing on the non-payment of Stamp Duty and, if the document of transfer is stamped at a later date, penalties will arise in relation to the original non-presentation for stamping of the document of transfer. There may also have been past transfers of non-UK shares which have come within the charge to Stamp Duty because of a document of transfer relating to a 'matter or thing to be done' in the UK. These latter cases are extremely difficult to identify in practice.

When performing a tax due diligence review of a company which holds interests in UK land and buildings, it should be remembered that such companies may have pre-SDLT assets falling within the old Stamp Duty regime. Stamp Duty on land and buildings was not a compulsory tax and there are many land interests upon which no Stamp Duty was ever paid because the document to transfer the land interest was never presented to the land registry.

Unpaid SDRT liabilities are generally a more serious tax due diligence risk. Because SDRT is assessable and reportable, it must either be paid or cancelled. SDRT may only be cancelled by stamping a document of transfer within six years of the original agreement giving rise to the liability. If SDRT remains unpaid, interest and penalties will apply which may not be cancelled by the subsequent stamping of a document of transfer.

SDLT is also assessable and reportable. Its comparatively recent introduction means that SDLT compliance mistakes are not uncommon. Where an inherent SDLT liability remains unpaid, interest may be accruing and penalties (in certain cases up to the amount of the SDLT due) may have arisen in relation to the late submission of a land transaction return.

There may also be inherent SDLT clawback charges within a target company. This may be the case, for example, if that target company has claimed an SDLT relief in the past and a clawback has already been triggered by the target company's separation from the transferor of the land interest in relation to which that group relief was claimed.

Another common cause of unpaid SDLT in a target company is the historical failure to identify assignments to that target company of leases to which *Paragraph 11 Schedule 17A Finance Act 2003* applies. See 9.16.5.

A generic/proforma information request for a stamp tax due diligence review is provided at 4.6.

10. Tax Due Diligence in Asset Acquisitions

It is often assumed that a purchaser of business assets (as opposed to shares) will not inherit the tax history of the business in which the assets were formerly employed and that accordingly tax due diligence is not strictly necessary in connection with an asset acquisition.

In the UK it is broadly true that the historical tax liabilities of a business do not pass to a purchaser of its assets[36]. However, there are still a number of pre-acquisition tax matters with regard to business assets which can affect the post-acquisition tax position of a purchaser and which a purchaser would be well-advised to investigate by way of pre-acquisition due diligence. Furthermore, purchasers of business assets in some jurisdictions outside the UK will find that they do automatically assume certain of the business' pre-acquisition tax liabilities. See 10.2.

10.1. Pre-acquisition tax matters with regard to business assets which can affect the post-acquisition tax position of a third party purchaser of those assets: UK

10.1.1. The seller's practices, processes and procedures in relation to tax compliance

Although the seller's tax liabilities will not generally pass to a purchaser of business assets, the seller's practices, processes and procedures in relation to tax compliance will often automatically be adopted by the purchaser. If these are defective to any extent, post-acquisition tax exposures could accrue if they are maintained by the purchaser. Accordingly, some level of pre-acquisition due diligence is often advisable in order to:

- understand the seller's practices, processes and procedures in relation to tax compliance;

[36]The VAT 68 procedure is an exception to this general principle but is rarely encountered in practice. When a business is transferred as a TOGC (see 10.1.3), the purchaser can apply to keep the seller's VAT registration number. Such application requires the submission to HMRC of a separate form (VAT 68), signed by both purchaser and seller, confirming that both parties agree to the consequences of the transfer of the VAT number. The principal consequence is the transfer of all VAT liabilities to the purchaser. The seller has no right to any repayments of VAT or unclaimed input tax even where these relate to periods before the transfer. Any entitlement to recover VAT on bad debts is also transferred to the buyer, even if the VAT was originally paid by the seller.

- identify any deficiencies within them, including any errors to which such deficiencies may have given rise; and
- amend or replace them accordingly.

Broadly, such due diligence will ask similar questions to those asked in relation to share acquisitions, but with emphasis on identifying weaknesses in procedures rather than on identifying historical exposures. This is particularly true of VAT, given that VAT will generally apply at every stage of a transaction, and in this regard such due diligence should focus in particular on:

- the VAT liability of the supplies made by the target business (i.e. standard-rated, zero-rated, exempt, or outside the scope); and
- assessments or surcharges issued by HMRC and any late submission of VAT returns (these can be indications of inadequate controls in the business).

See also 9.13, 'The general tax control environment of the target company or group.'

10.1.2. Tax treatment of the assets acquired in the hands of the purchaser

The purchase consideration agreed between buyer and seller for the acquisition of a business will need to be allocated to the various assets, or classes of assets, acquired, so that both purchaser and seller are able to bring into their respective tax computations/returns for the relevant period appropriate figures to reflect the transaction.

Any allocation of purchase price must be fair and reasonable and reflect economic and commercial substance. It is helpful to include details of the allocation of purchase price agreed between buyer and seller within the agreement for the sale and purchase of business assets. Strictly, this will not bind HMRC. In particular:

- *Section 52(4) Taxation of Chargeable Gains Act 1992* allows HMRC to apply any apportionment of the purchase price for capital gains purposes as they consider just and reasonable. See *Inland Revenue Capital Gains Manual at 14774* for further guidance;
- *Section 562 Capital Allowances Act 2001* allows HMRC to apply a different apportionment of the purchase price for capital allowances purposes from the apportionment agreed between buyer and seller; and
- where one or more intangible fixed assets are acquired or realised together with other assets, *Paragraph 105 Schedule 29 Finance Act 2002* allows HMRC to apportion the purchaser's expenditure (if no values are allocated to the particular assets in accordance with generally accepted accounting

practice), or the seller's disposal proceeds, on a just and reasonable basis.

However, where the purchase price allocation is agreed at arm's length between unconnected parties it will generally be respected for tax purposes unless it is manifestly artificial. The case of *Stanton (Inspector of Taxes) v Drayton Commercial Investment Co Ltd [1982] STC 585* endorsed the principle of earlier cases (*Osborne v Steel Barrel Co Ltd* and *Craddock v Zevo Finance Co Ltd*) that HMRC are 'not entitled to go behind the agreed consideration in a case where the transaction is not alleged to be dishonest or otherwise not straightforward...[P]rovided the agreed value has been honestly reached by a bargain at arm's length, it must... be final and it is not open to attack by the Crown.'

In a slightly different context, the case of *E.V. Booth (Holdings) Ltd v Buckwell (Inspector of Taxes) [1980] STC 578* lends weight to the importance for tax purposes of a purchase price allocation agreed at arm's length: '...where parties to a composite transaction have, as a result of negotiations between themselves, provided that part of the consideration is to be paid for one part of the transaction and part for another, they cannot subsequently seek to reallocate the consideration for tax purposes...' (per Browne-Wilkinson J.)

Agreeing the purchase price allocation is a matter for negotiation between the parties and will depend on their respective bargaining strengths. Often, purchasers are offered an allocation which ensures that any tax triggered by the disposal is minimised as far as possible for the seller; and the purchaser is left with little room to deviate from this position. However, as a starting point for this exercise, the purchaser's tax due diligence should, where possible, identify:

- the assets which will form the business to be acquired; and
- their tax treatment (and tax basis or tax written down value, if possible) in the seller's hands.

With this information, the purchaser's tax due diligence adviser will be able to advise the purchaser on the tax implications for both buyer and seller of whatever purchase price allocation is agreed between the parties. In turn, this will enable the purchaser to model the tax effect of a range of different purchase price allocations to guide the negotiations with the seller in this regard.

As a general guide for purchasers of business assets, the tax treatment of purchase consideration allocated to a range of typical assets is described in the following table.

Asset type	*Tax treatment of purchase consideration allocated to asset type*
Stock	Deductible for corporation tax purposes in the accounting period in which the stock is sold or otherwise disposed of.
Debtors	Acquired debts are potentially chargeable assets for capital gains purposes. Accordingly, if they are recovered at more or less than the purchase consideration allocated to them, a chargeable gain or allowable loss arises. In practice, debtors are often excluded from the purchase of business assets and are collected on the seller's behalf.
Fixed assets	Various classes of fixed assets qualify for tax relief by way of capital allowances (i.e. tax depreciation) at annual rates which vary according to asset type. The more important of these in practice are described in the following sections of this table.
Plant & machinery	20% (10% for fixtures integral to a building) per annum on a reducing balance basis.

Industrial buildings (including plant & machinery and fixtures & fittings which are fixed to the building)	With effect from 21 March 2007, the purchaser's qualifying expenditure is limited to the residue of the seller's unrelieved qualifying expenditure which is then written off over the remainder of the building's 25-year tax life (*Section 36 Finance Act 2007*), i.e. the purchaser will take over the same tax relief as the seller. However, tax relief for expenditure on industrial buildings is being phased out over four years such that unrelieved qualifying expenditure at 31 March 2011 will be lost altogether. Where the sale and purchase of business assets includes an industrial building, *Section 198 Capital Allowances Act 2001* allows the seller and purchaser by joint election to fix the amount of consideration allocated to fixtures & fittings within that industrial building. Stamp Duty Land Tax ('SDLT') will be payable by the purchaser on purchase consideration allocated to UK land at the following rates applied to the full consideration allocated (i.e. not just to the consideration in excess of the previous band): **Consideration** Up to £150,000: - Nil £150,001 to £250,000: - 1% £250,001 to £500,000: - 3% £500,001 or more: - 4%
Intangible fixed assets, including goodwill, as defined in *Paragraphs 2, 3 and 4 Schedule 29 Finance Act 2002*	Tax relief is available for intangible assets acquired from an unconnected party or created by a company on or after 1 April 2002 for use on a continuing basis in the course of the company's activities. In accordance with *Schedule 29 Finance Act 2002*, expenditure on such intangible

	fixed assets is relieved for tax purposes: • either as it is amortised or impaired for accounting purposes (N.B. under International Financial Reporting Standards the intangible fixed asset may not be amortised); or • at the fixed rate of 4% per annum where appropriate election is made within two years of the end of the accounting period in which the intangible fixed asset is acquired.
Land & buildings (including plant & machinery and fixtures & fittings which are fixed to the land and buildings)	With the exception of industrial buildings (see above), no tax relief is available for expenditure on land & buildings until they are eventually sold; at which point such expenditure (appropriately indexed) will be the tax base cost in the calculation of any chargeable gain or allowable loss. Where the sale and purchase of business assets includes land & buildings, *Section 198 Capital Allowances Act 2001* allows the seller and purchaser by joint election to fix the amount of consideration allocated to fixtures & fittings within those land & buildings. Stamp Duty Land Tax ('SDLT') will be payable by the purchaser on purchase consideration allocated to UK land at the following rates applied to the full consideration allocated (i.e. not just to the consideration in excess of the previous band): **Consideration** Up to £150,000: - Nil £150,001 to £250,000: - 1% £250,001 to £500,000: - 3% £500,001 or more: - 4%

Since SDLT replaced Stamp Duty with regard to transfers of UK land, Stamp Duty now only applies to documents transferring certain shares, securities, partnership interests and bearer instruments. In the event that any of these are included within a purchase of assets, stamp duty will be payable by the purchaser at the rate of 0.5% of the purchase consideration allocated to them.

10.1.3. VAT: Transfer of a going concern ('TOGC')

From a VAT perspective there is a significant difference between a transfer of assets and a transfer of shares.

A transfer of shares is generally an exempt supply which means that any VAT associated with the transfer will not be recoverable. Although this does not directly affect the purchaser, the seller may include the VAT in the sales price as a cost element; and the purchaser will take on the VAT history of the business, including any historical VAT liabilities whether identified or not.

In contrast, a transfer of assets is in principle a taxable supply, unless it is subject to the transfer of a going concern ('TOGC') provisions when it is treated as outside the scope of VAT, i.e. as neither a supply of goods nor a supply of services.

If the conditions for TOGC treatment are not satisfied, the seller will be required to charge VAT on the purchase consideration. The purchaser may be able to recover this VAT as input tax depending on whether the purchaser is fully taxable or partially exempt for VAT purposes. Even if recoverable in full, there may be a cash flow disadvantage for the purchaser if there is a delay in its recovery from HMRC.

If the conditions for TOGC treatment are satisfied, no VAT is charged on the value of the supply. (There is no TOGC in the case of a transfer of shares in a limited company from one person to another).

The UK conditions for TOGC treatment are contained within *Article 5 VAT (Special Provisions) Order (SI 1995/1268)*. The European Union legislation from which *Article 5* is derived does not prescribe any specific conditions for TOGC status and even makes the introduction of TOGC legislation optional for Member States. Those Member States which have introduced the TOGC concept have done so with varying qualifying conditions (the UK's conditions are relatively onerous), so it cannot be assumed that a transfer which would qualify as a TOGC in one jurisdiction will necessarily do so in another. There are currently no provisions for a single cross-border TOGC covering transfers of assets in more than one Member State as part of the same transaction. Accordingly, where a transaction comprises transfers of assets in more than one Member State, each transfer must be considered separately to determine whether or not it qualifies as a TOGC according to the local rules of the jurisdiction in which it takes place.

For a transfer of business assets to qualify as a TOGC in the UK:

- the transfer must put the new owner in possession of a business which can be operated as such;
- the business (or part thereof) must be a going concern at the time of the transfer;
- the new owner must intend to use the assets in carrying on the same kind of business as the previous owner;
- there must not be a series of immediately consecutive transfers of the business;
- where the seller is registered for VAT, the purchaser must also be registered for VAT, or at the date of the transfer must be required to be registered for VAT;
- there must be no significant break in the normal trading pattern before or immediately after the transfer; and
- if the transfer is only of part of a business, that part must be able to operate alone as a business.

If the acquisition qualifies as a TOGC, there is no taxable supply and VAT must **not** be charged on the assets, other than in the particular circumstances described below in relation to land and buildings. If VAT is charged on a TOGC, the tax will be due to HMRC but the purchaser will not be able to recover this amount as input tax because there was no underlying taxable supply.

The use of the TOGC provisions is mandatory. Prior to any transfer of assets it is therefore vital to determine if the transfer will qualify as a TOGC and to ensure that appropriate clauses are included in the contract for the sale and purchase of the business. These will normally include:

- a clause to the effect that, for the avoidance of doubt, the parties to the transfer will make all reasonable efforts to ensure that it is afforded TOGC treatment; and
- a clause to determine how any VAT liability will be borne in the event that the VAT treatment of the transfer changes after completion of the transaction, e.g. following an inspection by HMRC.

It is worth noting that, if the consideration clause in the contract for the sale/purchase of the target assets is silent on the question of VAT, then, in the event that VAT is due, the price paid is deemed to be the VAT-inclusive price. Accordingly, the seller will want to ensure that the consideration clause makes clear that the price is VAT-exclusive so that any VAT ultimately held to be due is then payable by the purchaser in addition to the price.

10.1.4. VAT: Options to subject land and buildings to tax

As explained above, VAT must not be charged on a TOGC. There are, however, extra rules if the TOGC includes a transfer of land and buildings. If the seller has opted under *Part 1 Schedule 10 Value Added Tax Act 1994* to tax an interest in land or a building falling within the TOGC, the purchaser must have given written notification to HMRC of his intention to opt to tax his interest no later than the 'relevant date'. HMRC take 'relevant date' to mean no later than the time of the supply, normally the date of the transfer. The purchaser must notify the seller that the seller's option to tax will not be disapplied. The purchaser must be satisfied that the transferred property will not become a capital goods scheme item (see 10.1.5) and that the purchaser's supplies of the land will not fall to be exempt supplies by virtue of the anti-avoidance rules which would result in disapplication of the option to tax *(Paragraphs 12 to 17 Schedule 10 Value Added Tax Act 1994).*

As part of any tax due diligence review of the target business, inspection should be made of written confirmation that the seller has opted to tax the seller's interest in any land and buildings forming part of the sale.

10.1.5. VAT: Capital Goods Scheme ('CGS')

The VAT Capital Goods Scheme ('CGS') applies to capital expenditure:

- of £50,000 or more on computers and computer equipment (excluding computerised equipment such as computerised telephone exchanges and computer software); and
- on land and buildings which cost £250,000 or more at the time of building or refurbishment.

VAT incurred in purchasing and bringing into business use such items may be recoverable either:

- in full, if attributable to the making of taxable supplies;
- not at all, if attributable to exempt supplies; or
- in part, if incurred for the making of both taxable and exempt supplies (in an indistinguishable proportion).

In the last case, only a percentage of input VAT (as agreed with HMRC) can be recovered. However, under the terms of the CGS, this input tax is recoverable over a prescribed number of years, with a proportion of the input VAT being treated as recoverable in each year. For computer equipment, the input tax is recoverable over a period of five years. For most land and buildings, the input tax is recoverable over a period of ten years.

As at the time of the purchase of a CGS asset, input VAT may be recovered according to the relevant proportion for that year, following a recovery percentage agreed with HMRC.

In the subsequent five or ten years after purchase, the company is obliged to adjust the input VAT recovery in respect of the year of purchase (and subsequent years) if the VAT recovery percentage changes in a subsequent year.

The VAT claimed in the year of purchase (and subsequent years) must therefore be adjusted either upwards or downwards, i.e. if the recovery percentage drops the business may have to repay input VAT to HMRC which it had previously reclaimed in previous years.

Where CGS assets are sold to a purchaser of a business by way of a transfer of business as a going concern ('TOGC'), the purchaser takes over the responsibility to make these CGS adjustments for the remainder of the adjustment period. Where the VAT recovery percentage of both the seller and the purchaser are the same this should not present any significant VAT problems for the purchaser. However, where the VAT recovery percentage of the purchaser is lower than that of the seller, then the purchaser would be in the position of having to pay over additional input VAT to HMRC which the seller had previously reclaimed.

In order to meet the obligations of the CGS following an asset acquisition, the purchaser therefore needs to establish through due diligence:

- when any CGS asset were purchased;
- how much input tax was incurred on the original purchase of these CGS assets; and
- in relation to each, how many annual adjustments have already been made by the seller and how much of the adjustment period remains.

The above information may then be interpreted in light of whatever information may be known about the purchaser's intentions for future use of the CGS assets. This should provide the purchaser with an early indication of any potential increases or decreases in the amount of VAT historically recovered.

10.1.6. VAT: Transfer of assets into a VAT group – anti-avoidance provisions

In addition to the CGS issues described at 10.1.5 above, there are also specific anti-avoidance provisions relating to the transfer of assets into a VAT group where the VAT group is not entitled to full recovery of input tax. If the TOGC provisions apply to such a transfer, and no VAT is charged accordingly, the purchaser may need to account for VAT on the purchase of assets as a self-supply (i.e. the purchaser charges itself VAT). The corresponding input tax reclaim would then be subject to the purchaser's VAT recovery percentage.

The assets being transferred to the VAT group as part of the going concern are subject to this anti-avoidance provision if they are 'chargeable assets'.

There are certain exceptions to this rule:

- where the purchaser is entitled to a full recovery of input VAT;
- where HMRC are satisfied that the seller held the assets for a period of more than three years prior to the sale; and
- where the assets consist of CGS assets (see 10.1.5 above).

10.1.7. PAYE liabilities: income tax and National Insurance contributions ('NIC')

On a transfer of the assets and employees of a target business, historical tax and NIC liabilities will generally remain with the selling company and it should not be possible for HMRC to recover any historical exposures to PAYE and NIC from the new employer or from employees who transfer to the new entity.

This follows from *Regulation 102(6) Income Tax (Pay As You Earn) Regulations 2003(SI 2003/2682)* which states that:

'The new employer is not liable for the payment of any tax which was deductible from relevant payments made to the employee –

(a) before the change [in the employer] took place, unless those payments were made by the new employer, or

(b) by the former employer after the change took place.'

However, a historical exposure to PAYE could be transferred where it is anticipated before the transfer of the assets and employees of a target business that income will be required to be paid after the transfer. In this situation, the obligation to pay the income passes under *Transfer of Undertakings (Protection of Employment) Regulations* (TUPE) to the new employer together with the associated PAYE liability. Where completion accounts are to be prepared, such liabilities should normally be expected to be included as liabilities in the completion balance sheet: the income tax and employee's NIC would be deductions from the gross income but the employer's NIC would be an additional liability.

10.1.8. Stamp taxes

An asset purchase will not normally involve Stamp Duty or SDRT assets. Accordingly, SDLT should be the principal focus of any stamp tax due diligence in relation to an asset acquisition. There are two areas of risk to be considered:

- the creation of a charge to SDLT as a result of the purchase of the target assets; and
- the assumption of any inherent outstanding SDLT charges already in existence in the company selling the target assets.

Creation of a charge

It is expected and accepted by purchasers generally that a charge to SDLT will arise on the purchase of most freehold and leasehold interests over UK land and buildings based on the consideration given. However, the following two factors can cause an apparently simple land or building purchase to be layered with complexities.

- The 'linked transaction' legislation was introduced as an anti-avoidance measure to prevent sellers splitting up what in essence is a single large land transaction or a series of large transfers into smaller transactions with the aim that each should fall within the SDLT nil rate band. Where land transactions form part of a single scheme or arrangement or a series of transactions between the same seller and purchaser, or persons connected with them, the transactions will be 'linked' (*Section 108 Finance Act 2003*) and all the transactions will be treated as a single transaction. Where transactions are linked and have the same effective date, the purchaser may make one land transaction return for all the linked land transfers. The chargeable consideration for all the linked land transfers will be consolidated and SDLT calculated on the total amount with only one nil rate band.
- Where a purchaser of assets is acquiring a leasehold interest, it will be important to identify whether the lease was granted under the old Stamp Duty regime or post-1 December 2003 under the new SDLT regime. If the lease was granted post-1 December 2003 and a SDLT relief was claimed on that grant (e.g. sale and leaseback relief), then the first assignment of the lease in relation to which no relief is available will be treated as the grant of such lease (*Paragraph 11 Schedule 17A Finance Act 2003*). In this situation, any SDLT liability will not be based on the consideration given, but will instead be calculated by reference to any premium given and the net present value of any rent. See 9.16.5.

Inherent liabilities

When an SDLT liability arises in connection with the transfer of a land interest, that SDLT liability remains with the transferee of the land interest to which it relates and does not attach to the land interest itself. Generally, therefore, where a sale of business assets includes a land interest, a purchaser will not assume any SDLT liabilities associated with the seller's own acquisition or ownership of the land interest.

However, special provisions apply with regard to the assignment of a lease. If the purchaser of business assets is being assigned a lease, there may be continuing obligations for the purchaser as assignee. Where a lease is assigned and, in the absence of such assignment, there would otherwise be a requirement for an amended return to be submitted by the assignor, the assignee is still required to fulfil this obligation. When purchasing a lease interest, it is therefore important for the purchaser to obtain the full lease history.

10.1.9. Tax warranties and indemnities in relation to an asset acquisition

In the UK, the purchaser of business assets will not generally inherit the historical tax liabilities of the business in which those assets were employed. Accordingly, no tax indemnity or covenant is provided to the purchaser in the context of an asset acquisition. The seller will, however, often provide limited tax warranties and these will typically include warranties in relation to the matters described at 10.1.1 to 10.1.8 above.

10.1.10. UK asset acquisition information request list

General

Is the UK business being acquired liable to tax (corporation tax, employment taxes or VAT) in any jurisdiction outside the UK?

If any of the assets being acquired relate to a business being carried on outside the UK where the target is registered or liable for non-UK tax, confirm whether historical tax liabilities relating to, or associated with, those assets will transfer on an asset acquisition.

Employment taxes

Provide details of any remuneration or bonuses relating to the UK business being acquired which will not actually be paid until after the acquisition.

VAT

With regard to the assets being acquired:

- has the seller opted to subject any land and buildings to VAT (see 10.1.4 - such option binds a purchaser); and
- is the seller obliged to apply the Capital Goods Scheme provisions to computer equipment with a value of £50,000 or more or, if relevant, land and buildings with a value of £250,000 or more (see 10.1.5 - such obligation affects a purchaser)?

Stamp taxes

See 4.6.

Other considerations

The following issues should be addressed in negotiation and/or covered in the agreement for the acquisition of the target business:

- allocation of the purchase price; and
- whether the transfer of the assets will be exempt from UK VAT as the transfer of a going concern.

10.2. Does a third party purchaser of business assets (rather than shares of a company) assume any tax liabilities of the business in which the assets were formerly employed by the previous owner (jurisdictions outside the UK)[37]?

In many jurisdictions, the general principle in relation to asset acquisitions (subject to the assumptions in footnote 37) is the same as that for the UK. In other words, a purchaser of business assets will not generally assume any

---

[37]Please note that the comments in this section are necessarily very general and for any particular circumstances, specific reference material should be consulted and advice obtained. For the purposes of this section, taxes which arise as a result of the actual purchase of business assets itself (i.e. transfer taxes) are not considered to be liabilities which the purchaser assumes from the previous owner, even though they may be liabilities of the purchaser. In other words a distinction is drawn between historical tax liabilities of the seller, which are the focus of tax due diligence, and transfer tax liabilities of the purchaser, which are more properly the focus of tax structuring. A seller may, of course, incur tax liabilities in connection with the sale of the assets and may try commercially to pass these on to the purchaser within the purchase price. However, these are not considered to be liabilities which the purchaser assumes from the previous owner, even though economically they may become liabilities of the purchaser via negotiations between seller and purchaser over the purchase price. This section excludes consideration of any employment law consequences of the sale of business assets and assumes: that the seller and purchaser are unconnected parties dealing at arm's length; that the sale of business assets takes place at fair market value; and that the selling entity is solvent, i.e. that it is not in liquidation, receivership, administration or the equivalent insolvency proceedings in any jurisdiction.

historical tax liabilities of the business in which the assets were formerly employed by the seller and such liabilities will remain with the selling entity.

However, this is not true of all territories in which a business may be acquired. There are many jurisdictions which impose secondary, joint and several or even primary liability on a purchaser of business assets for some or all of the business' tax liabilities relating to periods before its acquisition.

Although not always a pre-condition for such assumption of historical tax liabilities by a purchaser of business assets, some jurisdictions (e.g. Austria, France, Greece, Mexico, Poland, Spain) draw a distinction between:

- a pure acquisition of assets; and
- an acquisition of the whole of a business, business unit or division or of business assets which together comprise a going concern.

In the latter case, a purchaser will often assume some or all of the tax liabilities of the business' previous owner. The following examples illustrate this point:

- In Greece, where one or more separate and distinct assets are transferred which do not comprise the transfer of a business as a going concern, the purchaser will not assume historical tax liabilities. However, on the transfer of a business as a going concern[38], *Article 479* of the *Greek Civil Code* provides that the transferee is jointly liable with the transferor for the transferred business' unpaid debts, including its tax liabilities, up to a maximum of the value of the business.

- In Belgium, where the transfer of business assets results in the continuation of the same business by the purchaser, the Belgian tax authorities need not recognise the transfer until the end of the month following the month in which the tax authorities are notified of the contract for the transfer of the business. Until this date, the tax authorities can recover unpaid tax liabilities, including those accruing while the selling entity carried on the business, by requiring the business assets to be sold even if they are owned by the purchaser. After this date, the purchaser's liability for the unpaid tax liabilities of the seller is limited to the amount paid to the seller before the end of the month following the month in which the notification to the tax collector has taken place.

- In Germany:

---

[38]Transfers of a business as a going concern include transfers where the assets of a business are transferred in totality, e.g. in a transfer of business, or a business split-up or spin-off in accordance with the provisions of *Incentive Law 2166/1993* or *Incentive Law 1297/1972.*

- Under *Section 25 Commercial Code*, the purchaser is liable for the selling entity's historical corporate income tax, trade tax and withholding tax liabilities if an entire business (including its business name and all its assets) is transferred. The purchaser's liability can be waived by contractual agreement between purchaser and seller. Such waiver will be respected by third parties, including the tax authorities, if it is registered with the Commercial Register or if the third party is otherwise made aware of it by either purchaser or seller.
- Under *Section 75 General Tax Code*, the purchaser is liable for the selling entity's historical liability for business taxes (e.g. trade tax and withholding tax liabilities) if:

  a separate business or business unit is transferred to the purchaser;

  the tax liabilities relate to the period from the beginning of the calendar year preceding the calendar year in which the business was transferred; and

  the taxes have been assessed on, or declared by, the seller before the end of one full year following the registration of the business by the purchaser.
- Liability under *Section 75 General Tax Code* is a secondary liability which is capped at the value of the assets acquired by the purchaser but which cannot be waived by contractual agreement.
- Both *Section 25 Commercial Code* and *Section 75 General Tax Code* apply to the selling entity's historical VAT and employment/payroll tax liabilities.
- *Section 25 Commercial Code* applies to the selling entity's historical car tax and real estate transfer tax liabilities.

The tax law of some territories provides for a mechanism which affords some level of protection to a purchaser of business assets. For example:

- In Belgium, a purchaser will be free of liability for the tax debts of the seller if a certificate is obtained from the tax authorities confirming that the seller has no unpaid tax liabilities (such certificates must not be more than one month old as at the date of the transfer of business assets).
- In Italy, the purchaser of a going concern may obtain a release certificate, i.e. the seller and/or the purchaser may request the Italian tax authorities to confirm whether or not contingent liabilities have been recorded against the seller. The tax authorities should issue the release certificate within 40 days from the date on which the request is filed, failing which it is deemed to have been granted. Such certificates of release from successor liability

will not be granted if the tax authorities can prove that the transfer of the going concern was part of a tax fraud, i.e. a scheme intended to avoid the payment of taxes and penalties.

- In Poland, a purchaser may apply to the Polish tax authorities for a certificate setting out the amount of any tax arrears of the seller. The purchaser is not liable for any tax arrears which are not disclosed in the certificate. However, this protection does not extend to tax arrears and certain other liabilities (e.g. penalty interest) of the seller which arise after the date of issue of the certificate and before the date of acquisition if between those dates:

  30 days have elapsed, in the case of a transfer of the whole or an organised part of an enterprise; or

  three days have elapsed in the case of a transfer of assets.

- In Spain, to avoid incurring joint liability for all the non-statute barred tax liabilities related to the acquired assets, the purchaser can apply to the tax authorities for a certificate listing the transferor's tax liabilities. The transferor must agree to the application. The purchaser's liability is then limited to the tax debts listed in the certificate issued by the tax authorities. The tax authorities are obliged to issue the requested certificate within a three-month period. If they fail to do so, the purchaser is relieved of joint liability.

In many jurisdictions where historical tax liabilities do pass to a purchaser of business assets in certain circumstances, such liability is often:

- limited to tax liabilities relating to a specifically defined period before the transfer of assets (e.g. Austria, Italy);
- limited to those liabilities of which the purchaser was, or ought to have been, aware (e.g. Austria);
- capped at some measure of the value of the assets acquired (e.g. Austria, Greece, Italy, Poland).

Taxes associated with real estate attach to the real estate itself in some jurisdictions and pass to a purchaser of that real estate. For example:

- In Finland:

  there is a specific procedure for transfers of real estate (if included in the acquired business assets). This usually means that potential exposures in relation to VAT deductions made by the seller in connection with the real estate are, in effect, transferred to the purchaser; and if the acquired business includes real estate, the purchaser may become liable for any real estate transfer tax which has not been paid on earlier transfers of the property.

- Where Dutch real estate is acquired, the purchaser can potentially assume the seller's liabilities with respect to real property taxes, environmental taxes and other similar taxes.
- In Norway, real estate taxes are secured by statutory mortgage. Consequently, if a property is sold and there are any unpaid tax claims on the property, the tax authorities may collect the real estate tax from the new owner, i.e. by forcing a sale of the property. Municipal taxes, such as sanitation charges, are also by law secured by mortgage over real estate. Consequently, when the real estate is sold, the new owner is liable for any unpaid charges.
- A purchaser of Spanish real estate is in most cases secondarily liable for any unpaid transfer tax, stamp duty and local tax on real estate associated with the real estate acquired relating to periods before the purchaser's acquisition of it.
- In India, liability for excise (tax on the manufacture of goods) typically attaches to the factory registered under the excise regulations. Where a factory unit is sold, the liability for any unpaid excise arising during the seller's period of ownership would pass to the purchaser together with pending excise proceedings.

11. Disclosure of Due Diligence Reports to the Tax Authorities

11.1. UK

Finance Act 2008 introduces significant changes to HMRC's information and inspection powers with effect from an Appointed Day, expected to be 1 April 2009.

From that date:

- HMRC's information and inspection powers in relation to direct taxes will be broader than they are at present. Specifically, requests for information and documents need no longer relate to a specific enquiry; although, where a return has been submitted, HMRC will still need to open an enquiry or make a discovery before they can exercise their new powers.
- HMRC will need to demonstrate that the requested information or document is 'reasonably required' for the purposes of 'checking the taxpayer's tax position.' This will allow HMRC to enquire into present and future tax liabilities (and not just those for historical periods as is currently the case) the effect of which will be to give HMRC for the first time a real-time audit power for corporation tax and income tax. HMRC will not require the prior authority of the Commissioners (or first-tier tribunal) before exercising this new power; and there will be only limited rights of appeal.
- Currently, HMRC can only require third parties to provide **documents**, i.e. items which actually exist at the time when the notice is served and which, by definition, do not need to be created by the recipient of the notice, e.g. a list of all customers' names and addresses. Under the new *Finance Act 2008* powers, HMRC will have the ability to require **information** from third parties and not just documents.
- HMRC's VAT and PAYE powers to inspect records at business premises will be extended to direct taxes and will cover business premises, business assets and 'statutory' records. In particular, HMRC will have the power to inspect documents in relation to periods for which a tax return has yet to be filed. HMRC will normally need to give seven days' notice of an inspection.

Further guidance on HMRC's new powers and a Code of Practice are expected and should, among other things, clarify the meaning of 'statutory' records.

Under the new powers the circumstances in which HMRC can require production of a due diligence report will remain very limited. Generally, due diligence reports will not be 'reasonably required' for the purposes of 'checking the taxpayer's tax position' on the basis that they consist of opinion, recommendation and guidance to a potential purchaser of a target business, as opposed to pure fact. References in the due diligence report to the facts on which this opinion, recommendation and guidance are based are likely to represent the due diligence adviser's understanding of the actual underlying facts contained within, for example, the target's business records. Generally, only the latter are likely to be disclosable.

However, the possibility of a due diligence report being disclosable to HMRC cannot be completely discounted. For example, the definition of 'tax position' in the new powers includes tax-related penalties. When determining an appropriate level of penalty in relation to an error on the part of a taxpayer company, HMRC might wish to know whether the company had been aware of the error but had failed to act promptly to rectify it. In these circumstances, it is possible that HMRC could require disclosure of an earlier due diligence report to establish whether the error had already been identified at that time.

Reports commissioned by an overseas parent in relation to a UK company and kept abroad by that parent might not be required to be produced as they might not be within either the power or possession of the relevant taxpayer. This underlines the need to control, in the case of an inbound group, the amount of documentation kept in the UK if that documentation properly belongs to the overseas parent.

11.2. Jurisdictions outside the UK

Outside the UK, there is wide variation in the ability of tax authorities to obtain copies of due diligence reports as part of their powers of investigation into the tax affairs of taxpayers.

The tax authorities in most jurisdictions have information and inspection powers of some kind to require disclosure of the information necessary to determine the liabilities of taxpayers. These can sometimes extend to due diligence reports (e.g. Hong Kong, Turkey, United States[39]). However, in many

[39]The US Internal Revenue Service ('IRS') could request a copy of a tax due diligence report pursuant to an audit or litigation and may petition a court to enforce its subpoena if a taxpayer refuses to produce the report. The IRS could also subpoena a taxpayer's tax adviser in certain circumstances for the production of a tax due diligence report and can likewise petition a court to enforce its subpoena should the adviser decline to produce the report. Engagement letters generally reserve the adviser's right to disclose such material if the adviser is forced to do so. The ability of state and local

jurisdictions where the powers could technically apply to due diligence reports, they are rarely, if ever, used in practice to this effect (e.g. Australia, Austria, Ireland, Russia).

In some jurisdictions, the tax authorities'power to obtain due diligence reports is extremely limited or non-existent (e.g. Denmark, Greece, Luxembourg, Mexico, Spain); or confined to certain criminal proceedings (e.g. France, Germany, Hungary). In others, the power is unclear and largely untested (e.g. the Czech Republic, Finland, Poland).

The question of tax authorities' information powers in relation to due diligence reports can be further complicated by the facts that:

- in some jurisdictions such reports may be confidential or privileged in certain circumstances; or
- where such reports are in the possession of someone other than the subject of a tax audit, it may not be legally or practically possible for the tax authorities to require their disclosure.

---

tax authorities to require disclosure of tax due diligence reports varies by state and locality.

12. The UK Tax Treatment of the Costs of Due Diligence

12.1. Corporation tax

Tax relief for costs incurred in connection with due diligence (e.g. the professional fees of the due diligence provider) is potentially available on the following bases:

- under *Section 75 Income and Corporation Taxes Act 1988* as expenses of management incurred by a company with investment business;
- under *Section 84 Finance Act 1996* as a charge or expense incurred for the purposes of the purchaser's loan relationships;
- as expenditure incurred for the purposes of acquiring certain assets qualifying for specific tax relief;
- as an incidental cost of acquisition of the shares or assets of the target company which will form part of the tax basis of those shares or assets and relieved for tax purposes only when the shares or assets are eventually disposed of (unless the SSE applies to such future disposal in which case there is no effective tax relief).

12.1.1. Expenses of management of a company with investment business

Where the professional fees associated with a due diligence review of a target company are:

- incurred by a company which qualifies under *Section 130 Income and Corporation Taxes Act 1988* as a company with investment business; and
- debited in that company's accounts for a period of account in accordance with generally accepted accounting practice (*Section 75A(2) Income and Corporation Taxes Act 1988*);

then there is a possibility that those fees will be deductible for tax purposes as expenses of management under *Section 75 Income and Corporation Taxes Act 1988* as and when they are debited to the company's accounts.

Generally, however, capital expenditure will not be deductible as an expense of management (*Section 75(3) Income and Corporation Taxes Act 1988*) unless either:

- it gives rise to capital allowances under *Section 75(7) Income and Corporation Taxes Act 1988*; or
- it can be treated as an expense of management on the basis of tax legislation other than Section 75 Income and Corporation Taxes Act 1988.

The difficulty with claiming tax relief for due diligence costs as management expenses is establishing that they are incurred for the purposes of investigating and evaluating possible investment options and not for the purposes of acquiring the shares of a particular target company. If incurred for the latter purpose, due diligence costs are likely to be regarded as capital in nature and therefore excluded from management expenses under *Section 75(3)*. At some point, evaluation of a range of possible investment opportunities will identify a specific investment opportunity and a decision will be made to acquire the target company's shares. From this point on, expenditure incurred by a company with investment business in relation to investigating the target company is unlikely to qualify as an expense of management.

Precisely when such expenditure ceases to be an expense of management will depend on what is often subjective interpretation of the facts of each particular case. For example, it is sometimes argued that the change occurs on the date when:

- a potential purchaser is granted exclusivity in relation to the acquisition of the target company's shares; or
- an offer (including a conditional or indicative offer) is made.

The *Inland Revenue Company Taxation Manual* provides helpful guidance in this respect at *8190 and 8260* and in particular makes a distinction between:

- 'expenditure on appraising and investigating investments ...up to the point at which a decision is made to acquire a particular investment' (which could qualify as an expense of management); and
- expenditure incurred thereafter (which would be capital in nature).

In any event, claims that due diligence costs qualify as management expenses are often challenged by HMRC and can become the subject of protracted negotiation.

The principles outlined above should also apply to the costs of due diligence incurred in relation to an acquisition which does not in the event proceed. The deductibility of such costs as management expenses will depend on whether they have been incurred:

- for the purposes of investigating and evaluating possible investment options; or
- for the purposes of an acquisition (albeit an unsuccessful one) of the shares of a particular target company.

12.1.2. Costs of obtaining loan finance

Where an acquisition of a target company's shares is to be funded by bank-debt, pre-acquisition due diligence may have been carried out at least partly for the purposes of supporting the bank's lending decision. Where this is the case, it may be possible for the purchasing company to argue that at least some of the costs of that pre-acquisition due diligence should be tax deductible under *Section 84 Finance Act 1996* as 'charges and expenses incurred ...under or for the purposes of its loan relationships' (*Section 84(1)(b)* as qualified by *Section 84(3)(a) to (d)*). In particular, *Section 84(3)(a)* provides for tax relief under *Section 84(1)(b)* for expenditure 'incurred directly in bringing any of those loan relationships into existence.'

In determining the proportion of due diligence costs attributable to obtaining loan finance, some just and reasonable basis of apportionment should be used, e.g. the same proportion as the loan finance represents of the total acquisition funding.

Where due diligence costs are eligible for tax relief under *Section 84,* they will be deductible as and when they are recognised in determining a company's profit or loss for any particular period in accordance with generally accepted accounting practice (*Section 85A(1) Finance Act 1996* with further clarification in *Section 85B Finance Act 1996*).

Even where a transaction does not in the event proceed, due diligence costs which would otherwise have been deductible under *Section 84 Finance Act 1996* may still be deductible by virtue of *Section 84(4)*.

12.1.3. Due diligence costs incurred in relation to the acquisition of certain assets qualifying for specific tax relief

Where the business assets of a target company are acquired, rather than its shares, the costs of any due diligence will generally be directly attributable to, or apportionable on some just and reasonable basis across, the specific assets acquired. Their tax treatment will therefore broadly follow that of the underlying assets to which they have been allocated. See 10.1.2. Specifically:

- expenditure incurred for the purposes of acquiring or creating on or after 1 April 2002 an intangible fixed asset for use on a continuing basis in the course of the purchasing company's activities (*Paragraph 133(a) Schedule 29 Finance Act 2002*) is deductible for tax purposes under *Schedule 29 Finance Act 2002*:

  either as it is amortised or impaired for accounting purposes (N.B. under International Financial Reporting Standards, the intangible fixed asset may not be amortised); or

  at the fixed rate of 4% per annum, where appropriate election is made within two years of the end of the accounting period in which the intangible fixed asset is acquired;

- certain qualifying expenditure incurred in connection with the acquisition of an asset eligible for capital allowances (or industrial buildings allowances, although these are being phased out – see 10.1.2) should also qualify for capital allowances (or industrial buildings allowances) treatment.

12.1.4. Due diligence costs which do not qualify for tax relief on any of the above bases

Due diligence costs which do not qualify for tax relief on any of the above bases will generally be treated for tax purposes as an incidental cost of acquisition of the shares or assets of the target company and will form part of the tax basis of those shares or assets. Accordingly, such costs will only be relieved for tax purposes when the shares or assets are eventually sold or otherwise disposed of. If, however, the SSE applies to such future disposal, there will effectively be no tax relief at all.

12.1.5. Vendor or sell-side due diligence

The costs of vendor or sell-side due diligence will generally be incurred by a seller in relation to a disposal of shares. The costs of such due diligence will therefore be capital in nature and will constitute an incidental cost of the disposal of those shares for which relief should be available under *Section 38(1)(c) Taxation of Chargeable Gains Act 1992*, unless the SSE applies to the seller's disposal, in which case there will effectively be no tax relief at all.

In practice, the seller's vendor due diligence costs are often passed economically to the purchaser via the pricing mechanism. For the purchaser in such cases, they will form part of the tax basis of the acquired shares to be relieved for tax purposes when the shares are eventually sold or otherwise disposed of. If, however, the SSE applies to such future disposal, there will effectively be no tax relief at all.

12.2. VAT

A prerequisite for the recovery of VAT incurred in relation to the costs of due diligence is that the person paying/recovering the VAT:

- is a recipient of the due diligence services, as evidenced by being a party to the relevant engagement letter; and
- receives an invoice.

12.2.1. Share purchases

Pre-acquisition or buyside due diligence

The costs of due diligence in relation to a purchase of shares are treated as general business overheads of the purchaser. Accordingly, the recoverability of the related VAT will depend on the purchaser's VAT recovery profile, i.e whether the purchaser is fully taxable, partially exempt or makes only exempt supplies.

Vendor or sell-side due diligence

A sale of shares is an exempt supply for VAT purposes. VAT incurred in connection with the costs of vendor or sell-side due diligence is therefore exempt input VAT and is only recoverable to the extent that the sale of shares is to purchasers outside the EU.

Due diligence in relation to an issue of shares

An issue of shares, on the other hand, is not a supply at all for VAT purposes following the European Court of Justice decision in the case of *Kretztechnik A.G. v Finanzamt Linz (Case C – 465/03) [2005] STC 1118*. Accordingly, the costs of due diligence in relation to an issue of shares (e.g. due diligence carried out by a reporting accountant in relation to a rights issue or an IPO which includes the issue of new shares– see 2.3) are treated as general business overheads of the issuer. The recoverability of the related VAT will depend on the issuer's VAT recovery profile, i.e whether the issuer is fully taxable, partially exempt or makes only exempt supplies.

Following the decision in *Kretztechnik*, HMRC explained its position on the VAT treatment of share issues and related input VAT recovery in *Business Brief 12/05* and provided further guidance on the matter in *Business Brief 21/05*.

Specifically, *Business Brief 12/05* (as summarised in *Business Brief 21/05*) confirmed that 'companies making a new issue of shares to raise capital for their business, in circumstances identical to those in *Kretztechnik*'s case, were not making any supply but were entitled to treat the VAT on the costs of the issue as input tax. Companies that make both taxable and exempt supplies should recover a proportion of the input tax in accordance with their partial exemption method that applied at the time of the issue.'

Business Brief 21/05 explains HMRC's view of the VAT position of share transactions where the circumstances differ from those in the *Kretztechnik* case. In particular, the following will not be treated as supplies for VAT purposes:

- issues of all types of share (e.g. preference shares, special rights issues, bonus issues, scrip dividends);
- issues of shares by any type of company whose motivation for the issue is the raising of capital;
- issues of other types of security or financial instrument (e.g. bonds, debentures, loan notes, shares or units in collective investment funds) where the purpose of the issue is to raise capital for the issuer's business;

- issues of shares or securities which form part of wider arrangements (e.g. as part of a company takeover, merger, demerger etc.).

However, *Business Brief 21/05* confirms that sales of existing shares (as opposed to issues of new shares) will continue to be treated as exempt supplies with the consequences described above (see *Vendor or sell-side due diligence)* i.e. VAT on related costs is only recoverable to the extent that the shares are sold to purchasers outside the EU.

12.2.2. Asset deals

Pre-acquisition or buy-side due diligence

Where a purchase of business assets qualifies as a TOGC

Where a purchaser of business assets as a TOGC incurs VAT in connection with the costs of pre-acquisition or buy-side due diligence, the purchaser's ability to recover that VAT will depend on the VAT-status of the supplies to be made by the acquired business:

- if the acquired business assets are to be used exclusively in making taxable supplies, then the VAT will be fully recoverable;
- if the acquired business assets are to be used exclusively in making exempt supplies, then none of the VAT will be recoverable;
- if the acquired business assets are to be used in making both taxable and exempt supplies, then the VAT will be treated as residual input tax and will be recoverable only to the extent determined by the purchaser's partial exemption method.

Where a purchase of business assets does not qualify as a TOGC

Where a purchase of business assets does not qualify as a TOGC, it will comprise an acquisition of a number of separate business assets for VAT purposes. The purchaser's ability to recover VAT incurred in connection with the costs of pre-acquisition or buy-side due diligence will therefore depend on the VAT-status of the supplies to be made using the acquired assets:

- if the acquired business assets are to be used exclusively in making taxable supplies, then the VAT will be fully recoverable;
- if the acquired business assets are to be used exclusively in making exempt supplies, then none of the VAT will be recoverable;
- if the acquired business assets are to be used in making both taxable and exempt supplies, then the VAT will be treated as residual input tax and will be recoverable only to the extent determined by the purchaser's partial exemption method.

Vendor or sell-side due diligence

Where a sale of business assets qualifies as a TOGC

Where a seller of business assets as a TOGC incurs costs in relation to vendor or sell-side due diligence, those costs will be treated as general overheads of the business transferred. The seller's ability to recover VAT in connection with the costs of vendor or sell-side due diligence in these circumstances will therefore depend on the VAT-status of the supplies made by the business transferred:

- if the transferred business made only taxable supplies, then the VAT will be fully recoverable;
- if the transferred business made only exempt supplies, then none of the VAT will be recoverable;
- if the transferred business made both taxable and exempt supplies, then the VAT will be treated as residual input tax and will be recoverable only to the extent determined by the seller's partial exemption method.

Where a sale of business assets does not qualify as a TOGC

Where a sale of business assets does not qualify as a TOGC, it will comprise a sale of a number of separate business assets for VAT purposes. The seller's ability to recover VAT incurred in connection with the costs of vendor or sell-side due diligence in these circumstances will therefore depend on the VAT-status of the supplies of these separate business assets:

- if all of the supplies of the transferred assets are taxable supplies, then the VAT will be fully recoverable;
- if all of the supplies of the transferred assets are exempt supplies, then none of the VAT will be recoverable;
- if some of the supplies of the transferred assets are taxable and some are exempt, then the VAT will be treated as residual input tax and will be recoverable only to the extent determined by the seller's partial exemption method.

Acknowledgements

I am very much indebted to the following for their invaluable help with this book. This has included inspiration, advice and support; answering numerous questions; assisting with drafting (and in some cases contributing passages of text); and proof-reading.

Nadia Ali

Jonathan Anderson

Nilesh Ashar (India)

Richard Avery

Evgeny Bezlepko (Russia)

Robert Brockwell

Andrzej Broda (Poland)

Fiona Campbell (VAT)

Wilson Cheng (Hong Kong)

Richard Clarke

Florian Delisle (France)

Akshit Desai

Andrew Drysch

Ersin Erdem (Turkey)

Mark Evans

Suzanne Evans (stamp taxes)

Daniel Eyre

Graham Farquhar

Giuseppe Fiorella (Italy)

Julie Garside

John Goulias (Greece)

Kevin Griffin

Ana Gross (Mexico)

Leon Harris (Israel)

Sjoerd Hensen (Netherlands)

Steve Hextall

David Hobart

Magdalena Holland (Germany)

Lena Johnsen (Norway)

Stefan Kainberger (Austria)

Marc Korthoudt (Belgium)

Thomas Krämer (Denmark)

Rene Kulinsky (Czech Republic)

David Kuo (China)

Eric YH Lam (Hong Kong)

Kathryn Lawrence

Giovanni Lettieri (Italy)

Joackim Lundholm (Sweden)

Helder Matias (Portugal)

Josh McKniff (United States)

Pete Miller ('The New Disclosure Regime: Revised descriptions of disclosable arrangements', Tax Journal, 24 July 2006)

Gary Mills (transfer pricing)

Hiroyuki Nishida (Japan)

Caspar Noble

Rhys Novak

Chris Oates

David Oldknow

Derk Oosthoek (Netherlands)

Susanne Peppitt

Don Poar

Sriram Ramaswamy (India)

Peter Rayney

Susanne Renelt (Germany)

Juan Roda (Spain)

Lubica Rybarova (Slovak Republic)

Araceli Saenz de Navarrete Crespo (Spain)

Mika Sipilä (Finland)

Ondrej Topinka (Czech Republic)

Mark Treherne

Giuseppe Tuzze (Luxembourg)

Fionnuala Tyrrell (employee share/security ownership)

Peter Vaszari (Hungary)

Sam Wallis (PAYE)

Declan Walsh (Ireland)

Paul Warn

Matt Weerden (Australia)

Martin Wikborg (Norway)

Index

FSC
www.fsc.org
MIX
Papier | Fördert gute Waldnutzung
FSC® C083411

Kolibri 360 GmbH
Ferdinand-Jühlke-Straße 7
99095 Erfurt, Deutschland
produktsicherheit@kolibri360.de